*In memory of
Sheikh Zayed bin Sultan Al Nahyan
who led the archaeologists to Jebel Hafit,
to the mounds from "the Age of Ignorance"*

The Early Bronze Age Tombs of Jebel Hafit

Danish Archaeological Investigations in Abu Dhabi
1961-1971

by Bo Madsen

with a contribution by Margarethe Uerpmann
and Hans-Peter Uerpmann

Jutland Archaeological Society   Moesgaard Museum

Abu Dhabi Tourism & Culture Authority

The Early Bronze Age Tombs of Jebel Hafit

Danish Archaeological Investigations in Abu Dhabi 1961-1971
Bo Madsen © 2017

ISBN 978-87-93423-04-6
ISSN 0107-2854

Jutland Archaeological Society Publications vol. 93

Editing: Flemming Højlund
Layout: Narayana Press
Cover: Louise Hilmar
Drawings: Knud Thorvildsen, Arne Thorsteinsson, Vagn Kolstrup, Jens Aarup Jensen, Jørgen Lund, Michael Beck, Niels Axel Boas, Steen Andersen, Bo Madsen, Bente Fischer, Phine Wiborg, Peder Mortensen
Photos: Knud Thorvildsen, Arne Thorsteinsson, Vagn Kolstrup, Jens Aarup Jensen, Jørgen Lund, Michael Beck, Niels Axel Boas, Steen Andersen, Bo Madsen, Bo Lavindsgaard, Rogvi Johansen, Helle Strehle
Digitizing maps, plans and sections: Andreas Hegner Reinau, Phine Wiborg, Jonatan Rose Andersen
English revision: Lisa Yeomans
Printed by Narayana Press

Published by Abu Dhabi Tourism & Culture Authority in cooperation with Jutland Archaeological Society and Moesgaard Museum

Distributed by Aarhus University Press
Langelandsgade 177
DK-8200 Aarhus N
www.unipress.dk

Contents

Preface 7

1. Introduction 9
2. History of investigation 11
3. The landscape and the environment 23
4. Danish investigations in the Jebel Hafit area 31
5. Excavation procedures 37
6. The mounds on the northern plateau 39
7. The mounds along the eastern mountain ridge 63
8. The mounds on the western mountain ridge 89
9. The mounds on the southern plateau 173
10. The mounds on the eastern side of the mountain 193
11. The finds and their context 217
12. Human skeletal remains 223
13. Funerary architecture 225
14. Secondary burials and later burial forms 235
15. Concluding discussion 237

Bibliography 239

Appendix. The camel bones from Tomb 1308,
by M. and H.-P. Uerpmann 243

Preface

This book is the first of a series of planned publications resulting from an archaeological collaboration between the government of Abu Dhabi and archaeologists from the Moesgaard Museum in Denmark.

This remarkable relationship pre-dates the foundation of the United Arab Emirates in 1971, having been established by the late Sheikh Zayed bin Sultan Al Nahyan in the 1950s, and has been recently renewed through a new cooperation between Moesgaard Museum and the Abu Dhabi Tourism & Culture Authority (ADTCA).

The collaboration with Moesgaard Museum is intended to produce a series of peer-reviewed monographs on the historic work of the Danish team in Al Ain from 1961-1971. This series complements their earlier publications on the tombs and settlement on Umm an-Nar island. This new series is informed by the overall vision of ADTCA to provide the public not only with access to the archaeological sites and historic buildings within the cultural landscape of Al Ain but also detailed scientific information about its past produced by ongoing archaeological research and the publication of previous work. This strategy is guided by the vision of Abu Dhabi Tourism & Culture Authority. One of its main components is a programme of publication aimed at increasing public awareness and access to the Cultural Sites of Al Ain, the UNESCO World Heritage Site inscribed in June 2011. The World Heritage Site is composed of 17 sites, grouped into 4 distinct assemblages – Hafit, Hili, Bida Bint Saud & the Oases – that reflect both the interaction of Man and Nature within this unique cultural landscape and the long history of settlement in Al Ain over more than 5,000 years. The original exploration of these sites was conducted by the Danish team and the results of this work are the focus of this new series.

This first book in this series deals with the discovery and exploration of the earliest features of this sequence, the Early Bronze Age tombs clustered on the slopes of Jebel Hafit, the massive and timeless landmark of Al Ain rising 1000m above the surrounding plain. The exploration of these tombs provided important information on the pre-cursor to the Umm an-Nar civilization which was also made famous by the Danish excavations on the island of the same name off the coast of Abu Dhabi. The tombs at Jebel Hafit marked a fundamental transformation in the relationship between humans and the environment in the region and may coincide with the emergence of oasis agriculture at the nearby site of Hili 8. A wide range of artifacts was discovered and indicate long-distance trade and the exploitation of local and imported resources, such as copper. Many of these artifacts can be seen in al-Ain National Museum, the first museum opened in the UAE.

The publication of this book is particularly timely in that it coincides with ongoing ADTCA work to develop the eastern slopes of Jebel Hafit as Mezyad Desert Park, thereby preserving and presenting the diverse elements of the natural and cultural landscape of Al Ain. Some of the tombs excavated by the Danish teams will form an integral part of this project.

Aside from the detailed archaeological description of the pioneering exploration of the tombs between 1961-1971 and the discussion of their typology and the various finds made during the work, the book also showcases a fascinating series of photographs that capture a unique moment in time for Al Ain, poised between the ancient landscape and the massive urban expansion which it has experienced in the past fifty years since those first explorations by the Danish archaeologists of Moesgaard Museum.

H.E. Mohamed Khalifa Al Mubarak
Chairman
Abu Dhabi Tourism & Culture Authority

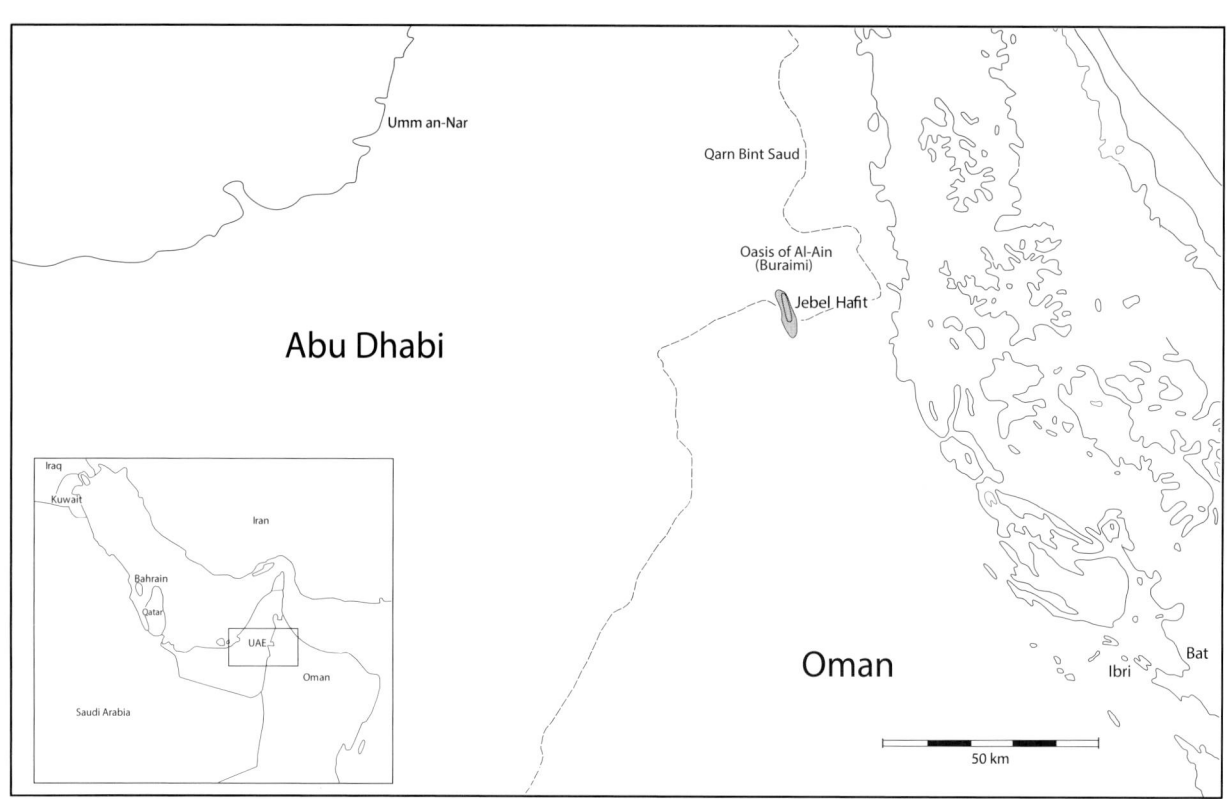

Fig. 1. Map of Abu Dhabi with excavation localities indicated.

1. Introduction

The burial monuments from Jebel Hafit published in this volume were investigated by teams from the Danish Moesgaard Museum between 1961 and 1971 (fig. 1). Through preliminary publications by Karen Frifelt (1971, 1975a-b, 1979, 1980, 2002), the finds from Jebel Hafit have become the foundation of our understanding of the beginning of the Bronze Age in South-East Arabia and it is the eponymous site of the *Hafit period*, which can be broadly dated to c. 3100-2700 BC.

The Jebel Hafit tombs consisted of "cairns of stones built up around a central corbelled chamber approached by a narrow entrance passage through the thickness of the mound, a length of up to two meters" (Bibby 1965 p. 105). Excavation of the chambers produced an assemblage of gravegoods, including pottery, copper objects and personal ornaments which alluded to the dating and cultural affinity of their occupants. Of special interest were a series of pottery vessels in shape and decoration identical to pottery from the Jemdet Nasr period in Mesopotamia. In some instances, preserved skeletal material has given an insight into the funerary practices of the monument builders. The investigations have also yielded important information on burial architecture, building techniques and materials, and the environmental setting of the tombs. The accumulation of hundreds of monuments in extensive mound fields points to the organizational capabilities of the communities responsible for the erection of these impressive monuments and is evidence of the pivotal role of tomb building in the funerary practices around 3000 BC.

The concentration of tombs around Jebel Hafit and their imported Mesopotamian gravegoods probably indicate the importance of this area in establishing the first trade in copper from the interior Oman peninsula to present day Iraq. As such, the Hafit culture stands as the precursor of the subsequent Umm an-Nar culture (c. 2700-2000 BC) that represents the floruit of Bronze Age civilization in Southeast Arabia (Carter & Tikriti 2004).

The Hafit tombs were sporadically used for secondary burials in the following periods, the Umm an-Nar period (c. 2700-2000 BC), the Wadi Suq period (c. 2000-1600 BC), the Late Bronze Age (c. 1600-1250 BC), the Iron Age and later pre-Islamic period (c. 1250 BC-c. 600 AD).

The extant volume contains 15 chapters and can be roughly divided into three parts: an introduction, chapters 1-5, which presents the historical events that led to the uncovering of such exceptional funerary remains; a second part, chapters 6-10, in which individual funerary structures are thoroughly described, and a third part, chapters 11-15 in which the components from descriptions of the individual tombs are synthesized in order to generate a more coherent interpretation of mortuary practices in early 3rd millennium BC. A camel's burial is dealt with in an appendix.

The basic field documentation is housed in the archives of the Oriental Department, Moesgaard Museum, Denmark. It consists of field plans and note books, black- and white photos and colour-slides in different formats. The find objects have been listed and briefly described on index cards by Frifelt. A small portion of the artefacts recovered at Jebel Hafit is still stored in the collections at Moesgaard Museum, but the majority was returned to Abu Dhabi in 1969-1971 after conservation, photographing, drawing and analysis.

Subsequent to the termination of each excavation season reports as well as find lists were submitted to the Ruler's Office in Abu Dhabi and later to the Department of Antiquities & Tourism, Al-Ain. Recently, several thousands of photos taken during the archaeological campaigns have been digitized and transferred to Abu Dhabi following a grant from the Abu Dhabi Authority for Culture and Heritage (*ADACH*), now Abu Dhabi Tourism and Culture Authority.

In 1968 Sheikh Zayed bin Sultan Al Nahyan, Ruler of Abu Dhabi, gave instructions to create a national museum in Al-Ain next to the historic Sultan Fort. This task was entrusted to the newly established Department of Antiquities &Tourism, which arranged the exhibition in cooperation with Frifelt and other staffmembers from Moesgaard Museum. In 1971 the new exhibition, including the finds from the Jebel Hafit tombs, was presented to a wider audience (Rahim 1979).

The preparation of the present manuscript by Bo Madsen took place in 2009-2010 and was made possible under the terms of an agreement of cooperation signed in 2008 between *ADACH* and Moesgaard Museum. The manuscript was edited by Flemming

Højlund in 2016. Other early excavations, e.g. the Hili-1 Bronze Age Tower, the Grand Tomb at Hili, and burials and rock art at Qarn (Bidaa) Bint Saud are also being prepared for publication (Madsen forthcoming a and b).

In 2011 Moesgaard Museum prepared an exhibition detailing the early years of archaeological exploration of Abu Dhabi. The exhibition, *The Dawn of History. Revealing the Ancient Past of Abu Dhabi*, was hosted at Al-Jahili Fort in Al-Ain and included a section dedicated to the Jebel Hafit burials (Anon. 2011). In 2011 the Hafit tombs were inscribed on UNESCO's World Heritage List as part of the *Cultural Sites of Al-Ain (Hafit, Hili, Bidaa Bint Saud and Oases Areas)*.

For the support to publish the investigations at Jebel Hafit thanks are due to Sultan bin Tahnoon Al Nahyan, Chairman of ADACH; the Late Mohammed Khalaf Al-Mazrouei, Director General of ADACH; and Dr. Sami El Masri, Deputy Director General of ADACH. In addition, we are indebted to Muhammed Amer Al-Neyadi, Director of the Historic Environment Department of Abu Dhabi Tourism & Culture Authority, for granting the funds for editing and printing the present volume. Thanks are also due to members of the staff of Abu Dhabi Tourism & Culture Authority, Dr. Walid Yasin Al Tikriti, Head of Archaeology Section and Peter Sheehan, Head of Historic Buildings & Landscapes Section, and to an anonymous reviewer for reading the draft text and offering constructive comments.

Special thanks go to the members of the teams who excavated at Jebel Hafit and established the foundation for the study of the Hafit Culture. For all of us who participated in the expeditions to Abu Dhabi, the excavations not only opened a door to the ancient and long forgotten Hafit Culture, but equally meeting the people and the landscape of Abu Dhabi gave us magnificent experiences and lifelong memories.

2. History of investigation

Archaeological explorations in Abu Dhabi were initiated in 1958 when P.V. Glob and T.G. Bibby were invited by the Ruler, Sheikh Shakhbut Bin Sultan Al Nahyan, to conduct an archaeological survey (Glob 1959a). At that time the Danish Gulf expeditions had spent four years investigating the archaeology and documenting the vanishing traditional cultures of Bahrain and Qatar. The operational base in Denmark was the provincial museum in Aarhus, later to become Moesgaard Museum. Professor P.V. Glob was Director of the museum, and he was assisted by T.G. Bibby, who had previously worked in Bahrain. The museum also acted as the Chair of Archaeology under the University of Aarhus. This was a most fruitful arrangement that provided a framework for the ongoing projects in the Arabian Gulf.

Sheikh Shakhbut Al Nahyan had described the existence of ancient structures and idols or imagery on the island of Umm an-Nar and through a liaison with the local oil company invited the Danes that were excavating on Bahrain to come for a survey in 1958. Sheikh Shakhbut encouraged the archaeologists to take a closer look at Umm an-Nar (Glob 1959a, Frifelt 1991, Højlund 2013). By the following year excavations had commenced on the island. Glob asked Harald Andersen to be in charge of the fieldwork. He was a meticulous excavator who at the time had a reputation for developing excavation methodology (Glob 1959b, Thorvildsen 1962, Frifelt 1991, 1995).

When members of the ruling family came to see the excavation of the first uncovered tomb at Umm an-Nar, Sheikh Zayed Bin Sultan Al Nahyan, then governor of the Eastern Province of Abu Dhabi, invited Glob and Bibby to come to Al-Ain (fig. 2). Sheikh Zayed wanted them to see places with even more mounds than the already impressive mound field at Umm an-Nar (Bibby 1969).

A week later Glob and Bibby with an experienced driver advanced through the sand tracks and dunes to Al-Ain to visit the legendary governor. In the early morning the Sheikh took them out to the prehistoric grave-mounds. Sheikh Zayed's interest in the country's ancient past and his strong personality left a deep impression. Both Glob and Bibby have vividly described the significant event (Glob 1968 p. 174, Bibby 1969 p. 211).

"…promptly at seven two open jeeps roared up before (the guest house), with Zayid himself, looking spruce and wide awake, driving the leading vehicle. We climbed into our two land-rovers and followed behind, along the steep-sided wadi which skirts Al-Ain, and out on the rough track along the valley leading toward Jebel Hafit.

On our left rose steep crags, and on our right a gentler rocky slope led up to a bluff overlooking the green valley. And as we approached the bluff we could see that the whole slope was covered with burial-mounds, steep-sided cairns of stones clustering most thickly along the very edge of the bluff. Zayid's jeep turned up the slope and stopped in the middle of the largest group of mounds. We dismounted and looked around.

Zayid's boast of hundreds of mounds was not idle. Around us on the ridge stood quite that number and as our eyes accustomed themselves to the landscape we could see mounds on every crag and crest and spur, all the way to Mount Hafit itself. Zayid turned to us with a lift of his eyebrows. "Yes", we said, "gravemounds, from the Age of Ignorance." (Bibby 1969).

The archaeologists loosely counted some 200 stone burial cairns at a first glance (fig. 3). They noted a diameter of roughly 12 m for the largest (a very preliminary measurement) and a height of more than 2 m for the tallest. It was immediately obvious that the as yet unexplored structures looked quite different from the tombs at Umm an-Nar, which were constructed with an outer cladding wall of well hewn or pecked ashlars. These tombs were constructed from un-worked, but somewhat selected stone blocks. They were seemingly situated or had mainly been preserved in more stony terrain. The first impression was that they lay exposed on raised plateaus, on hillocks and on the adjacent mountain slopes. The tombs were soon named after Jebel Hafit, the very prominent mountain raising its silhouette almost like a whaleback some ten kilometres south of Al-Ain and representing a notable marker in the landscape (Glob 1959b) (figs. 4-5, 9 and 12).

The excavations on the island of Umm an-Nar, especially the tombs, were given first priority until 1961. Afterwards the work was concentrated on the large settlement on the island, as well as investigations of the interior of Abu Dhabi. In these years an identification of the Umm an-Nar culture was

Fig. 2. The Ruler, Sheikh Shakbut Bin Sultan Al Nahyan, Sheikh Zayed Bin Sultan Al Nahyan, and other members of the ruling family with their retainers visit the excavations on Umm an-Nar in 1959.

Fig. 3. The northern plateau as it looked in 1961 seen from the north, with "mounds on every crag and crest and spur, all the way to Mount Hafit".

established, and it was tentatively placed within the early part of the third millennium BC on the basis of a range of grave pottery either imported from the Iranian plateau or imitating such pottery (Thorvildsen 1962, Tosi 1989). Later these dates were modified to the middle of the millennium. The next challenge lay within the Hafit tombs at Al-Ain.

During the next two campaigns, 1961/62 and 1962/63, the excavation team started digging on Umm an-Nar and at the end of the winter season moved up to Al-Ain, where the climate was cooler and less humid.

At the time of their archaeological recognition, half a century ago, many of the prehistoric tombs of Abu Dhabi were already well known to local people. For generations they had observed them while riding by or when grazing their animals on the shrubs among them. The ruined mounds looked like no more than a heap of stone blocks and rubble and were considered to be ancient ruins or graves from a time before Islam.

In those years new materials began to replace traditional mud-brick architecture. A small scale production of cement for new housing, channels and roads had begun in Abu Dhabi as a consequence of a growing economy and a rising population. An increased need for limestone blocks to use in this industry started to take a heavy toll on monuments built from un-worked stones that most people could move and handle (fig. 6). The introduction of small trucks and the first low price pick-ups, which could drive almost everywhere, similarly made it easy for the local villagers in need of foundation stones to fetch them in still more distant areas where suitable stones were easily accessed. In consequence, the early excavations in the Hafit area were carried out not just as research but also as rescue investigations.

For the first ten years, beginning in 1958, the excavations were supported by *Abu Dhabi Marine Areas Ltd* and the *Abu Dhabi Petroleum Company*. Moesgaard Museum also provided its own budget money and the Gulf investigations were supported from a range of institutions and foundations in Denmark, with the Carlsberg Foundation as the major supporter. At the end of the 1960s the Department of Antiquities & Tourism was established by a decree from the Ruler, Sheikh Zayed bin Sultan Al Nahyan, who closely followed the archaeological research. From then on the fieldwork received additional support from the Government of Abu Dhabi and logistically by the new department.

During the early years the results of the excavations were mainly reported in *Kuml*, yearbook of the

Jutland Archaeological Society. The discoveries from Abu Dhabi and other Gulf countries at the same time reached a wide international audience with the release of Bibby's *Looking for Dilmun* in 1969. The book became a bestseller and was translated into many languages, including Arabic. Two chapters, from one of which the above excerpt is taken, were devoted to the archaeology of Abu Dhabi.

The excavation campaign 1961/62

Knud Thorvildsen was in charge of the two major excavation campaigns on Umm an-Nar in 1960 and 1961 (fig. 7). At the end of the second season, the team moved up to Al-Ain, where they arrived shortly before New Year. Thorvildsen was an experienced archaeologist and conservator, an efficient excavator and a specialist on monumental stone tombs of the north European Neolithic. He was on secondment from the Danish National Museum and on behalf of Glob and Bibby was sent to the more unexplored part of the Gulf after excavating for a few weeks in Bahrain. The small excavation team in Abu Dhabi furthermore consisted of Arne Thorsteinsson (a Faroese archaeologist) who had worked previously in Kuwait and Bahrain and already had spent a season on Umm an-Nar. Vagn Kolstrup was in the Gulf for the first time. Elise Thorvildsen, the wife of Knud, herself an experienced excavator and organizer, had left before Christmas to take care of the family back home.

Over the course of 12 days, based in a small hotel in Al-Ain, the team excavated Hafit tombs and carried out surveys in the northern Hafit area and at Hili where Thorvildsen made the first description of a ruined structure, Site 1059, which was later to be known as the Hili Grand Tomb.

It was a short but efficient campaign. A handful of local men assisted with the practical work. The mission charged to the team was to excavate some typical tombs, investigate the burial structure and the context of possible finds.

"Five mounds were excavated and proved to be of a completely different structure from the round sepulchral buildings of Umm an-Nar. They consisted of cairns of stones built up around a central corbelled chamber approached by a narrow entrance passage through the thickness of the mound, a length of up to two meters. The graves appear to have been plundered, but two large bronze pins were found, together with fragments of steatite bowls and two complete pottery vessels. These latter were completely different from those of Umm an-Nar, being small round-bodied vases of biscuit-colored ware with flat collar-rims. No conclusions could at this stage be drawn concerning the date of these tumuli." (Bibby 1965 p. 104-105)

The excavation campaign 1963

The following year another excavation team arrived in Abu Dhabi after briefing and acclimatization in Bahrain. The task was to commence excavation in the settlement layers on Umm an-Nar and at the end of the season to continue the excavation of Hafit tombs.

The investigations south of Al-Ain took place in January 1963 (fig. 8). Excavation was based on the rather simple strategy of rescuing as many finds and recording as much information as possible from the tombs which were being damaged by increasing stone robbing for building purposes. Finds that could provide dating evidence and comparisons to the Umm an-Nar burials and their grave furniture were of high interest. Also further surveys, now mainly of the eastern and western sides of Jebel Hafit formed part of the work (Bibby 1965 p. 109). The team set up their tent camp with a couple of conspicuous Scandinavian frame tents in blue and orange on the plain at the southern fringe of Al-Ain in the vicinity of the tombs they intended to excavate (fig. 9).

The young team was headed by Jens Aarup Jensen with earlier experience from Kuwait and Qatar. He was joined by Vagn Kolstrup from the previous campaign and Jørgen Lund (fig. 10), a newcomer but already a competent excavator, trained by Harald Andersen, who headed the first excavations on Umm

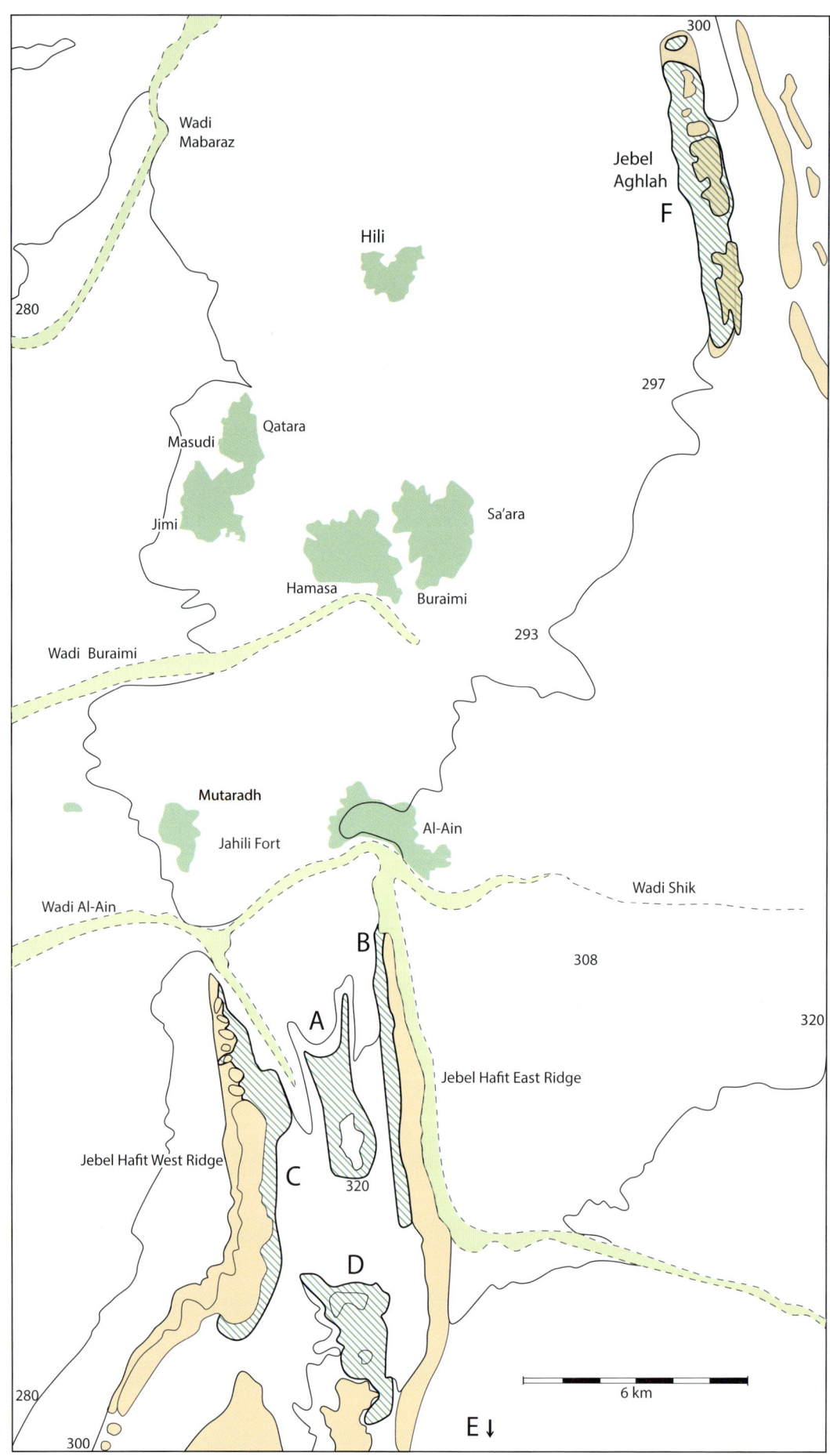

an-Nar in 1959. During two weeks 20 tombs were excavated with the assistance of six local workers. The archaeologists split up, so that around three tombs were in the progress of excavation at any one time. Most of the tombs that were chosen for excavation were damaged by recent stone robbing.

"… They all proved to be of the same construction as those excavated in the centre of the valley in the 1961/62 season: cairns built up of loosely heaped local stone around a false dome over a round or slightly oval chamber, constructed upon the original ground surface and approached by a narrow entrance passage on the southern side ….

After the completion of the excavating programme a number of reconnaissance trips were made within Abu Dhabi territory. These revealed that similar cairns, though some up to three times the size of the largest at Al-Ain, were to be found along the eastern side of Jebel Hafit, though none were to be seen along the west side. To the east of the villages of Sa'ara and Hili several hundred cairns could be counted…" (Bibby 1965 p. 109).

The role of secondary finds in the Hafit tombs was not appreciated during the first campaigns, and the discovery in one of the cairns of a bronze sword with parallels from Luristan dating to the 13th and 14th centuries BC, was taken by Bibby as an indication of the date range of the Hafit tombs (1965 p. 109. 1969 p. 215).

While working in the field, the team saw traces of fresh excavations in some of the tombs where the chambers had been emptied. In the field report from 1963 it was noted that several tombs had been opened since the previous campaign in 1961/62. "As far as we could find out some of these excavations are carried out by someone from the Trucial Oman Scouts stationed at Fort Jahili on the south side of Al-Ain. The whereabouts of the finds are unknown", wrote Aarup Jensen.

These "amateur digs" are known from later publications of the tomb furniture (During Caspers 1971, Mitchell 1972). One of the finds, a ceramic vessel (British Museum BM 134314: 1963), is reported to have been found c. 4.5 km south of Fort Jahili. This is approximately where the Danish team observed traces of fresh digging. Another fine painted vessel has the limited provenance "Buraimi" (British Museum BM 134636). Buraimi was at the time the traditional name for all the oases including Al-Ain. Most likely the second find came from the same area where the officers of the Trucial Oman Scouts knew that there were good finds to be made. The more distant area with dense spreads of Hafit tombs east of Hili, at Jebel Aghlah in neighbouring Oman, was outside the normal domain of the Trucial Oman Scouts stationed at Fort Jahili, as noted by Frifelt (1975b p. 66).

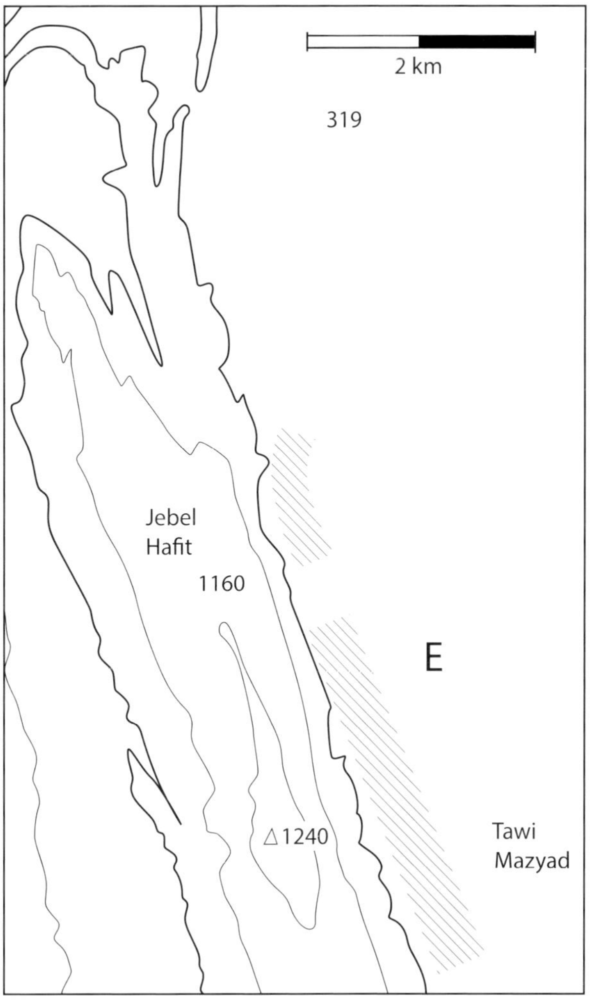

Fig. 5. Map of eastern Jebel Hafit with tomb areas northwest of Mazyad indicated in hatched lines.

« Fig. 4. Map of the northern part of Jebel Hafit and the Al-Ain oases (formerly known as the Buraimi). Areas with Hafit tombs mentioned in the text marked in hatched lines: A) Northern plateau. B) East ridge. C) West ridge. D) Southern plateau. E) Mazyad. F) Jebel Aghlah.

Fig. 6. From the southern outskirts of Al-Ain 1965. Wagon loads of stone blocks taken from nearby Hafit tombs.

Fig. 7. Field Director Knud Thorvildsen at the Umm an-Nar digging camp in 1961.

Fig. 8. The Ruler, Sheikh Shakbut Al Nahyan with Sheikh Muhammed bin Khalifa and followers visit the camp south of Al-Ain in January 1963. In front of them finds from the excavation of Hafit tombs.

Fig. 9. The camp in 1963, near the tombs to be excavated south of Al-Ain. In the background the silhouette of Jebel Hafit.

Fig. 10. Archaeologist Jørgen Lund during a briefing with Professor P.V. Glob (with head-cloth) in Bahrain before commencing excavations in Abu Dhabi in 1962.

Discovering Jemdet Nasr in Abu Dhabi 1970

After her campaigns in Abu Dhabi 1968-1970, Frifelt began in the summer of 1970 to analyse the finds from the first 25 tombs, excavated at Jebel Hafit by Moesgaard teams in 1961 and 1963. Her purpose was to give an overview of what the Danish expedition had discovered in Abu Dhabi as her contribution to the *Festschrift* that was being prepared on the occasion of Glob's 60th birthday on February the 20th 1971. In the process of this study she identified the enigmatic pottery from the tombs as Mesopotamian Jemdet Nasr ware. She gave the following description of the most significant pots (1971 p. 378):

"They are… covered with a dark plum-coloured paint, also under the base and inside, down the neck as far as the shoulder. Beside the pronounced carination between the upper and lower parts of the body, there is a second carination just below the neck, and below that the shoulder or upper part of the body is divided up into trapezoidal panels with designs.

One jar has apparently had a creamy slip applied all over, after which it has been covered in red paint, leaving every second panel on the shoulder in reserve outlined in black and filled out with cross-hatching in black or a stylized plant motif in red and black. Circling black bands frame this ornamental frieze….Closely related, almost identical jars are known from Ur, Jemdat Nasr, Tell Uqair, and Khafajah, where they are dated to the end of the Jemdat Nasr period. The Hafit pots are in fact Jemdat Nasr ware."

The first outline of a novel typological horizon, already well-established as a distinct chronological period in Mesopotamian archaeology, was hereby introduced. More documentation was provided by During Caspers (1971) who published Jemdet Nasr types in the shape of the previously mentioned two ceramic vessels found in tombs dug by amateurs on the northern plateau south of Al-Ain in 1962.

The excavation campaign 1971

The years following the 1962-63 excavation campaign witnessed new development in Abu Dhabi as oil production quickly improved the economy, and Sheikh Zayed Al Nahyan in 1966 became ruler (Mann 1969). The excavations in Abu Dhabi were resumed in 1968, and in 1971 the archaeologists returned to the Hafit tombs prompted by the identification of the Jemdet Nasr pots (Frifelt 1971).

The new development of Al-Ain also affected archaeology with an increased pressure on the environment where archaeological sites were endangered by construction. On the organizational side, the excavations were now planned under the auspices of Sheikh Tahnoon bin Mohammed, the Ruler's Representative in the Eastern Province of Abu Dhabi, and in cooperation with the Department of Antiquities & Tourism.

Bibby appointed Karen Frifelt (fig. 11), a former student of Glob with several years of experience from Bahrain, to be in charge of the Danish fieldwork in Abu Dhabi from 1968 and the following years (Blau 2004). In 1971 Frifelt was accompanied by a team of four archaeologists. Michael Beck had previous experience from Bahrain, whereas Niels Axel Boas, Steen Andersen and Bo Madsen brought their excavation experience from Denmark and other Nordic countries. The team was settled very comfortably in a house in the new public housing project near Al-Jimi west of Al-Ain.

During the 1971 campaign, 21 tombs were excavated and three ruined tombs recorded. In addition, surveys and field walks were conducted, and a large panel with ancient cup-marks was discovered. During the last month of the four month long season the team moved north of Al-Ain into the desert to Qarn Bint Saud. This isolated limestone outcrop was surveyed and a very rich early Iron Age tomb was excavated. Some Hafit type tombs were also identified on Qarn Bint Saud, as well as flint scatters, and inside a cave on the NE side of the outcrop rock art was discovered. Near Qarn Bint Saud an adjacent settlement with mudbrick remains was located (Madsen forthcoming b. Al Tikriti 2011b).

In 1971, it was decided to investigate some of the least damaged Hafit tombs more carefully. The purpose was to document the context of the earliest Bronze Age interments in relation to possible sec-

Fig. 11. Field Director Karen Frifelt and T.G. Bibby at Hili, spring 1969.

ondary burials. However, some rescue excavations became unavoidable. Contrary to the previous campaigns, it was decided by the team not to use any supplementary untrained labour. The excavations benefitted from more time and better practical conditions when compared with the previous campaigns. The team split in two, once in a while re-grouping, and during any one week two, or occasionally three, tombs were in the process of being excavated. The clearing of the outer periphery of the tomb was often done by the whole team when a resolute effort was necessary. Like in 1963, the team surveyed selected parts of the plains near the mound fields in order to locate contemporary settlements, but in vain. Some minor flint parts (mainly Neolithic) were found on the eastern side of Jebel Hafit and some larger flint scatters and flint outcrops east of Umm Ghafa approximately 20 km east of Jebel Hafit.

3. The landscape and the environment

The area of investigation is situated in the Eastern Province of Abu Dhabi south of the town of Al-Ain, north and east of Jebel Hafit (figs. 1, 4-5, 12-22). This prominent mountain stretches c. 29 km north-south, c. 5 km east-west, and reaches 1260 m above sea level. Jebel Hafit and lesser mountains form a series of anticlines that are part of the westernmost foreland and high plains of the Hajar Mountains of Oman (Aspinall & Hellyer 2004).

Towards the south and west of Jebel Hafit lie vast desert stretches of Al-Khattam which merges into the Rub al-Khali in the south-west. Extensive dune formations reach the western side of the mountain. To the north, a large complex of oases, with Al-Ain and Buraimi as the most important, is situated between the desert and the plain of Al Jaww at some 280-290 m above sea level. It is a most fertile area with fresh water occurring abundantly. The British traveller, Colonel S.B. Miles, visited the area in 1875 and noted: *"there is an apparent equality of property throughout; their dwellings being mostly palm leaf and mat huts, there being very few houses constructed of stone. They are not dependent on the annual rainfall, which is small, but are able to irrigate their fields by means of their felejes or aqueducts drawn from the hills, as well as from wells, water being plentiful and at no great depth."* (Miles 1919).

The oases were, in the era before cars, a hub with caravan routes leading across the desert to the Arabian Gulf coast or through the mountain canyons of Wadi al-Jizzi to the Gulf of Oman and the Arabian Sea. A network of trails along the mountains led north to the plain of al-Madam, to Dubai and south to Ibri. In early Islamic time the oases were described as the capital of the west as opposed to Sohar on the coast of the Indian Ocean (Williamson 1973).

The palm gardens today lie within the boundaries of the town of Al-Ain, which has engulfed part of the area where the Danish excavations took place.

The dominant feature of the plains and foothills around the mountain of Jebel Hafit are waterborne, alluvial deposits which have primarily formed since the Late Glacial. On the western side, dune sand covers these surfaces, to the east and north stretch vast plains of alluvial material, which has been transported westward from the neighbouring Oman Mountains. On the north-western side of Jebel Hafit, at Ain al-Fayda, the alluvial deposits from Jebel Hafit reach a depth of more than 15 m below the surface as observed in a lake deposit during construction work. In other deposits investigated southwest of Ain al-Fayda the existence of ancient lakes has been proven through the dating of freshwater snails living in these during prehistoric times, 7.000-4.000 BC (Gebel et al. 1989).

The mountain of Jebel Hafit has two narrow low ridges extending north like two arms towards Al-Ain (fig. 4). The *eastern mountain ridge* stretches like a 30-80 m high wall from the massif of Jebel Hafit almost eleven km north to the Al-Ain Oasis. Here a major wadi system runs east-west leading surplus water from Wadi Shik through Wadi Al-Ain. Towards the southern end of the ridge there is a pass through the ridge.

The *western mountain ridge* consists of a row of almost separate small mountain peaks interrupted by mainly east-west orientated valleys and escarpments (fig. 4).

The two km wide valley between these two ridges rises from c. 280 m to 320 m above sea level towards the south. It separates into two plateau landscapes: The *northern plateau* is mainly eroded surfaces appearing as varied intercut gravel hills whereas the *southern plateau* has a much more rocky and composite relief. In between the plateau and the mountain ridges, ran half a century ago, two major north-south going trails. Tombs were excavated along both ridges of Jebel Hafit as well as on the northern and southern plateau (fig. 4A, B, C, and D). The tombs appear as clusters or "mound fields" inside which smaller groups and alignments occur.

A further group of tombs were investigated on the eastern side of Jebel Hafit northwest of the village of Mazyad, 12-14 km south of Al-Ain (fig. 5). Here hundreds of stone built tombs could be observed either in small groups or as irregular alignments along the foothills, on terraces as well as on more isolated rocky hillocks. Other parts of the steeper eastern side of

Fig. 12. The eastern arm of Jebel Hafit and Jebel Hafit viewed from Al Murabba Fort, from NNE in 1959. This is where P.V. Glob and T.G. Bibby slept when they first visited Sheikh Zayed. In the foreground lies the Sultan Fortress, later to become part of the Al-Ain Museum. Next to the fortress, the Department of Antiquities was established in 1968-69.

Fig. 13. The gravel terraces with tomb clusters viewed from NW.

Fig. 14. The southern plateau viewed from the north.

Jebel Hafit were searched for graves but none were discovered.

Several archaeological teams have reconnoitred the areas outside these zones repeatedly, but failed to find any sign of tombs.

When the first archaeological surveys and excavations took place the land was still exploited in the ways of the traditional subsistence economy. Herds of goats and sheep were moved around for grazing. Firewood was collected for cooking, and occasionally travellers would pass by on camel back bringing their cargo for the suq in Al-Ain or passing by on their way to Dank and Ibri in the opposite direction.

The northern plateau and the valley were referred to as *Nudud al-Jahal* by Glob (1959b p. 237 and 239) and Bibby (1969). This is where Sheikh Zayed first showed them the large cairn fields. The name is, however, not a real place name. It does not appear on early maps and has not been recorded by Al Tikriti during his survey of the area (Al Tikriti 1981 and pers. comm.). It translates into *Mounds from the Age of Ignorance* and is rather a reference to the character of the area, which had plenty of grave mounds from the earliest time.

Fig. 15. The western arm of Jebel Hafit towards Al-Ain.

Fig. 16. The western arm of Jebel Hafit viewed from NW.

Fig. 17. Looking north from Jebel Hafit

Fig. 18. Jebel Hafit viewed from Jebel Aglah east of Hili.

Fig. 19. On way from Al-Ain to Mazyad following ancient paths along the Bronze Age tomb fields north of Jebel Hafit.

Fig. 20. Bedouin encampment east of Jebel Hafit.

Fig. 21. Goats grazing at the western arm of Jebel Hafit.

Fig. 22. On survey at eastern Jebel Hafit, a stop at the village of Mazyad 1963.

4. Danish investigations in the Jebel Hafit area

An overview of sites recorded in the field by Danish teams in the Hafit area from 1961 to 1971 is listed in the following section. The tombs are described according to the year of excavation and main topographic zone where they are situated. The site numbers correspond to the Oriental Department's archive system at Moesgaard Museum and are presented in this order. They are numbered in a discontinuous series as many other sites were excavated or surveyed during the same seasons in Umm an-Nar, Hili and Qarn Bint Saud and elsewhere in what is now the United Arab Emirates. Due to the lack of information on local place names, the excavations are related to the main topographic features. The tombs have in previous reports been listed respectively as Hafit graves, "mounds" or "burial cairns" (cairn is a Celtic word for a human-made pile of stones). The main areas with tombs are shown in figs. 4-5.

The investigations in 1961 suffered from a lack of proper maps in a scale usable for plotting archaeological sites, and due to the short campaign no sketch map was made in the field, so the five mounds excavated during this season can only be given a general location in the northern plateau (fig. 4A). In 1963 the excavated mounds were approximately placed on a map of the area (fig. 23). However, by scrutinizing the angles of the many excellent 6 × 6 cm field photographs it has been possible roughly to determine in which topographic area the tombs were located and to assess their altitude from later maps. Not till the campaign in 1971 were more detailed maps available in the field (figs. 24-26).

In 1961-62: 5 tombs were investigated, site numbers 1030-1034 (fig. 4A) (field numbers mound 1 to 5, cf. Frifelt 1971 p. 380-382).

In 1963: 20 tombs were investigated, site numbers 1035-1054, including one with two chambers (fig. 23) (field numbers mound 6 to 25, cf. Frifelt 1971 p. 380-382).

In 1971: 22 tombs were investigated, site numbers 1300-1321 (figs. 24-26) (field numbers mound 1, 1a-21). Additionally, three demolished tombs (1055.B, 1055.D and 1055.L) were recorded with their associated finds.

A total of 50 tombs were recorded, of which 47 were systematically excavated.

The excavation campaign 1961/62 (fig. 4A)

Tomb 1030, northern plateau, near the gypsum quarries at Al-Ain
Tomb 1031, northern plateau, near the gypsum quarries at Al-Ain
Tomb 1032, northern plateau, near the gypsum quarries at Al-Ain
Tomb 1033, northern plateau
Tomb 1034, northern plateau

The excavation campaign 1963 (fig. 23)

Tomb 1035, eastern ridge
Tomb 1036, eastern ridge
Tomb 1037, eastern ridge
Tomb 1038, eastern ridge
Tomb 1039, eastern ridge
Tomb 1040, eastern ridge
Tomb 1041, foothills of eastern ridge
Tomb 1042, foothills of eastern ridge
Tomb 1043, eastern ridge
Tomb 1044, eastern ridge
Tomb 1045, eastern ridge
Tomb 1046, western ridge
Tomb 1047, western ridge
Tomb 1048, western ridge
Tomb 1049, western ridge
Tomb 1050, western ridge
Tomb 1051, western ridge
Tomb 1052, western ridge
Tomb 1053, western ridge
Tomb 1054, western ridge

The excavation campaign 1971 (figs. 24-26)

Tomb 1055.B, western ridge
Tomb 1055.D, western ridge
Tomb 1055.L, western ridge
Tomb 1300, western ridge
Tomb 1301, western ridge
Tomb 1302, western ridge
Tomb 1303, western ridge
Tomb 1304, western ridge
Tomb 1305, western ridge
Tomb 1306, western ridge
Tomb 1307, western ridge
Tomb 1308, western ridge
Tomb 1309, western ridge
Tomb 1310, western ridge
Tomb 1311, western ridge
Tomb 1312, western ridge
Tomb 1313, southern plateau
Tomb 1314, southern plateau
Tomb 1315, southern plateau
Tomb 1316, southern plateau
Tomb 1317, Jebel Hafit east side, northwest of Mazyad
Tomb 1318, Jebel Hafit east side, northwest of Mazyad
Tomb 1319, Jebel Hafit east side, northwest of Mazyad
Tomb 1320, Jebel Hafit east side, northwest of Mazyad
Tomb 1321, Jebel Hafit east side, northwest of Mazyad

Fig. 23. Tombs excavated in 1963 along the west and east ridges of Jebel Hafit.

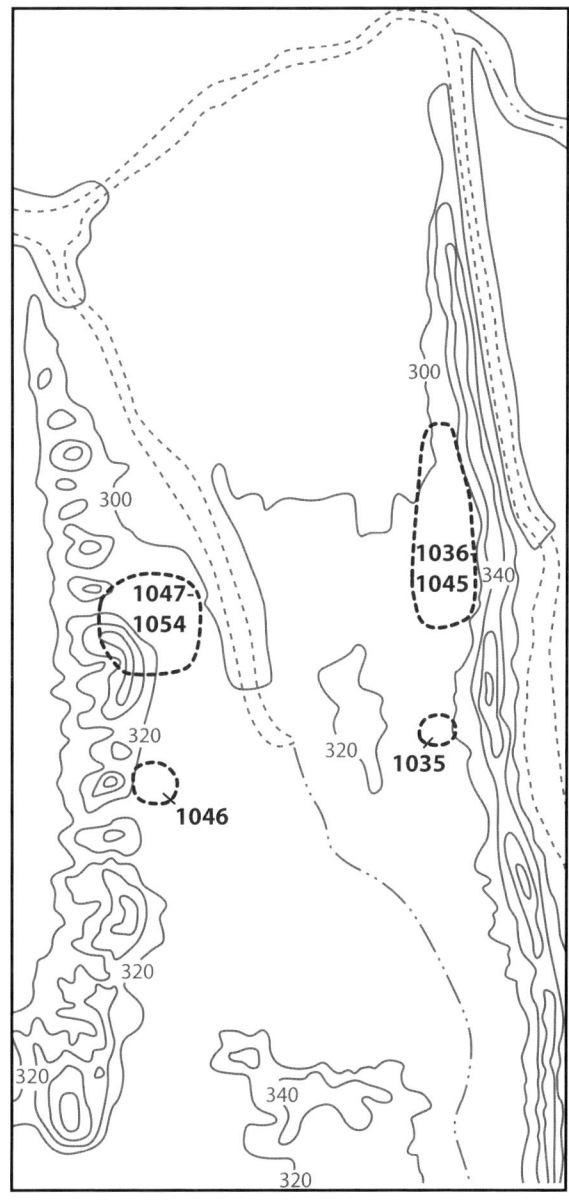

During the excavation campaigns, the areas around Jebel Hafit were surveyed. No settlements contemporary with the Hafit tombs were located, but on elevated terraces along the eastern side of the mountain three flint sites with no traces of structures, mudbrick or pottery were found some kilometers north of the village of Mazyad (sites no. 1057, 1058 and 1083). The lithic inventories were a mix of mainly debitage and very few tool fragments in both flint and flint-like rocks. No secure typological dating could be given to the artefacts, except that they may have elements of the Qatar C complex (Kapel 1967) as well as some possible Bronze Age knapping traces and historical gun flint production. The sites were later relocated and mapped by the French team, which found additional sites during their surveys (Cleuziou 1977 p. 9 and 36). Besides, a rock art site was located (site no. 1084).

Sites 1057, 1058 and 1083. Jebel Hafit eastern side. Settlements with scattered lithic artefacts. Probable date: Neolithic, Bronze Age, Historic. Surveyed in 1965 and 1971.

Site 1084. Rock art site situated at the northern end of the western ridge of Jebel Hafit, close to Al-Ain. A slightly inclined rock panel with numerous large cup marks, found in 1971 (fig. 27).

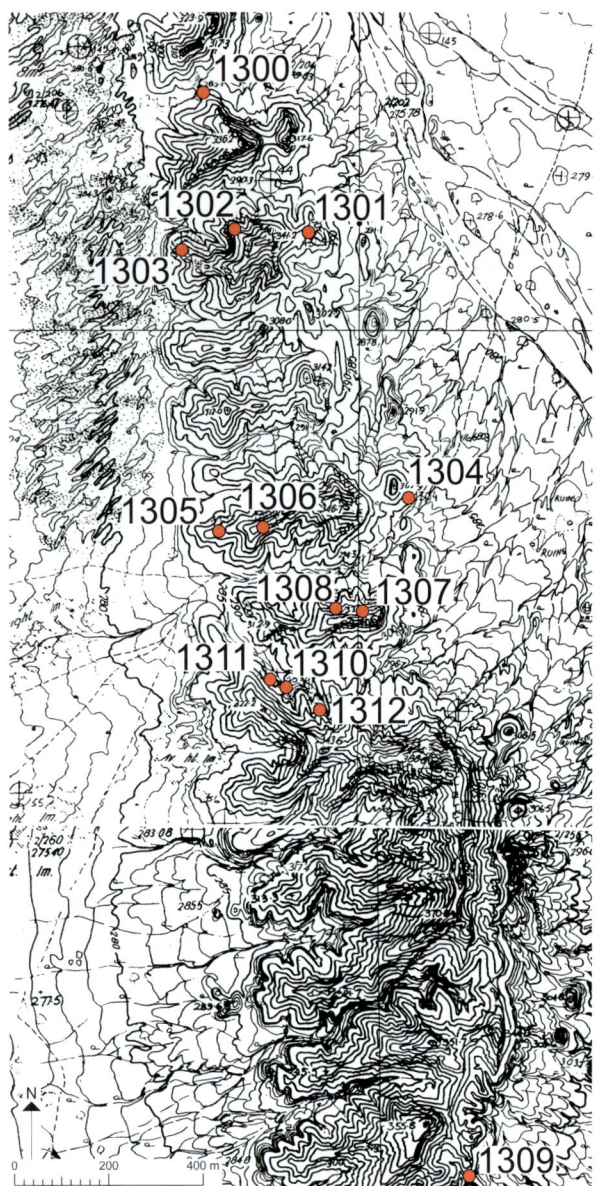

Fig. 24. Tombs excavated in 1971 along the west ridge of Jebel Hafit.

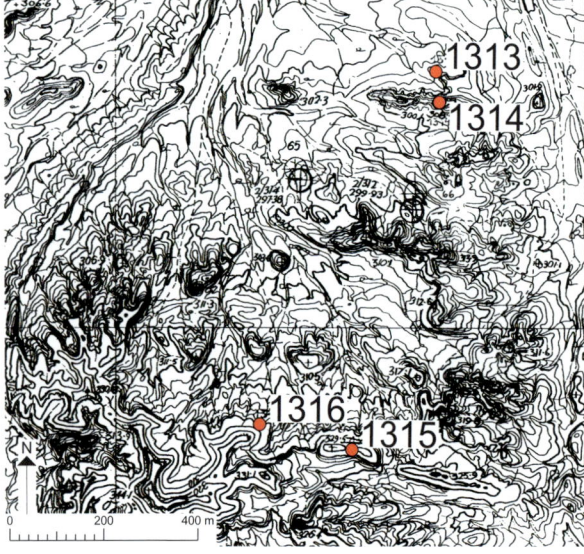

Fig. 26. Tombs excavated in 1971 on the east side of Jebel Hafit, northwest of Mazyad.

◂ Fig. 25. Tombs excavated in 1971 on the southern plateau between the west and east ridges of Jebel Hafit.

Fig. 27. Rock panel with cup marks, site 1084, looking N.

Fig. 28. Removing half of the ring wall of tomb 1035 in order to establish a cross section, a snapshot from the fieldwork in 1963.

5. Excavation procedures

The excavation methods varied during the ten years of fieldwork. In the two first campaigns the investigations were rapidly conducted rescue digs, and local labour was hired in order to speed up the work and save as much as possible from destruction (fig. 28). In 1971 all excavation work was conducted by the archaeologists without the assistance of unskilled labour.

In 1961-63 only black and white photographs were taken, but during the 1960s colour slide film and cameras became more accessible despite limited excavation budgets, so in 1971 two cameras were used for colour slides and black and white. Processing of films was done upon returning to Denmark, apart from some trial films that were mailed shortly after arriving to Abu Dhabi to check the quality.

Photography included, in most cases, an overview of the site before excavation commenced. This often included the surrounding landscape. In case of *in situ* finds, some interim photographs would be taken. As a principle, all structures were photographed after their excavation was finished.

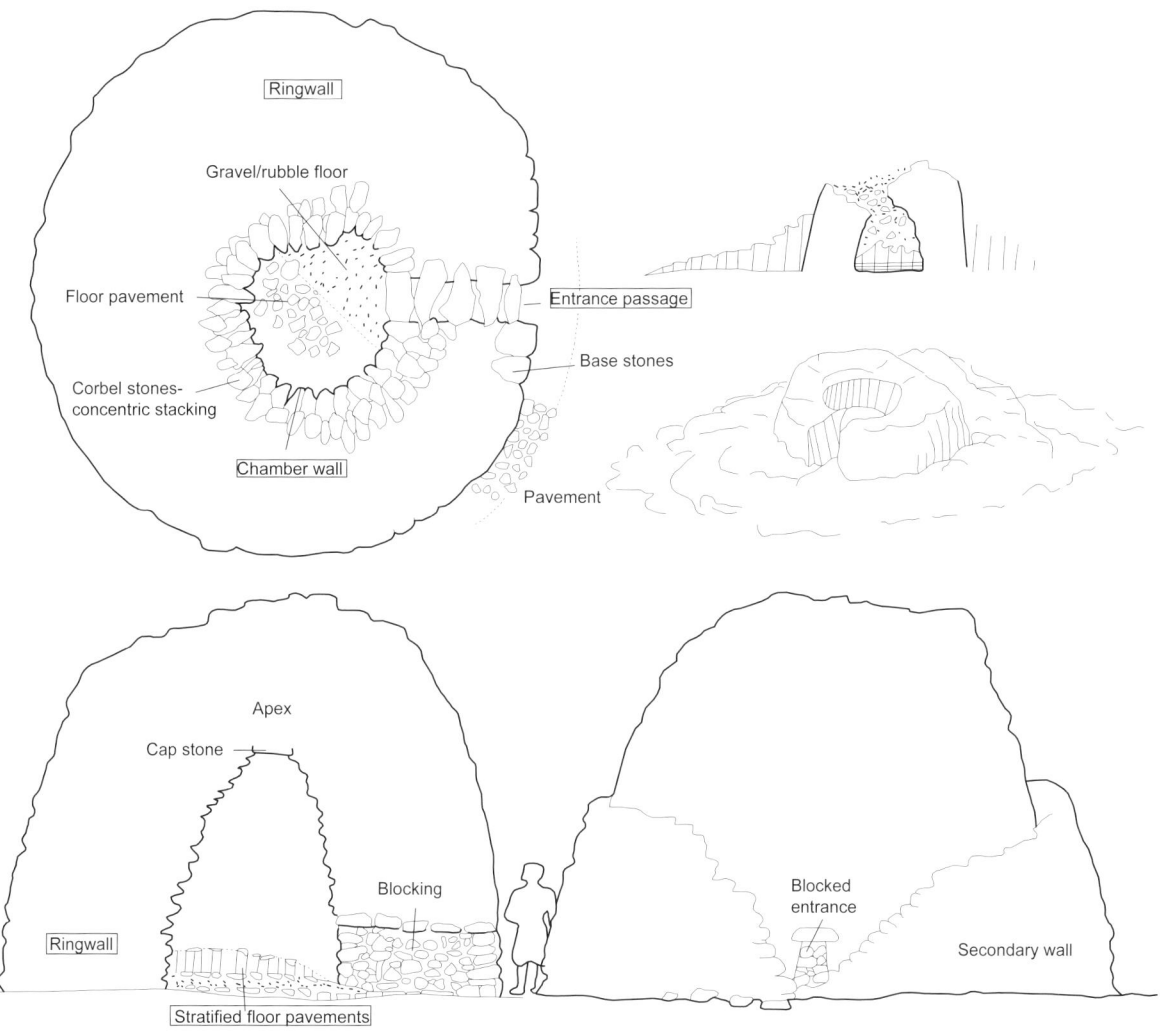

Fig. 29. The terminology applied to a Hafit type tomb (BM del).

When commencing excavation a local north/south grid system was established with the aid of strings stretched over the entire tomb in order to ensure that all finds and features could be mapped and spatially related to the structure. In the burial chambers the grid was projected down by plumb bob. The elevations of individual finds, stratigraphic cuts, layers or features were taken with a dumpy level using a temporary benchmark.

The standard procedure included mapping the overall tomb structure at a scale of 1:20, the grave chamber and entrance at a scale of 1:10. In some cases grave furniture and skeletal elements were drawn in more detail at a scale of 1:5.

The field drawings from 1971 were redrawn in black ink during the 1970s and some of them published by Frifelt (1971, 1975a, 1975b). The remaining plans were scanned and digitized in 2010-11 and appear for the first time in print in this volume. Some artefacts have previously been published by Frifelt (1971, 1975a-b, 1979, 1980) and a number of ceramic vessels were included in Waleed Al Tikriti's dissertation (1981) and in Sophie Méry's work (Méry 2000 p. 169-189).

In the following five chapters, the structural features of the tombs are described according to a basic terminology (fig. 29). The finds are listed, described and in most cases illustrated as line-drawings or photographs within the presentation of each tomb. The morphology and context of the finds are elaborated in chapter 11.

6. The mounds on the northern plateau

TOMB 1030

Location. The tomb was situated in the north-eastern part of the northern plateau (fig. 30). Tombs 1030-1034 formed part of 78 mounds positioned as linear groups and clusters on the central plateau. Tomb 1030 was the northernmost of the mounds selected for investigation. It was placed on level ground at the edge of a bluff estimated to be 295-300 m above sea level (cf. Frifelt 1971 p. 380: Cairn 1).

The excavation. The excavation of the tomb commenced in 1961 on New Year's Eve before the start of 1962. The investigation was carried out by the full team of three archaeologists with Knud Thorvildsen as field director and draughtsman. Vagn Kolstrup and Arne Thorsteinsson and six local men formed the rest of the excavation team (fig. 31). The mound initially looked like a heap of large stones as no structure, walls etc. were visible. It was cleared from the top and downwards-outwards by hand, hoe and trowel. After removing stone and rubble the remains of an unknown grave type appeared.

Structural remains. The tomb was damaged by stone robbing. What remained was preserved to a height of 0.75 to 0.90 m, but still gave a good indication of plan and construction and yielded important finds as well. The slightly oval mound measured 5.8 m north-south and 5.4 m east-west. It contained a grave chamber with an entrance passage facing SSE. The whole structure was built of stone in dry wall technique, i.e. without mortar.

The grave chamber was pear-shaped, 2 m long and 1.8 m wide at the entry side (fig. 32). The inside of the surrounding ring wall was constructed by larger (0.4 to 0.6 m) stones in the lower courses, predominantly in the western part. The building material used was specifically selected angular stone blocks and slabs with the flattest and most regular side facing the grave chamber. The inward inclination of the walls showed that the chamber had been roofed by a corbelled construction.

The chamber, or the lower preserved part of it, was filled with stones from the collapsed roof and chamber walls lying above a layer of fine sand. The sand covered a pavement of irregularly placed stone slabs measuring up to 0.2 × 0.3 m (figs. 32-33). The pavement was disturbed or removed in an area along the chamber wall towards the entrance.

The field photographs show that the pavement was constructed above a more gravelly layer with scattered small stones and rubble creating a level surface for the floor.

The entrance passage was a continuation of the chamber's longitudinal axis and had a length of c. 2 m and a width of 0.4 m, when measured in the middle of the entrance. It widened slightly towards the chamber as well as towards the outer wall. The entrance was constructed predominantly of regular slab-like blocks in contrast to the inner ring wall that was made from smaller stones with less overlap. The entrance was blocked by smaller stones carefully aligned with the inner and outer faces of the ring wall (fig. 34).

The ring wall was preserved at the east side to a height of 4 or 5 courses. The excavators noted that some of the preserved walling was removed during the excavation before the shape of the construction was realized. The lowest course of the ring wall's exterior face followed an almost circular line. It was made from larger, rather angular un-worked blocks of up to 0.7 × 0.6 × 0.3 m. The stacking of the stones in the exterior wall above the large blocks appeared random (fig. 35).

Fig. 30. Tomb 1030 looking NE.

Fig. 31. Excavation in progress.

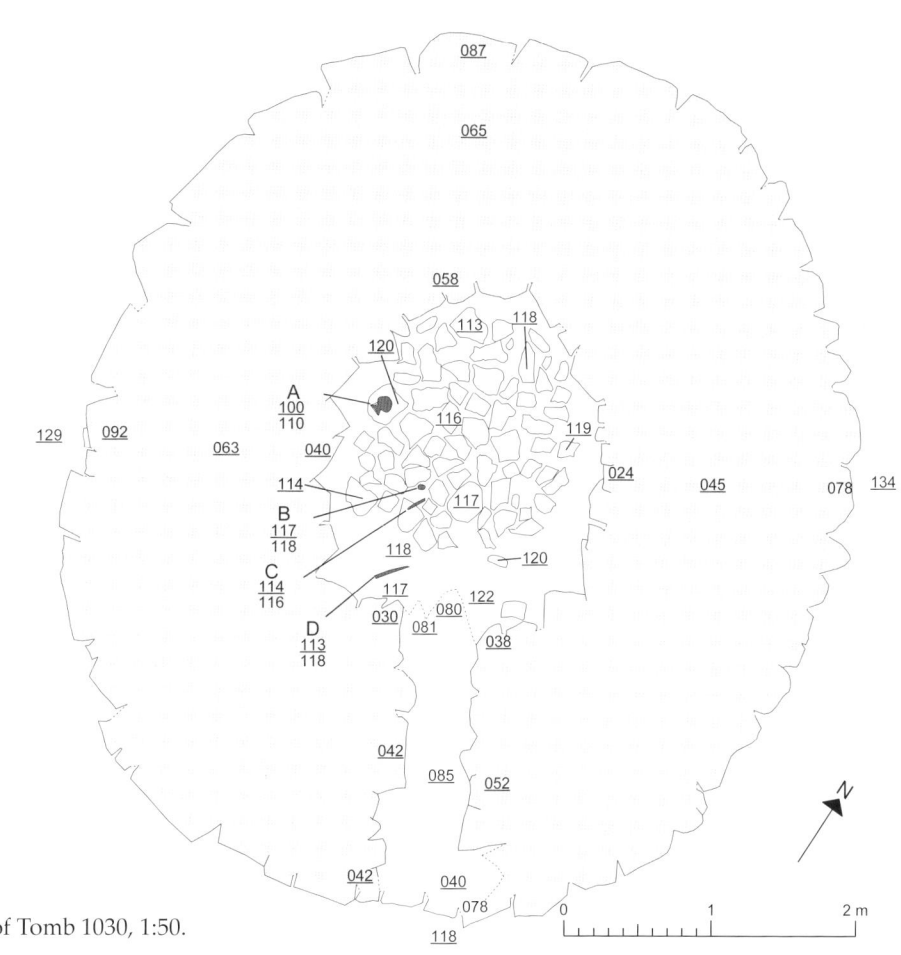

Fig. 32. Plan of Tomb 1030, 1:50.

Fig. 33. The floor pavement with pottery vessel, shell and two copper pins, viewed from the entrance passage.

Fig. 34. The blocked entrance viewed from the chamber with shell and two copper pins on the floor.

Fig. 35. The excavated tomb looking S.

Finds. A ceramic vessel and two copper pins were found in the sand just above the pavement (figs. 32-34). The vessel was found on its side in the western part of the chamber a few centimetres above one of the floor's stone slabs. The two pins and a cowry shell were closer to the entrance, the pins in an oblique position, and one of them, 1030.D, in a disturbed part of the floor. No human skeletal remains were noted, but the finds must indicate at least one primary burial.

1030.A: Biconical ceramic vessel with carinated shoulder of Jemdet Nasr type, in yellow-brown sand-tempered ware, painted in plum-red with a cream-coloured slip confined to the shoulder, where in two panels it is the background for oblique black lines, while two other panels may have had black cross-hatching; the panels are bordered by vertical black bands (Frifelt 1971 p. 378) (fig. 36).

1030.B: Cowry shell modified by grinding (*Cypraea Annulus*, Reese 1991) (fig. 37).

1030.C: Copper pin, with a round cross section, 10.8 cm long (fig. 38).

1030.D: Copper pin or very large needle with an oval hole, 24.1 cm long (fig. 39).

Fig. 36a. Pottery vessel with polychrome painting, 1030.A, 1:1.

Fig. 36b. Pottery vessel with polychrome painting, horizontally hatched = red, white = cream, black = black, 1030.A, 1:1

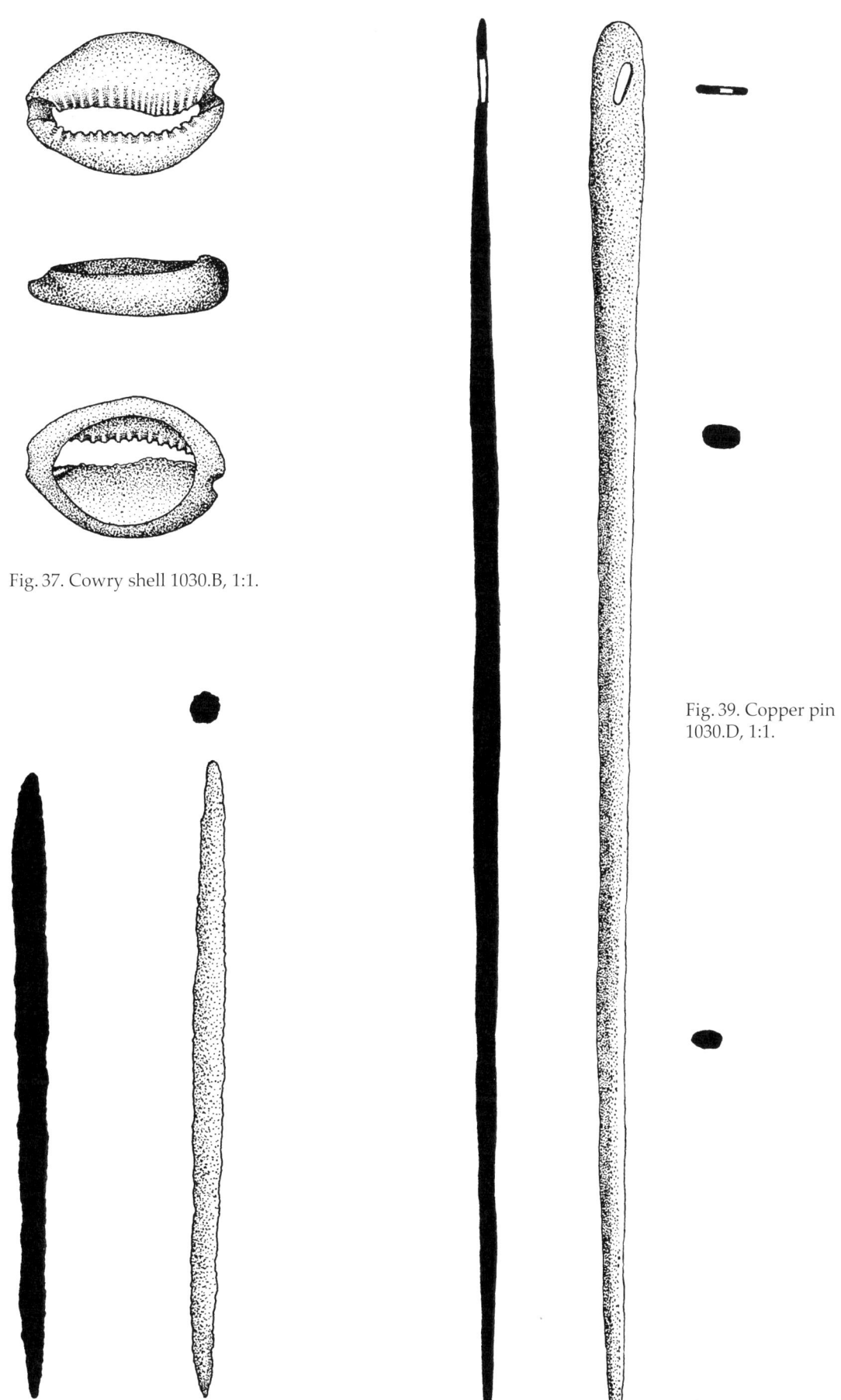

Fig. 37. Cowry shell 1030.B, 1:1.

Fig. 38. Copper pin 1030.C, 1:1.

Fig. 39. Copper pin 1030.D, 1:1.

TOMB 1031

Location. The tomb was situated on the northern plateau 125 m south of mound 1030 at an altitude of close to 300 m above sea level. It was placed on even ground next to a slope (fig. 40) (cf. Frifelt 1971 p. 381: Cairn 2).

The excavation. Vagn Kolstrup was in charge of the excavation, which was carried out in 1962. The top and periphery of the mound were cleared from loose stones and rubble by hand and hoes (fig. 41). The entrance and chamber area were excavated with trowels.

Structural remains. The tomb contained a central chamber and entry passage leading from the SSE side (fig. 42). The grave had been damaged by stone removal and was preserved to a height of 1.2-1.3 m. The oval asymmetrical chamber was aligned on the same axis as the direction of the entrance passage. Its length was 2.4 m with a width of 2.2 m. The chamber wall had a gradual inwards inclination of c. 0.5 m for the lower first meter, clearly indicating a corbelled construction (figs. 43-44). In the northern part of the central chamber remains of a floor pavement survived that was made of stone slabs of varied size, the largest measuring 0.40 × 0.25 m (fig. 45).

The entrance passage had a length of 1.8 m and a width of 0.7 m, slightly tapering towards the outside. The floor in the passageway was constructed from irregular stones set 0.2 m higher than the chamber floor. The entrance passage was filled with stones. Two courses of very regular blocks had been laid in line to seal and most likely hide the entrance.

The mound had an oval plan with the largest diameter close to 6 m. The external wall face was somewhat irregularly built. Part of the western wall had collapsed. The building material consisted of mainly rounded to angular blocks up to 0.6 m size with no evidence of having been shaped. The ring wall around the chamber, c. 1.8 m thick, seemed to be constructed by four to five concentric lines of stone. These were also rather haphazardly stacked.

Finds. One group of finds were found directly on the chamber floor. These comprised of two pottery vessels, badly preserved human remains including part of a cranium and a few scattered bone fragments found in the south-eastern side of the chamber.

A secondary burial (or re-burial) was found in the upper part of the entrance passage, c. 0.5 m above the floor, and close to the opening, just inside the sealing stones and the line of the outer wall face (fig. 44). The skeletal remains consisted of very badly preserved bones, a cranium/calvaria and un-specified limb bones. These bones were clearly disarticulated and heaped around the cranium.

1031.A: Biconical ceramic vessel with carinated shoulder of Jemdet Nasr type, in grey-yellow sand-tempered ware, plum-red paint on neck and body and faint traces of vertical black bands on the shoulder (fig. 46).
1031.B: Small ovoid jar with pointed base of Jemdet Nasr type, reddish-brown ware tempered with coarse sand (fig. 47).
1031.C: Charcoal found close to ceramic vessel 1031.A.
1031.D: Fragments of cranium.
1031.E: Secondary burial.

Fig. 40. Tomb 1031 looking S.

Fig. 41. Clearing the ring wall for disturbed material.

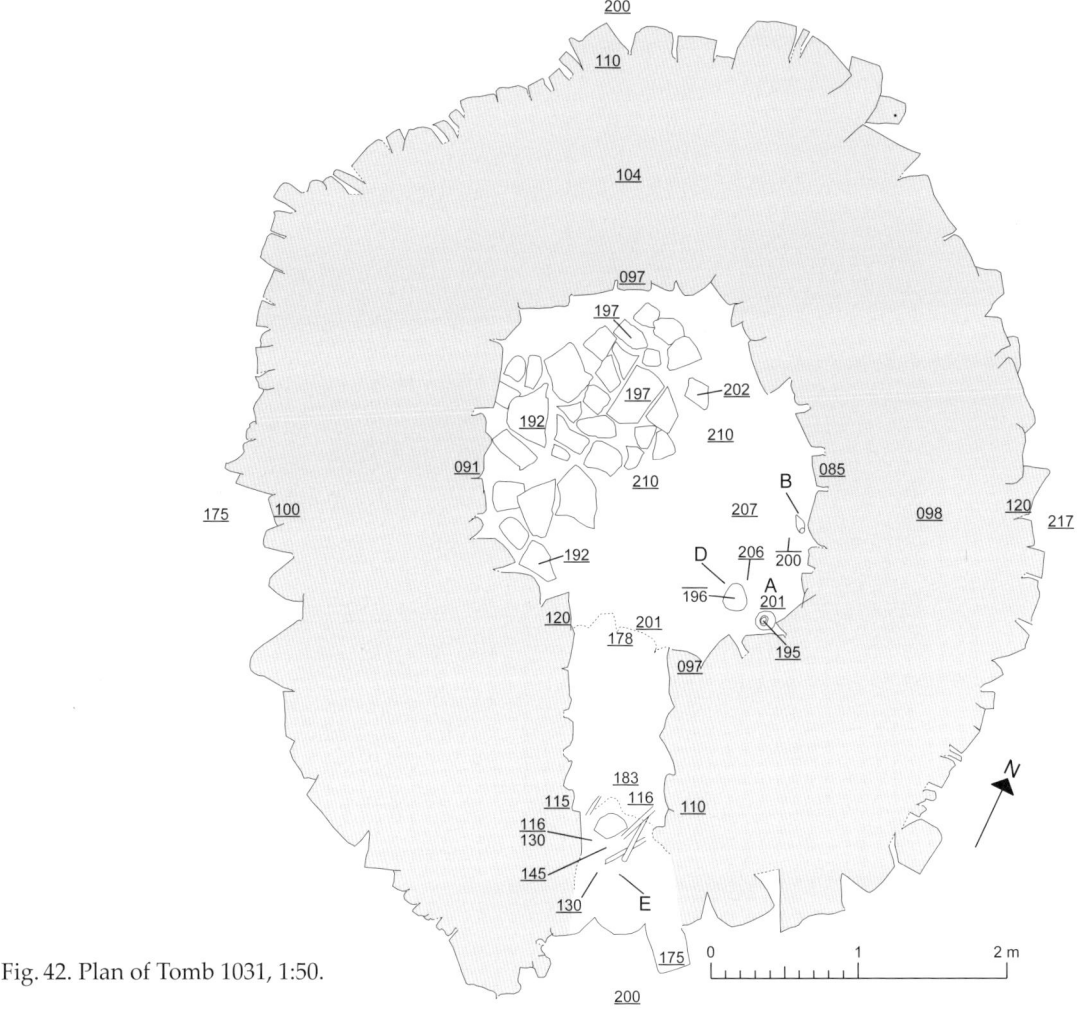

Fig. 42. Plan of Tomb 1031, 1:50.

Fig. 43. The chamber with impression of cranium 1031.D and vessel 1031.A.

Fig. 44. The excavated chamber and entrance passage.

Fig. 45. The entrance blocking aligned with the outer ring wall.

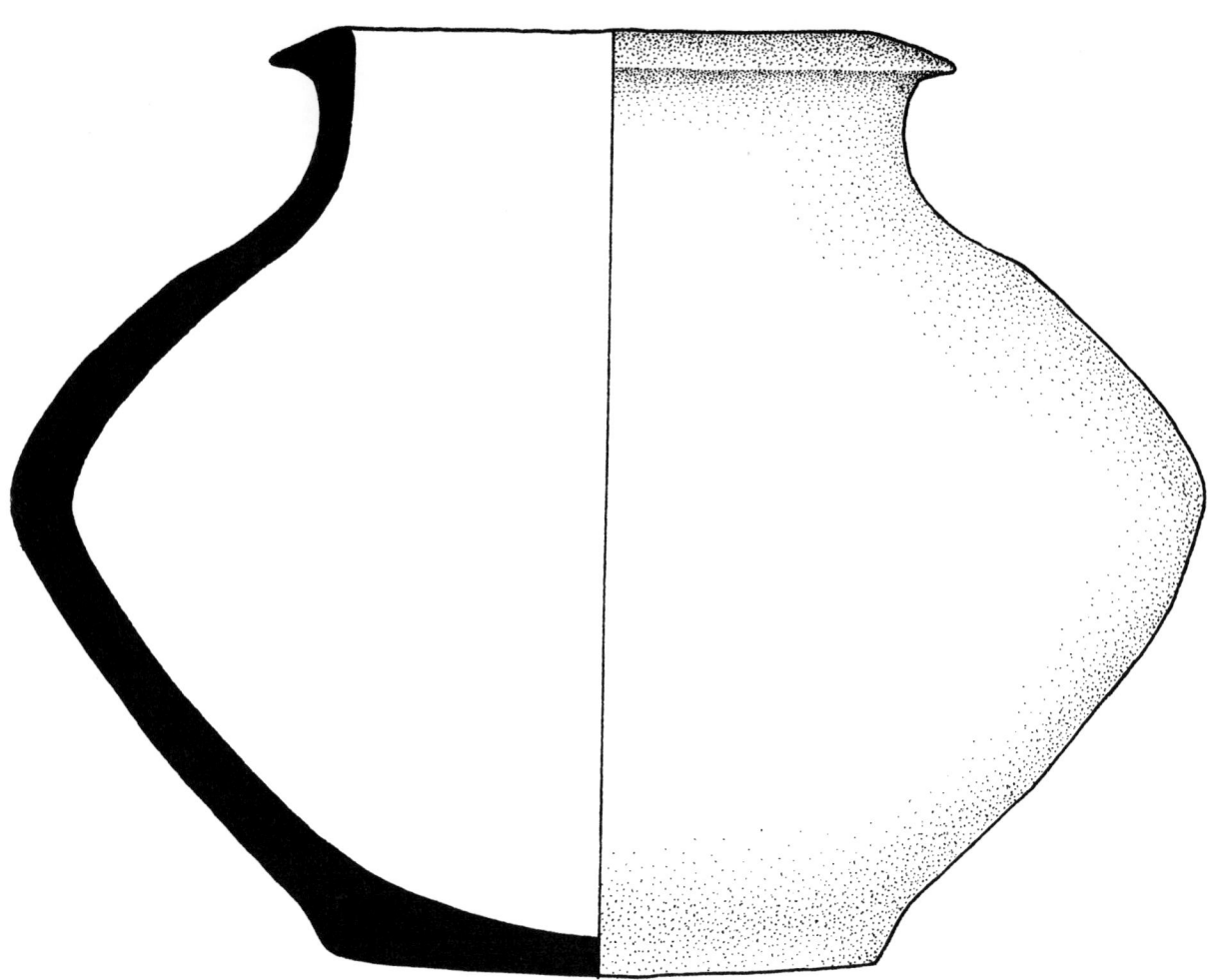

Fig. 46. Pottery vessel with traces of polychrome painting 1031.A, 1:1.

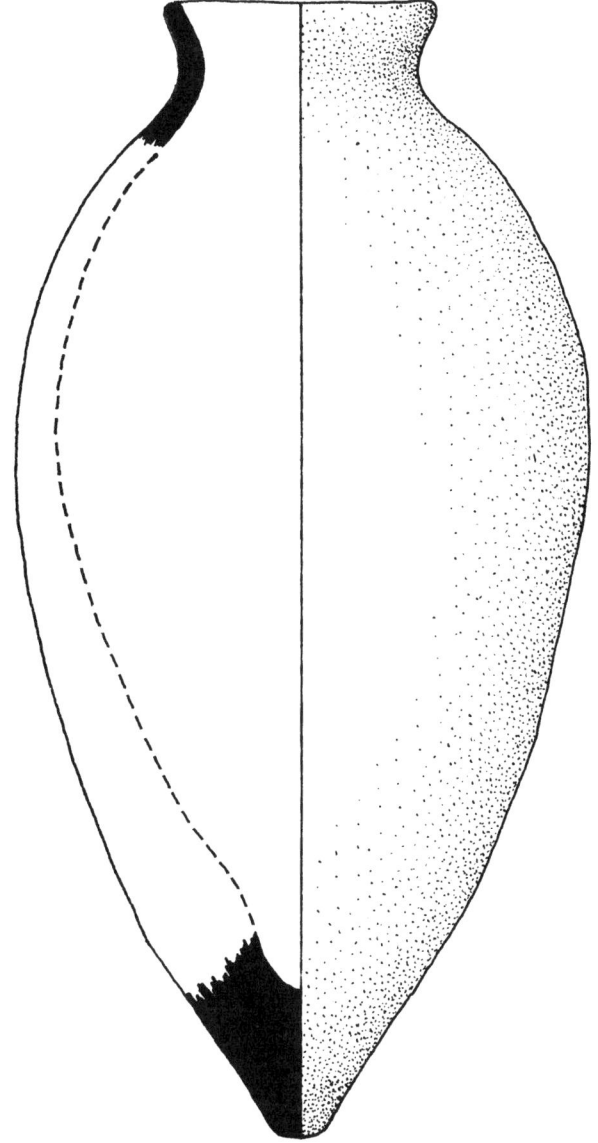

Fig. 47. Pottery vessel 1031.B, 1:1.

TOMB 1032

Topographic position. The tomb was situated in the middle of the alignment of mounds and groups of mounds on the northern plateau, being itself part of the largest group at an altitude of c. 300 m above sea level (figs. 48-49) (cf. Frifelt 1971 p. 381: Cairn 3).

The excavation. Arne Thorsteinsson was in charge of the excavation carried out in 1962. All loose stone and rubble were removed and after locating the outer face of the ring wall and the central chamber, the latter and the entrance passage were emptied of collapsed stones, while the fill in the grave area was excavated with trowel.

Structural remains. Before excavation Tomb 1032 appeared as a low mound with a sunken centre, 0.75 m high and with a diameter of 7 m (fig. 50). This mound had suffered from intense stone quarrying that had removed most of the four concentric stone lines that made up the ring wall around the chamber. Only a couple of meters of the external wall face were present on the eastern side indicating a diameter of around 6 m for the original tomb (fig. 51).

The excavation revealed a central chamber with a short entrance from the SSE side of the tomb (fig. 52). The almost circular chamber, with a diameter of 1.8-2 m, was placed in line with the entrance passage. The angled wall of the chamber indicated that the grave originally had a corbelled roof. On the western side a stone paved floor was preserved and was constructed from regular stone slabs of varied size up to 0.3 × 0.3 m.

The surrounding ring wall consisted of un-worked stones of different sizes. In the entrance area and in front of it the stone robbers had left large and flat stones with a length up to 0.4 to 0.5 m. Most probably these were cap-stones from the entrance and some stones from the outer wall face that were pulled out from the construction by stone robbers to be loaded later onto a truck.

The entrance passage was 0.5 m wide. It had a preserved length of 1 m but would have been longer before the monument was plundered for stone.

Finds. The chamber was empty except for a bead found at a high level in the secondary fill.

1032.A: Small, white, barrel- or ring-shaped bead of shell, L 3.4 mm, D 4.9 mm (fig. 53).

Fig. 48. Tomb 1032, number two from left, looking E.

Fig. 49. A look towards the south from Tomb 1032.

Fig. 50. The tomb before excavation.

Fig. 51. The tomb after excavation.

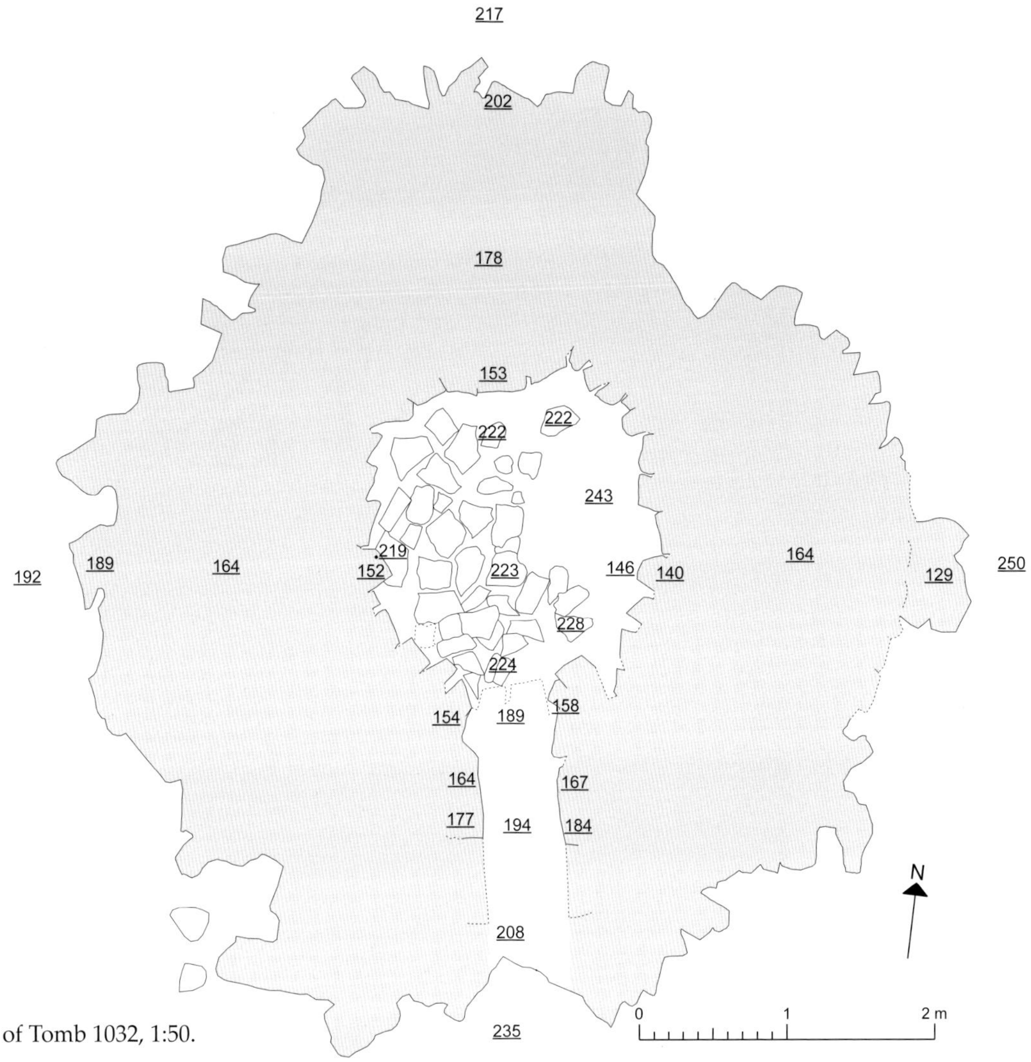

Fig. 52. Plan of Tomb 1032, 1:50.

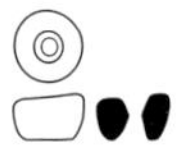

Fig. 53. Bead of shell 1032.A, 1:1.

54

TOMB 1033

Location. The tomb was situated about 20 m east-northeast of Tomb 1032 and was part of the same large group of mounds (figs. 54-55) (cf. Frifelt 1971 p. 381: Cairn 4).

The excavation. The tomb was excavated in 1962 by Vagn Kolstrup. Like the previous investigations all loose stone and rubble were removed after locating the outer face of the ring wall and the central chamber. The chamber and the entrance passage were carefully emptied of stone collapse (fig. 56). The fill in the chamber extended to a lower level and was excavated by trowel in horizontal layers.

Structural remains. In most respects Tomb 1033 looked like the previous examined graves, with a ring wall around a central chamber and an entrance passage oriented to the SSE (fig. 57).

The mound was heavily damaged by stone quarrying mainly focused on the external wall and extending inwards but some quarrying had also taken place at the top of the mound. It appeared that part of the chamber wall was still standing to a considerable height (fig. 58). The large chamber had an oval to asymmetrical plan orientated in the same axis as the entrance passage. It measured 2.3 m in length and 1.9 m in width. The western chamber wall was preserved to a height of c. 1.5 m. The chamber wall was almost vertical showing that the corbelling started high up and indicating a taller chamber construction than in the previous graves. Thorvildsen remarked in his field notes "that the grave chamber must have stood with a tall pointed corbelling". The lowest stone course of the wall was made from larger selected blocks of a rounded-flat shape up to 0.6 m wide. No traces of floor pavement were observed.

Due to the damage to the outside of the grave the full length of the entrance passage could not be observed; what was left had a length of 1.2 m, a width of 0.6 m and a height of c. 0.7 m. The chamber-entrance interface was carefully made of large, but un-worked blocks with an unusually large lintel measuring 0.8 × 0.4 × 0.2 m (fig. 59). The opening to the chamber was thus quite wide compared to the other tombs.

No definite remains of the outer ring wall face were observed. The outer diameter was possibly 6 m.

Finds. 1033.A: Bowl of grey softstone decorated with two rows of dotted circles above bunches of oblique lines (fig. 60). It was found in the northern end of the chamber, in a secondary position, 0.8 m above the chamber floor, which tallies with its typological dating to the Wadi Suq period.

No skeletal remains were noted.

Fig. 54. Tomb 1033 looking SE with the eastern ridge in the background.

Fig. 55. The tomb before excavation.

Fig. 56. The entrance side of the tomb after excavation.

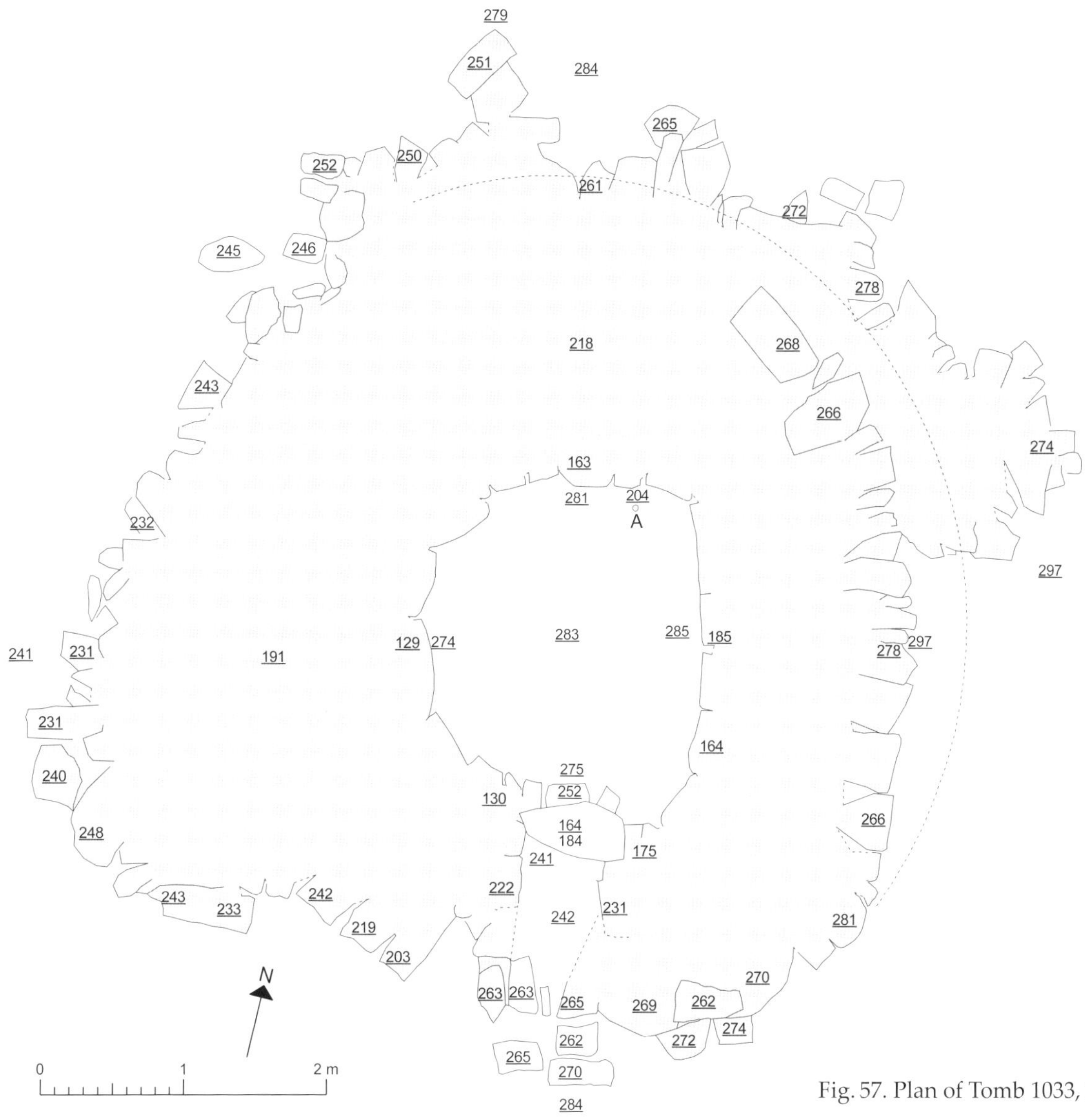

Fig. 57. Plan of Tomb 1033, 1:50.

Fig. 58. A look into the excavated chamber with remains of the corbelled wall.

57

Fig. 59. The innermost cap-stone in the entrance passage of Tomb 1033.

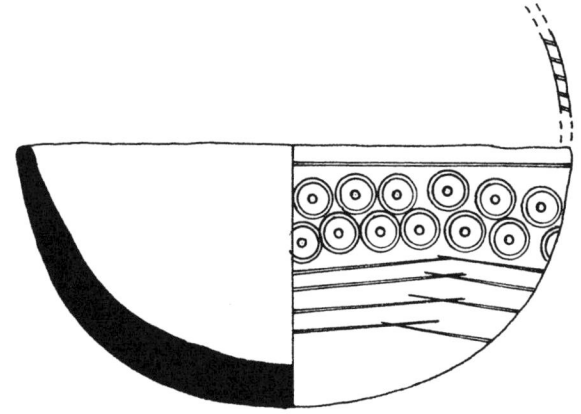

Fig. 60. Softstone vessel 1033.A, 1:1.

TOMB 1034

Location. The grave mound was placed c. 200 m west of Tombs 1032 and 1033 on a level part of the gravel plateau at an estimated altitude of 300-315 m above sea level (figs. 61-62) (cf. Frifelt 1971 p. 381: Cairn 5).

The excavation. The tomb was excavated in 1962 under the direction of Arne Thorsteinsson. It followed the procedures of the previous excavations, where the robust parts of the tomb were cleared by hoes and by hand. The lower parts of the chamber and entrance were excavated by trowels and brushes. As time was limited only the chamber and entrance area and the adjacent outer wall face were fully excavated and mapped. The remaining mound was partially cleared and the outline of the disturbed ring wall recorded.

Structural remains. The grave mound contained a large central chamber and an entrance passage oriented towards the south (fig. 63). The chamber was damaged by stone robbing, it resembled the chamber in Tomb 1033 and had an oval plan forming a continuation of the entrance. The eastern chamber wall was almost straight and its length was 2.4 m, and the maximum width of the chamber was 2.2 m. The wall still stood to a height of 1.4 m above the floor (fig. 64). The floor was un-paved or any paving had been removed by secondary activities.

The entrance passage was 0.6 m wide and seemed to have been 1.8 m long. The passage wall was preserved for about 0.8 m. Further towards the entry there was just a suggestion of the passageway and remains of a blocking door at the entrance. The out-

Fig. 61. Tomb 1034 looking NNW.

Fig. 62. Tomb 1034 before excavation.

ermost lowest course indicates an almost unbroken stone line, possibly with three secondary stones filling the entrance. There is though no secure evidence of a secondary wall.

The exterior ring wall at the entry-side measured 1.8 m in thickness and indicated a mound diameter of c. 6 m (fig. 65). The ring wall was constructed from medium (c. 0.4 m) to small un-worked stones with some elongated blocks placed in the corbelled inner wall face. The lowest course of stones in the outer wall face consisted, at least in the investigated area, of selected smaller blocks measuring some 0.3 × 0.3 m.

Finds. The only find was part of a thin-walled pottery vessel lying in an apparently secondary level, 0.10-0.15 m above the floor. A few potsherds were found higher up in the disturbed layers from the robbing of the grave.

1034.A: Fragmented pottery vessel (fig. 66) with remnants of wavy hatched black bands on the shoulder, in Black on Red-buff sandy ware, exfoliating, badly preserved, comparable to pottery from the Umm an-Nar settlement (Frifelt 1991 fig. 16 and p. 127) and Hili (Méry 2000 fig. 87).

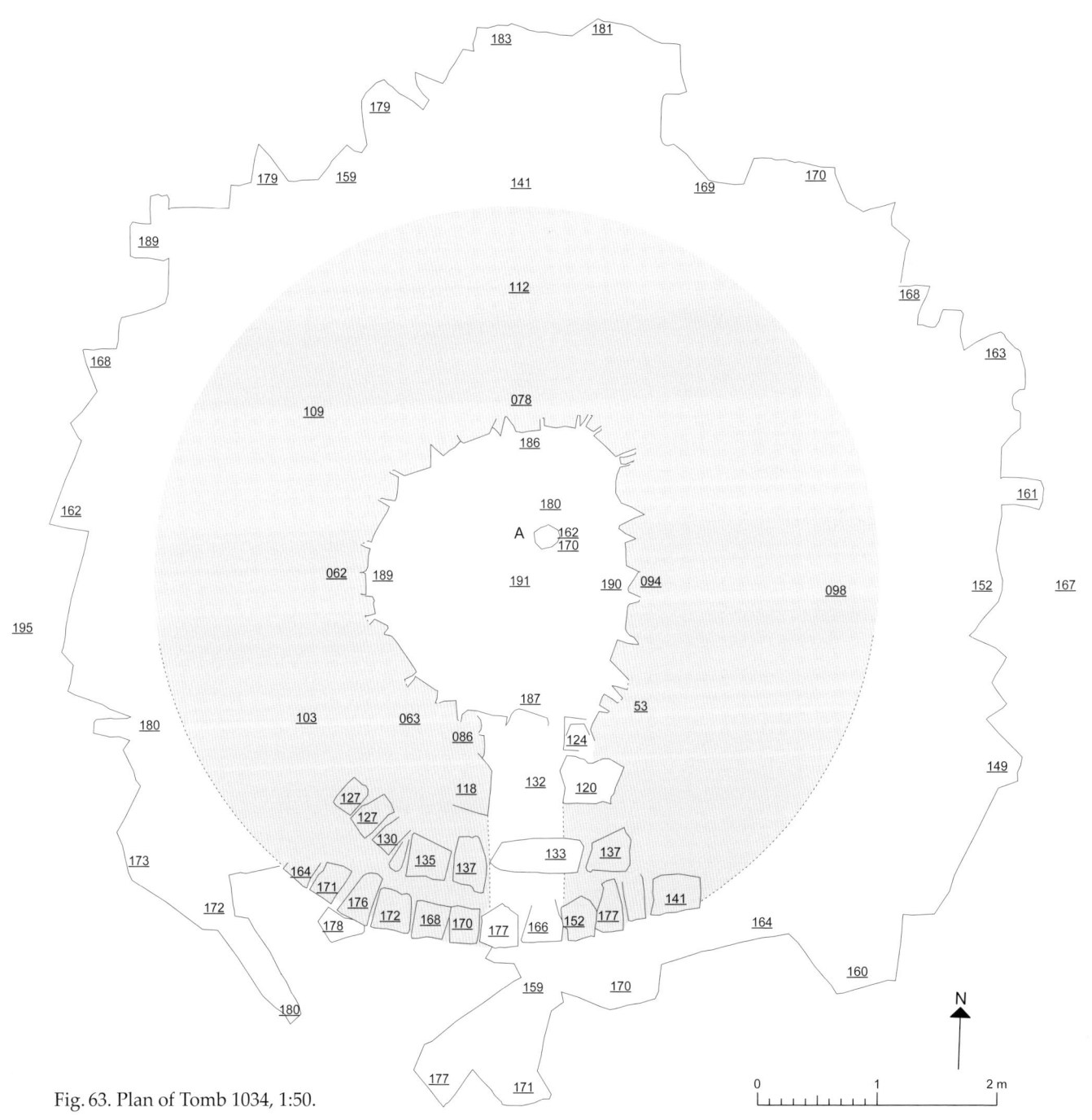

Fig. 63. Plan of Tomb 1034, 1:50.

Fig. 64. Preserved courses of corbelled construction in the chamber.

Fig. 65. Remains of ring wall on the NE-side.

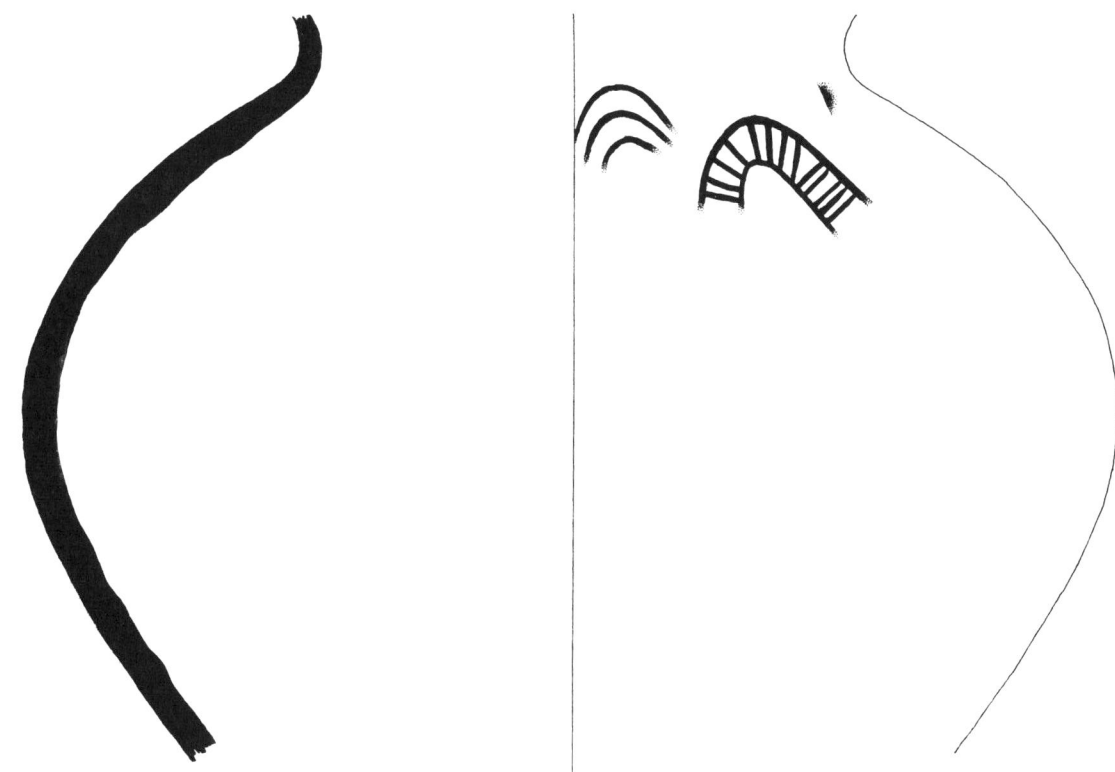

Fig. 66. Umm an-Nar period ceramic vessel 1034.A, 2:3.

Fig. 67. Tomb 1035 looking E.

7. The mounds along the eastern mountain ridge

TOMB 1035

Location. The tomb was lying at the west foot of the eastern ridge approximately in the middle of the valley. The estimated altitude is 295-300 m above sea level (fig. 67).

The excavation. Tomb 1035 was investigated as the first of 20 mounds during the second excavation campaign in the area south of Al-Ain in January 1963. The excavation of this mound was led by Jens Aarup Jensen, assisted by Vagn Kolstrup and Jørgen Lund. The team also comprised of four local workers. What remained of the grave was cleared with hoes, trowels and brushes. It was decided to remove most of the southern half and establish a cross section in order to investigate the ring wall construction in section as well as in plan (fig. 28).

Structural remains. The tomb appeared as a conical mound of stones and rubble and the outer stone construction had recently been removed by stone quarrying. The chamber was breached from the top. The entrance pointing to the south was visible (fig. 68).

In the chamber area the height was preserved to almost two meters above the floor (fig. 69). The slightly oval chamber was orientated in line with the entrance passage. It had a length of 2.6 m and a width of 2.2 m (fig. 70).

The entrance passage measured 2.5 m. The width at floor level was 0.5 m and the height, measured to the underside of the three preserved cap-stones, was 1.35 m. At the ceiling, the passage narrowed in to 0.25 m and was therefore not fully corbelled. The lintel-stones consisted of large, flat slabs, the largest measuring 1.05 × 0.55 × 0.25 m. The passage was densely packed with smaller stones measuring 0.15-0.30 m.

The ring wall was estimated to have had an outer diameter of c. 8 m, although stones in secondary position were spread out in a wider scatter. The adjacent terrain dropped away approximately one meter west of the chamber which probably explains the oval outline of the deflated mound. The ring wall was made from irregular flattish stones up to a size of half a meter.

Finds. The only finds consisted of small scattered fragments of human bone including some cranial fragments found in the fill above the disturbed chamber floor.

Fig. 68. Tomb 1035 looking N.

Fig. 69. Tomb 1035 looking N.

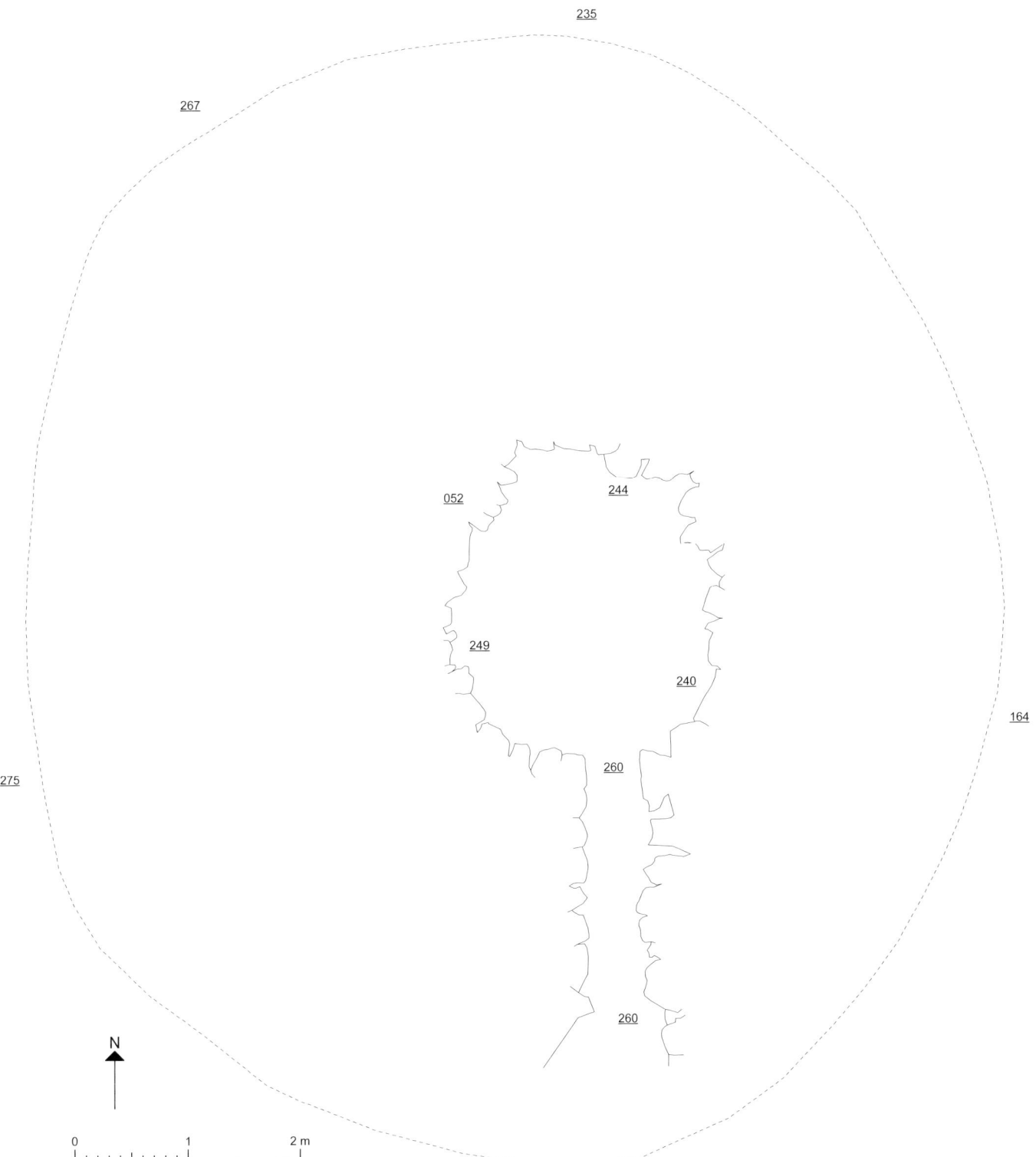

Fig. 70. Plan of Tomb 1035, 1:50.

TOMB 1036

Location. The mound was located on the western foothills of the eastern mountain ridge at an estimated altitude of 300-310 m above sea level. It was situated on a rocky terrace next to Tomb 1037 (figs. 71-72) (cf. Frifelt 1971 p. 381: Cairn 7).

The excavation. The excavation in 1963 was led by Jørgen Lund. The remaining mound surface was cleared from loose blocks and rubble. From the robber's hole in the top, the inner part of the construction was explored. The last part of the chamber area was carefully excavated by trowel and brushes. The entrance passage was only partially excavated.

Structural remains. The mound contained a central chamber surrounded by a ring wall with an entrance passage oriented towards the south (fig. 73). The structure was very damaged by the removal of stones; seven to eight courses were preserved of the ring wall, all were rather large rounded blocks to judge from the one photo. At the highest point it reached 1.3 m above the chamber floor. The chamber was round to pear-shaped, 2 m long and 2.2 m wide, and formed a continuation of the entrance passage. The latter was 1.3 m long, but had probably been longer with a height at the chamber of 1.1 m. No remains of a stone pavement were observed.

The damaged mound had a diameter of c. 7 m. The external diameter of the ring wall could not be determined with certainty, but must have been smaller. The building material used were rounded stone blocks of varying size.

Finds. Beside a few splinters of skeletal material from the chamber and entrance area, the only find was a large flint artefact.

1036.A: Knife from a large flint blade with lateral retouch along the edges, 10.9 cm long (fig. 74).
1036.B: Skeletal fragments.

Fig. 71. Tomb 1036 (foreground left) and 1037 looking W.

Fig. 72. Tomb 1036 (right) and 1037 looking E.

Fig. 73. Plan of Tomb 1036, 1:50.

67

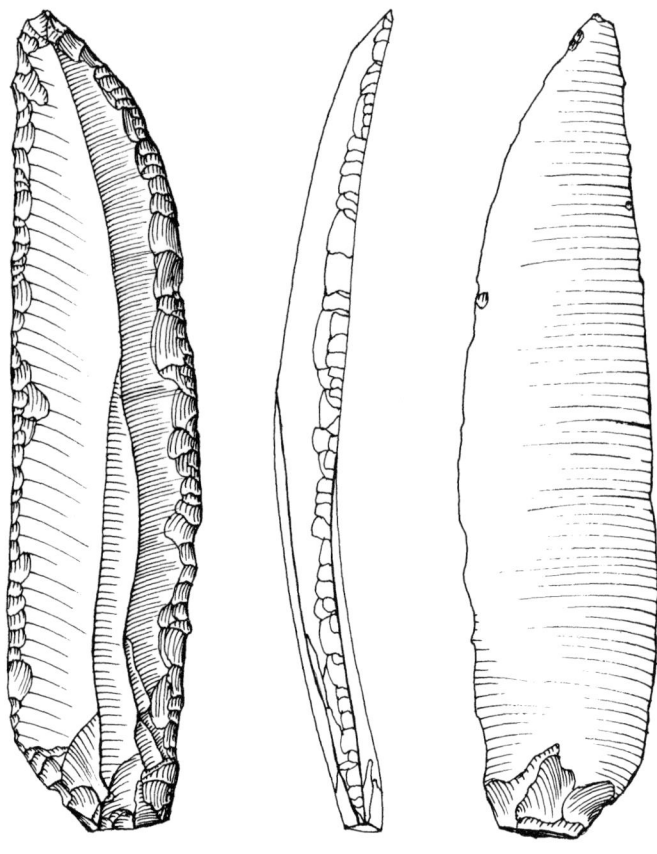

Fig. 74. Knife from retouched flint blade 1036.A, 1:1.

TOMB 1037

Location. This tomb was located on the western foothills of the eastern mountain ridge, 8 m north of Tomb 1036 (figs. 71-72) (cf. Frifelt 1971 p. 381: Cairn 8).

The excavation. The tomb was excavated in 1963. All rubble and loose blocks were cleared from the surface of the heavily damaged grave in order to locate the chamber and an entrance passage. The remaining fill in the chamber was carefully excavated with trowels and brushes.

Structural remains. The excavation recovered the remains of a round to oval mound with a central chamber and an entrance facing almost due south (fig. 75). The chamber was of oval shape and formed a continuation to the entrance passage. The length was c. 2 m and the width 1.8 m. Only four courses of the internal wall were preserved to a height of 1.3 m.

The entrance passage was not excavated further. It could be followed for a length of 1.3 m, but must have been longer.

The ring wall was scattered to form an irregular low mound with a diameter of 8 m. The original diameter of the tomb must have been less. The building materials used were rounded stone blocks in varying sizes ranging up to 0.4-0.5 m.

Finds. The only find from the floor level of the chamber was a painted ceramic vessel. A small bead came from the disturbed fill in the upper part of the mound.

1037.A: Biconical ceramic vessel with carinated shoulder of Jemdet Nasr type in yellow-brown sand-tempered ware (fig. 76) with a creamy slip applied all over, covered with red paint, leaving every second panel on the shoulder in reserve outlined in black and filled out with cross-hatching in black or a stylized plant motif in red and black (Frifelt 1971 p. 378).
1037.B: Spherical green glass bead, L 3.9 mm, D 4.1 mm (fig. 77).

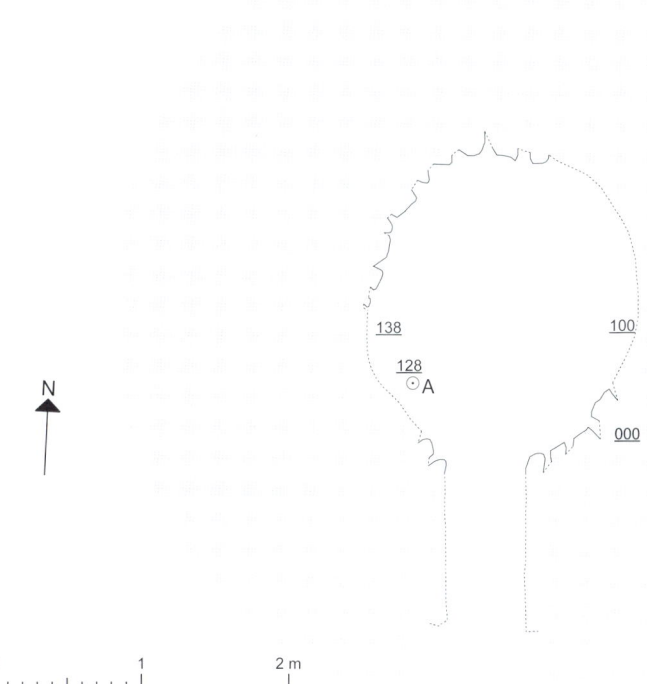

Fig. 75. Plan of Tomb 1037, 1:50.

Fig. 76a. Ceramic vessel with polychrome painting, 1037.A, 1:1

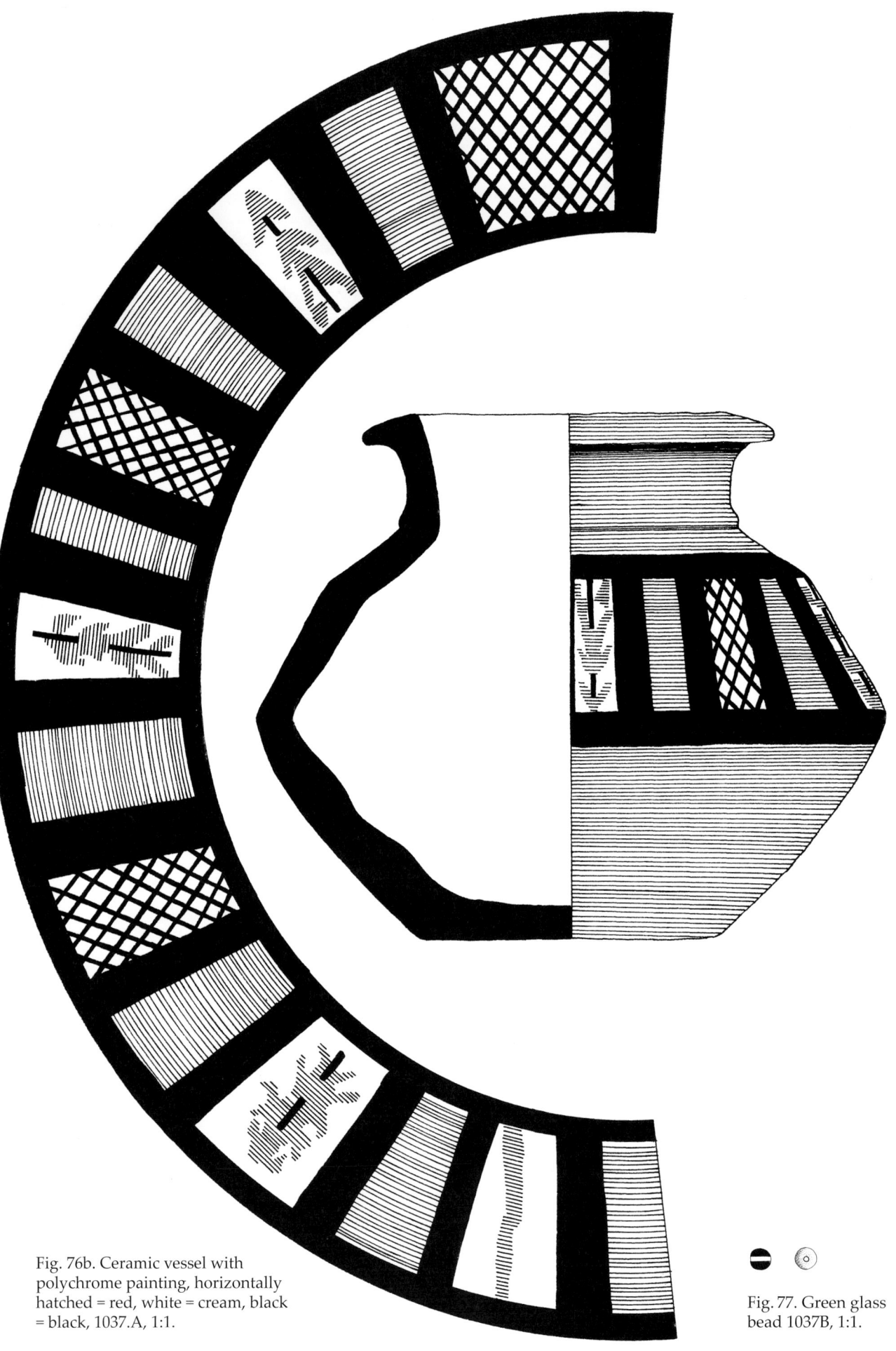

Fig. 76b. Ceramic vessel with polychrome painting, horizontally hatched = red, white = cream, black = black, 1037.A, 1:1.

Fig. 77. Green glass bead 1037B, 1:1.

70

TOMB 1038

Location. The mound was located in a rather high position, one third up the western side of the eastern mountain ridge. The altitude can be estimated to be 320-330 m above sea level (cf. Frifelt 1971 p. 381: Cairn 9).

The excavation. The excavation in 1963 was led by Vagn Kolstrup. The top of the mound was cleared and through the entry pit made by grave robbers the chamber and then the entrance passage were gradually emptied by digging horizontal layers by trowel.

Structural remains. A tomb with a central chamber and an entrance passage towards the south was uncovered (fig. 78). The chamber had an oval to round shape 1.9 m long and 1.8 m wide by the entrance and was almost symmetrically positioned to the axis of the entrance passage. Part of the eastern wall face was demolished, but the wall closest to the entrance passage still had six to seven intact stone courses reaching approximately 1 m above the base level of the tomb (fig. 79). The incline of the chamber wall indicated that the chamber had been corbelled. The floor consisted of sandy fill on the flat bedrock.

The entrance passage was preserved in a length of 1.4 m and was 0.4 to 0.5 m wide (fig. 80). The ring wall was badly preserved and its scattered stones made up a mound of c. 9 m in diameter. The building material was medium stones of varied size and shape, but mainly rather irregular blocks, with those of an oblong and flat shape used in the chamber wall. The original ring wall diameter may have been around 5 m judging from the better preserved tombs with a similar size of chamber.

Finds. Several artefacts were found in the western side of the chamber. A ceramic vessel and a white pendant were discovered on the floor. Two fragments of corroded, rather thin copper sheet, curved in their longitudinal section as well as in their cross sections, were found 0.35 to 0.60 m above this level. They may be parts of the same object, perhaps a shallow bowl.

1038.A: Oblong pendant of white shell, L 29.1 mm, W 8.1 × 12 mm (fig. 81).
1038.B: Fragment of curved copper plate (fig. 82).
1038.C: Biconical ceramic vessel with carinated shoulder of Jemdet Nasr type in reddish-brown sand-tempered ware with a greyish slip and traces of plum-red paint on neck and shoulder and black vertical bands on the shoulder (fig. 83).
1038.D: Fragmented cylindrical bead in black stone with red spots, L 11.9 mm, D 16.1 mm (fig. 84).
1038.E: Fragment of curved copper plate (fig. 85).

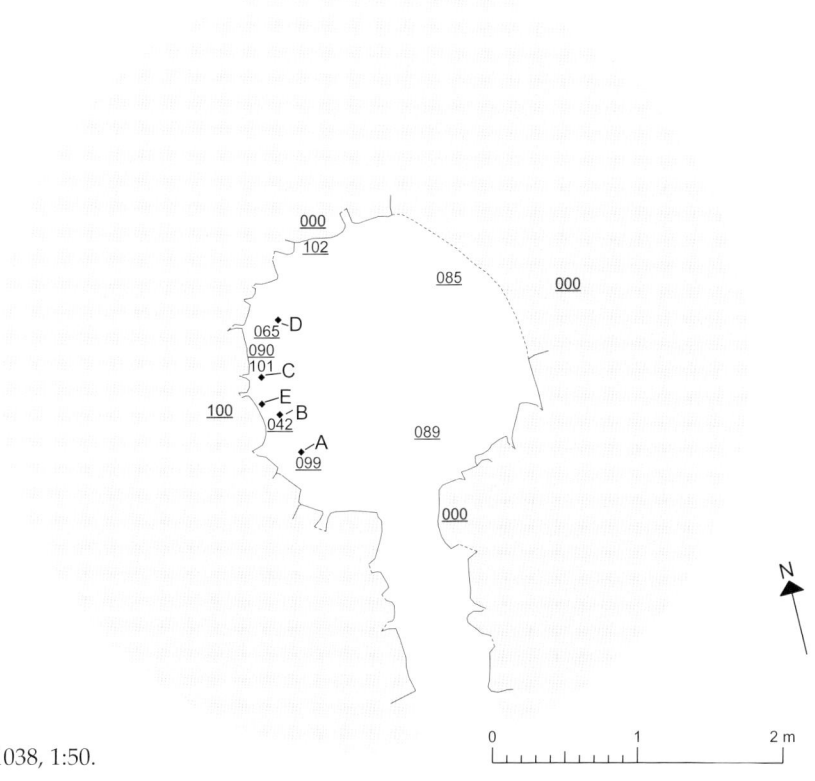

Fig. 78. Plan of Tomb 1038, 1:50.

Fig. 79. Tomb 1038 looking W.

Fig. 80. The entrance passage of Tomb 1038.

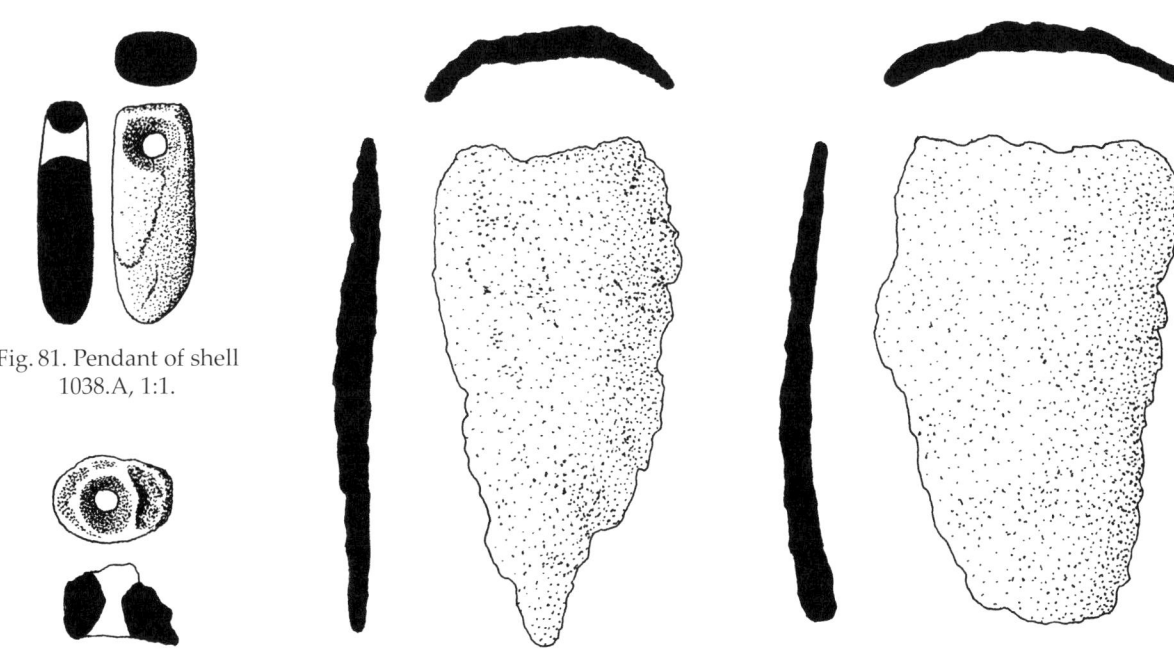

Fig. 81. Pendant of shell 1038.A, 1:1.

Fig. 84. Bead of black stone 1038.D, 1:1.

Fig. 82. Copper object 1038.B, 1:1.

Fig. 85. Copper object 1038.E, 1:1.

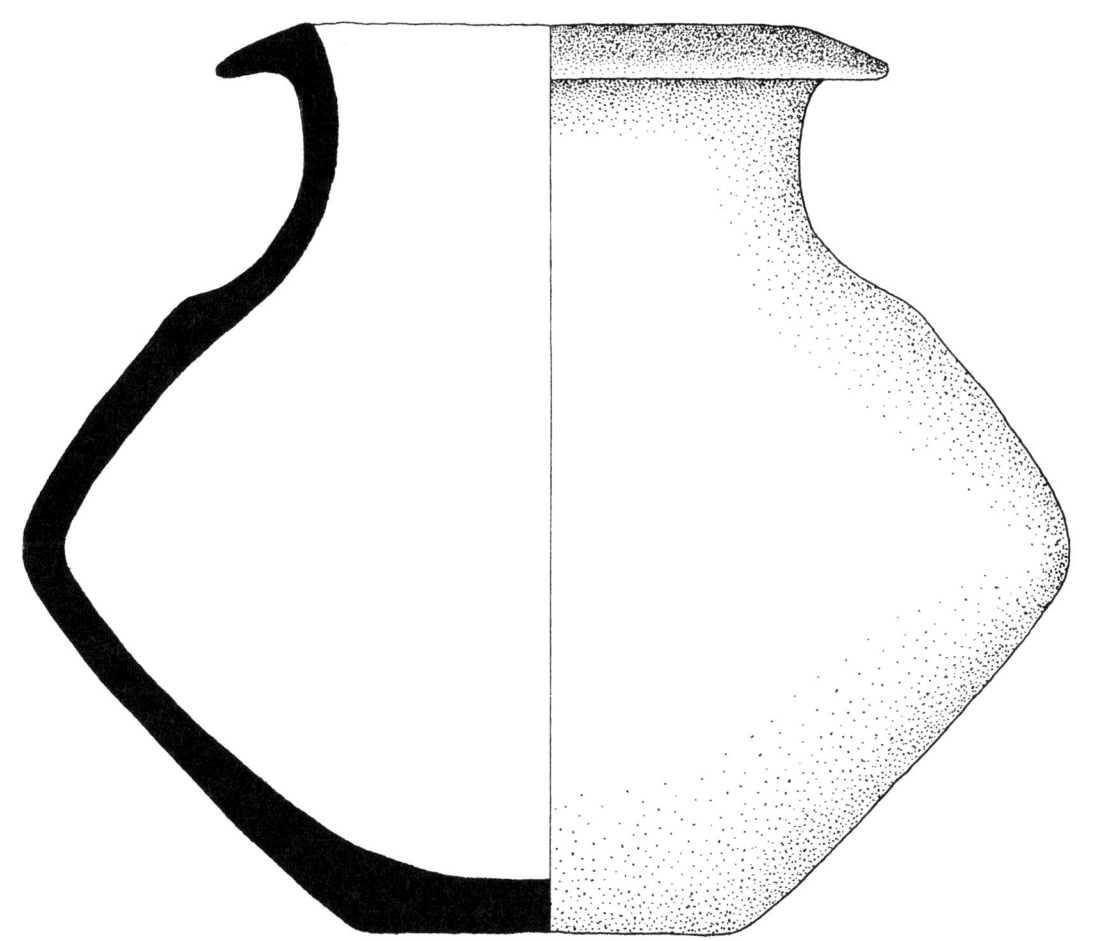

Fig. 83. Ceramic vessel with traces of polychrome painting 1038.C, 1:1.

TOMB 1039

Location. The tomb was situated on the western foothill of the eastern mountain ridge, the altitude loosely estimated to be 310-320 m above sea level (fig. 86).

The excavation. The investigation in 1963 was led by Jørgen Lund. The mound was cleared from rubble and loose stones giving priority to the central pit left by grave robbers. The chamber and entrance passage were emptied by scraping with trowels down to bedrock.

Structural remains. The excavation revealed a rounded tomb that had been heavily damaged by secondary intrusions and stone removal. From a central chamber a short entrance passage led towards the south (figs. 87-88).

The chamber had a circular to oval, irregular shape. It was 1.8 m long and 1.9 m wide. The wall was c. 1 m tall with some four stone courses remaining. The incline indicated a corbelled construction. No remains of a floor pavement were recorded.

The entrance passage was preserved to a height of 0.6 to 0.7 m. The preserved length was 1.4 m and the width expanded from 0.4 m at the chamber to 0.6 m by the entrance.

The ring wall was demolished with the resulting stone scatter spreading in a diameter of c. 7 m; the original mound probably measured closer to 6 m in diameter. The building material was irregular stone blocks of varied size, with some of the largest, being up to 0.6 m wide, flanking the entrance passage.

Finds. No finds were observed.

Fig. 86. Tomb 1039 looking N.

Fig. 87. The entrance passage, set from large blocks.

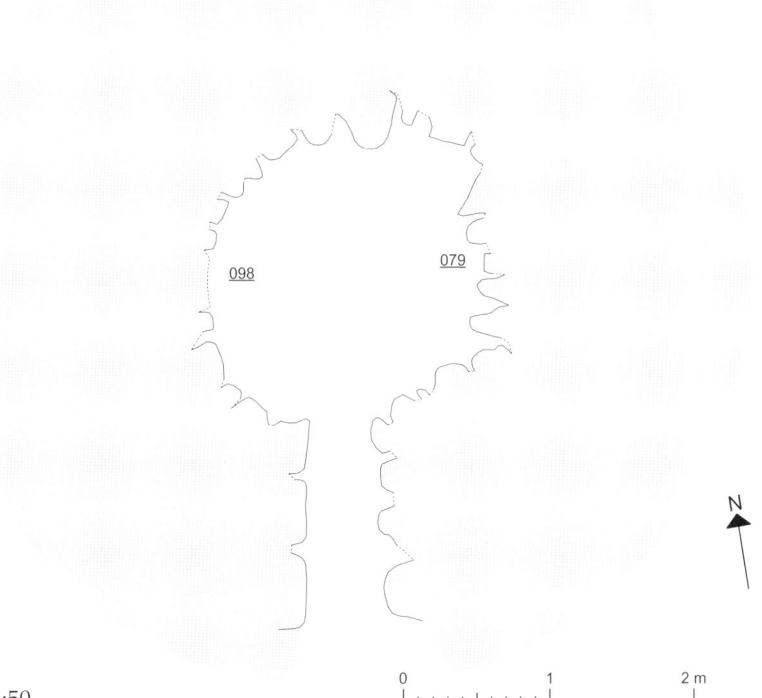

Fig. 88. Plan of Tomb 1039, 1:50.

TOMB 1040

Location. The mound was found at the foothills some meters east of Tomb 1039 at an estimated altitude of 330-340 m above sea level (fig. 89) (cf. Frifelt 1971 p. 381: Cairn 11).

The excavation. Excavation in 1963 was led by Jørgen Lund. Starting from a recent robber's pit in the middle of the mound, the chamber area and the entrance passage was explored by horizontal excavation below secondary fill and rubble. The remains of the ring wall were only superficially cleared.

Structural remains. The excavation resulted in the identification of a tomb with a ring wall, a small central chamber and an entrance passage towards south (figs. 90-91).

The remains of the chamber had a height of 0.7 m. Only five stone courses of the wall were preserved. The incline of the wall indicated a corbelled chamber construction. The chamber was almost semi-circular and lay slightly off the axis of the entrance passage. The length was 1.2 m, measured in this direction and the width was 1.4 m.

The chamber floor consisted of sand and bedrock. The entrance passage measured 1.6 m in length and 0.6 m in width with parallel sides. It was preserved to only 0.4 m in height.

The disturbed ring wall had a diameter of c. 5 m. The building material was irregular stones of varying sizes, with some larger blocks up to 0.5 m placed in the entrance and in the base course of the chamber wall.

Finds. The scarce finds were recovered in the eastern side of the chamber and included a copper pin and fragments of probably human bone.

1040.A: Corroded fragments of copper pin, 4.5 cm long.
1040.B: Bone fragments.

Fig. 89. Tomb 1040 with Jørgen Lund and the crew looking W. On the plain several large cement kilns.

Fig. 90. The chamber and entrance passage looking NW.

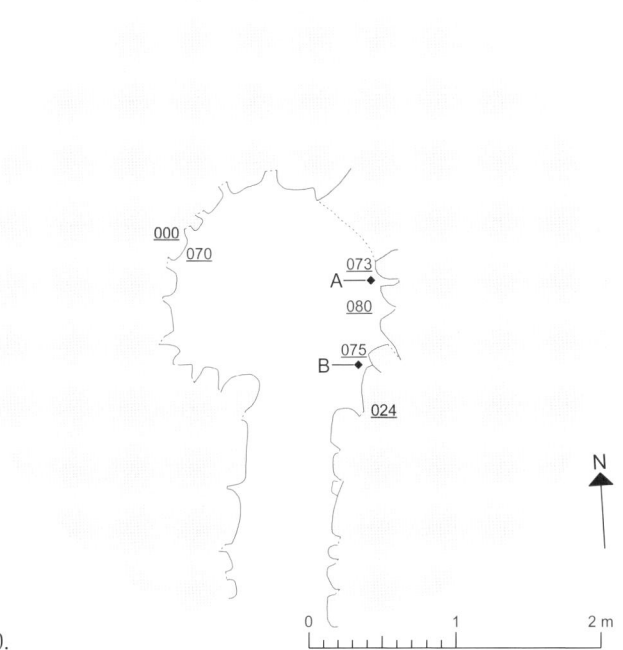

Fig. 91. Plan of Tomb 1040, 1:50.

TOMB 1041

Location. The mound was located on the western foothills of the eastern mountain ridge at an estimated altitude of 300-320 m above sea level (fig. 92) (cf. Frifelt 1971 p. 381: Cairn 12).

The excavation. The excavation in 1963 was led by Vagn Kolstrup. It commenced by clearing the top around the robber's entry hole and then tracing the outline of the chamber wall and the entrance passage. The fill under the disturbed zone, comprised of stone collapse, rubble and sand was excavated by trowel. The entrance was similarly emptied outwards until stones blocking the passage were reached.

Structural remains. The excavation revealed a tomb with a ring wall, a central chamber and an entrance passage leading towards the SSE (fig. 93). The chamber had a symmetrical pear-shaped plan. It measured 2 m in length and 2.2 m in width along the axis of the entrance passage. Six courses of the chamber wall were preserved, the remaining chamber being 1.22 m high. A photo from the inside of the chamber, showing the entry area in the south side, clearly shows the wall incline of a corbelled construction (fig. 94). The floor consisted of mixed sand spread on the bedrock.

The entrance passage was estimated to be c. 1.5 m long, but could have been longer as the outer periphery of the tomb was demolished by stone removal. It was still covered by three large, flat lintel stones, the largest measuring 1 × 0.35 × 0.25 m. The passage was sealed with a packing of stone blocks up to a size of 0.6-0.4 m. Inwards to the chamber the blocking did not reach the roof, but an empty space of c. 0.35 m was left.

The outer diameter of the disturbed tomb was c. 7 m.

Finds. A carnelian bead was found and a few fragments of a human cranium, besides some scattered bone splinters above the level of the chamber floor.

1041.A: Ring-shaped carnelian bead, L c. 3 mm, D c. 7 mm (fig. 95).
1041.B: Cranial fragment and scattered bone fragments.

Fig. 92. Tomb 1041 looking NNE before excavation.

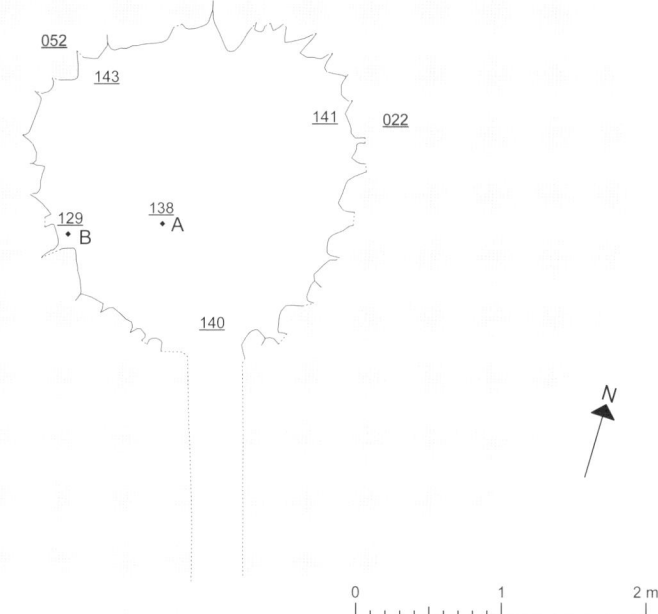

Fig. 93. Plan of Tomb 1041, 1:50.

Fig. 94. The excavated chamber and entrance with large lintel stones.

Fig. 95. Carnelian bead 1041.A, 1:1.

TOMB 1042

Location. The tomb was located at the foot of the eastern mountain ridge. The estimated altitude of the tomb is 300-310 m above sea level (fig. 96) (cf. Frifelt 1971 p. 381: Cairn 13).

The excavation. The investigation in 1963 was led by Jørgen Lund. The central part of the mound was cleared. Only the remains of the chamber's lower levels were excavated due to the poor condition of the tomb.

Structural remains. The excavation revealed the remains of a tomb with a central chamber and an entrance passage towards the south (fig. 97). The chamber was almost round and measured 2 m in length along the axis of the entrance passage and 1.8 m in width. It was preserved with only three courses or 0.7 m in height on the south side by the entrance. The preserved wall was constructed of larger elongated stone blocks, up to 0.6 × 0.3 m, stacked with their longitudinal axis pointing towards the centre of the chamber, indicating that the tomb most likely once had a corbelled roof.

Finds. The finds were located on the extreme northern side of the chamber. A ceramic vessel stood upright next to a copper object and must have been part of a primary burial. Approximately 1 m away a large bead was recovered. In the centre were bone fragments.

1042.A: Rounded biconical ceramic vessel with a faint marked shoulder and a broad base in buff sand-tempered ware (fig. 98).
1042.B: Corroded fragments of copper pin, 8.5 cm long.
1042.C: Cylindrical bead from dark-green soft stone, L 15 mm, D 6 mm (fig. 99).
1042.D: Bone fragments.

Fig. 96. Tomb 1042 looking S.

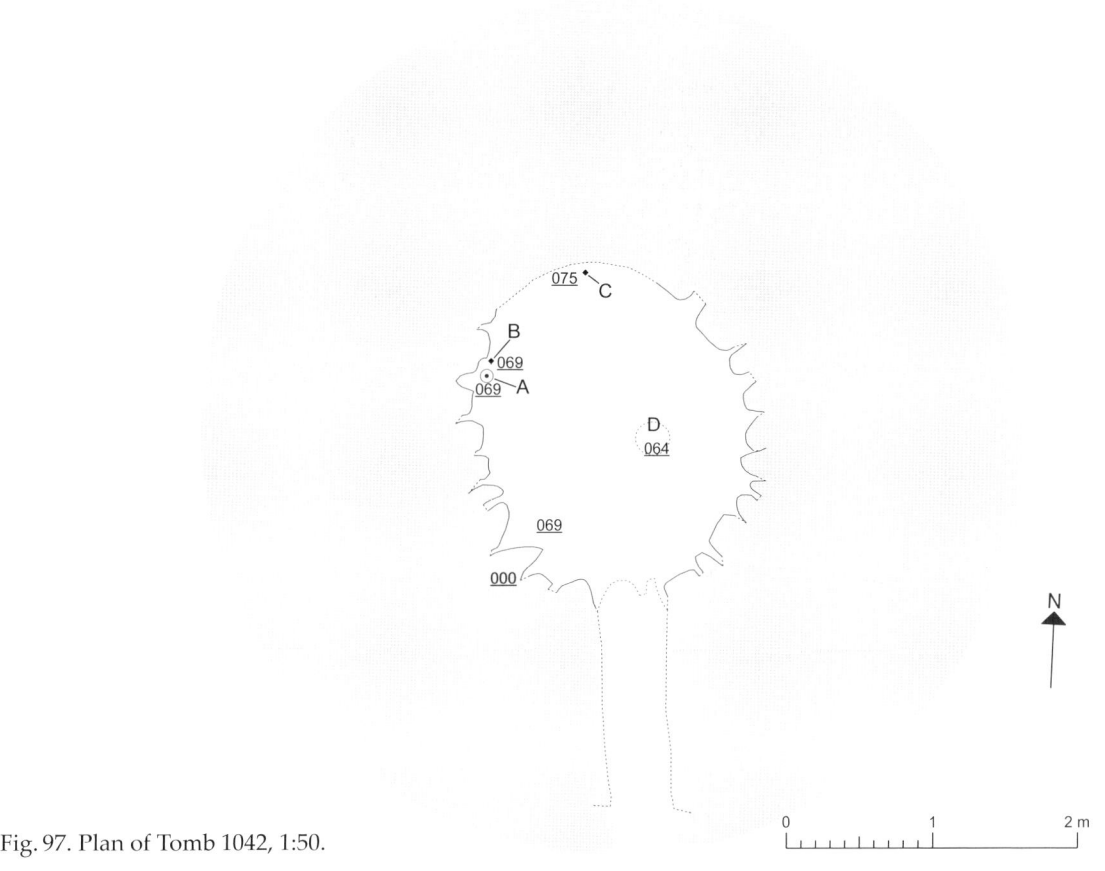

Fig. 97. Plan of Tomb 1042, 1:50.

Fig. 98. Ceramic vessel 1042.A, 1:1.

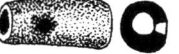

Fig. 99. Dark stone bead 1042.C, 1:1.

81

TOMB 1043

Location. The tomb was positioned on the foothill of the eastern mountain ridge some meters south of and above Tomb 1044, in a cluster containing Tombs 1043, 1044 and 1045 (fig. 100). The altitude, about one third up the cliff, is estimated to be 320-330 m above sea level. This group of mounds were the northernmost investigated in the valley south of Al-Ain. Their position was around 1500 m from the northern end of the eastern mountain ridge (where it meets Wadi Shik and Wadi Al-Ain). A photo taken towards the west, shows that processing of limestone/gypsum in large kilns had already commenced in the valley south of Al-Ain by early spring 1963 (fig. 89) (cf. Frifelt 1971 p. 381: Cairn 14).

The excavation. The tomb was excavated in 1963 led by Jørgen Lund. The flat-topped mound with traces of entry by robbers was cleared. On the photo taken before excavation one can see part of the line of stones in the chamber wall and some rather large elongated blocks that have been pulled out from the chamber area.

Structural remains. The excavation of the tomb exposed the damaged ring wall surrounding a central round grave chamber with an entrance passage towards the south (figs. 101-102). The length, in line with the axis of the entrance, was almost 2 m and the width was 1.7 m. The wall was preserved to a height of 1.1 m with up to six courses of stones still standing. The stones used in the wall were elongated irregular blocks oriented lengthwise towards the chamber indicating a corbelled roof construction. The floor consisted of a sandy layer on bedrock.

The entrance passage was not emptied of its stone blocking. It was preserved to a length of 1.5 m, but may have been longer due to the condition of the ring wall. The width was around 0.5 m and the height was 1.1 m at the entry to the chamber. The field report does not mention how the passage was covered, if it was corbelled or whether flat stone blocks were used.

The ring wall was badly preserved and not investigated further since the outer perimeter was damaged by stone removal. The scattered building material comprised of rather small irregular blocks. The diameter of the remaining mound was 5 m.

Finds. The grave contained one ceramic vessel which was standing upright along the western side of the chamber. In three places skeletal remains were found (fig. 103). All finds (1053.A-C) were positioned at floor level and were severely crushed by the actions of looters or stone robbers. The sherd 1043.E was found out of context.

1043.A: Biconical ceramic vessel with a faint marked shoulder of Jemdet Nasr type in brownish sand-tempered ware with traces of plum-red paint on neck and body and inside the rim (fig. 104).
1043.B: Fragments of cranium.
1043.C: Fragments of cranium.
1043.E: Rim sherd from a coarse hand-made pot in red sand-tempered Iron Age ware (fig. 105).

Fig. 100. Tomb 1043 looking NE.

Fig. 101. The excavated chamber looking SE.

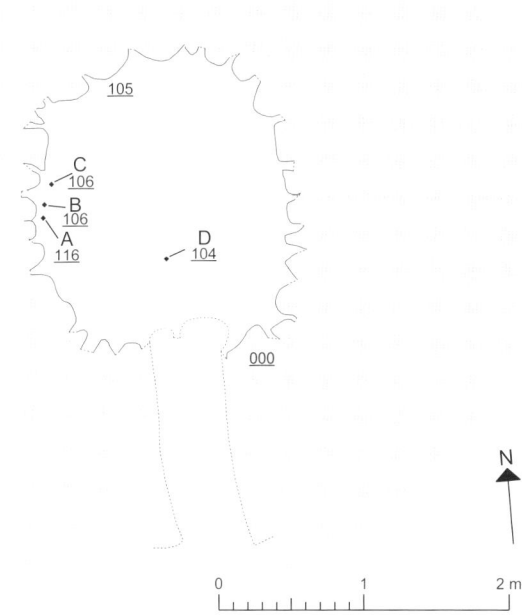

Fig. 102. Plan of Tomb 1043 with possible outline of ring wall indicated, 1:50.

Fig. 103. Interior of chamber with part of cranium and vessel 1043.A.

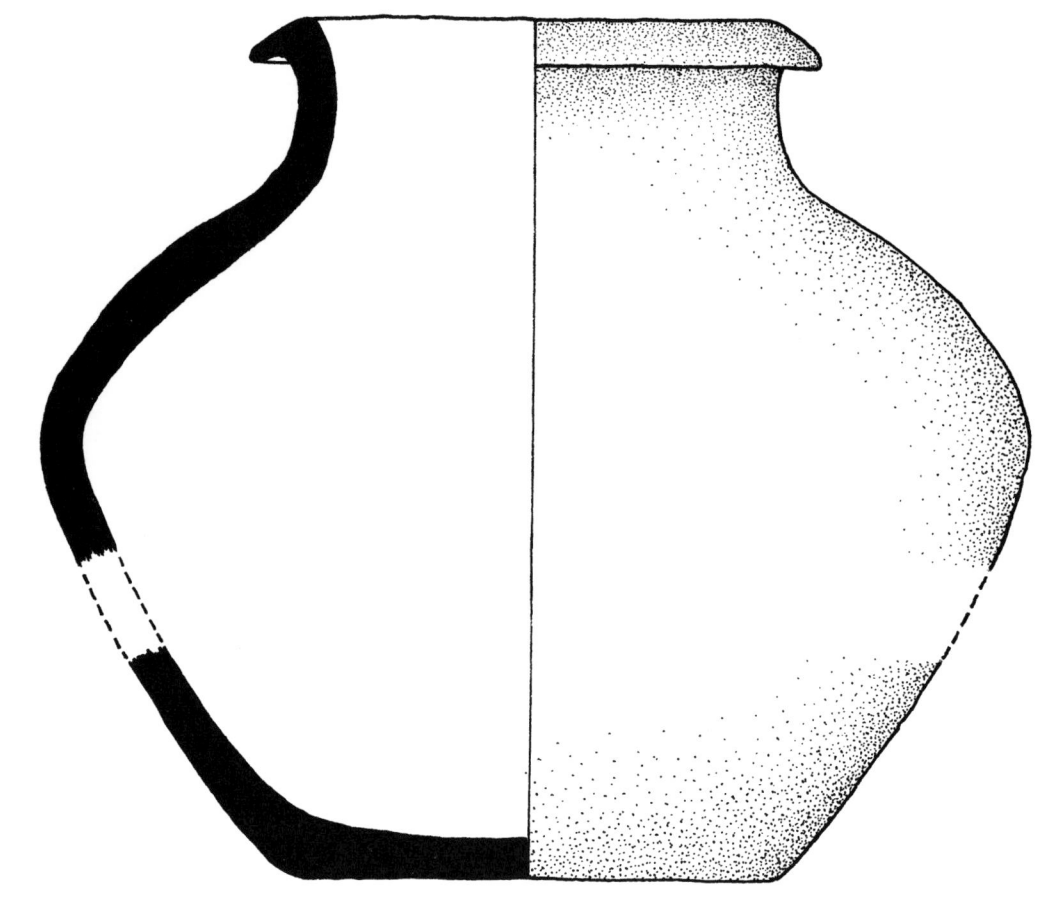

Fig. 104. Ceramic vessel 1043.A, 1:1.

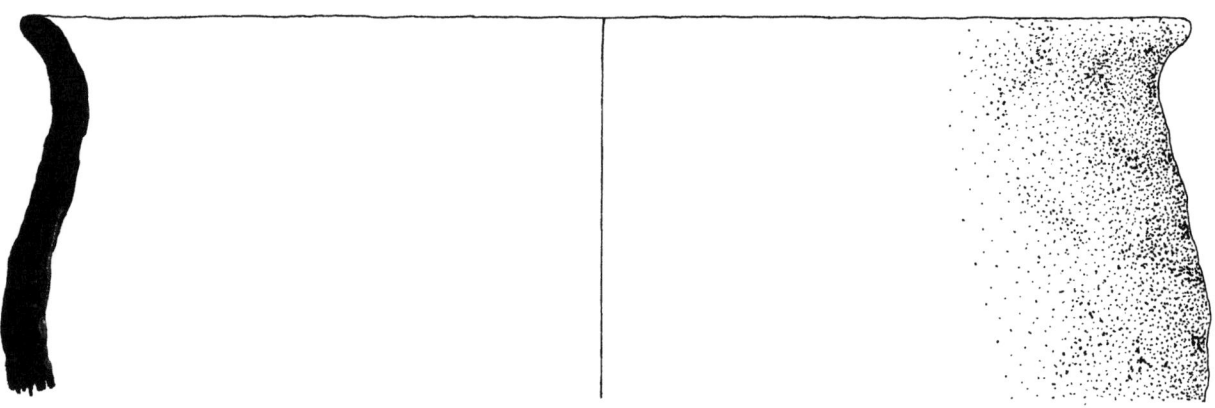

Fig. 105. Upper part of ceramic vessel 1043.E, 1:1.

TOMB 1044

Location. The mound lay on the foothills of the eastern mountain ridge a few meters north of Tomb 1043 (fig. 106). The altitude is estimated to be 310-320 m above sea level.

The excavation. The tomb was excavated in 1963 under the charge of Jørgen Lund. Only the chamber floor was excavated due to the ruined state of the mound. The remains of the tomb structure were not mapped, only photographed.

Structural remains. The excavation revealed the remains of a tomb with a central chamber (fig. 107). No trace of an entrance passage was found. The chamber wall was represented by just one course around a floor of sandy fill on top of the bedrock. The chamber measured 1.5 m north-south and 1.6 m east-west. The outer diameter of the mound was c. 4.5 m. No finds were observed.

Fig. 106. Tomb 1044 looking W.

Fig. 107. The ruined chamber.

TOMB 1045

Location. The tomb, excavated in 1963, was situated on the western flank of the eastern ridge together with mounds 1043 and 1044 (fig. 108) (cf. Frifelt 1971 p. 381: Cairn 16).

The excavation. Vagn Kolstrup was in charge of the investigation. Only the chamber area was excavated due to the highly disturbed state of the tomb. The remains of the tomb structure were not mapped, only photographed.

Structural remains. The low mound contained a severely damaged ring wall around a central chamber (fig. 109). The chamber walls were too collapsed to be identified and an entrance was not located. The chamber (or a part of it) measured 1.3 m north-south and 1.5 m east-west. The floor level was approximately 1.1 to 1.2 m under the highest point of the mound. It consisted of a sandy spread on the bedrock. The mound had a diameter of 5 m.

Finds. Just above the floor level a fragment of a fine painted ceramic vessel was found, which must have been part of a primary burial. At a higher level, in a mixed fill, c. 0.75 m above the floor, was a large base from a pottery vessel. Some scattered bone splinters were recovered from the disturbed fill.

1045.A: Fragment of hand-made pottery base in a reddish, coarse, sand-tempered ware (fig. 110).
1045.B: Biconical ceramic vessel with shoulder carination of Jemdet Nasr type in a reddish grey ware, painted red with black diamond pattern on a cream slip (fig. 111).
1045.C: Fragments of bone.

Fig. 108. Tomb 1045 looking NW.

Fig. 109. The chamber looking NE.

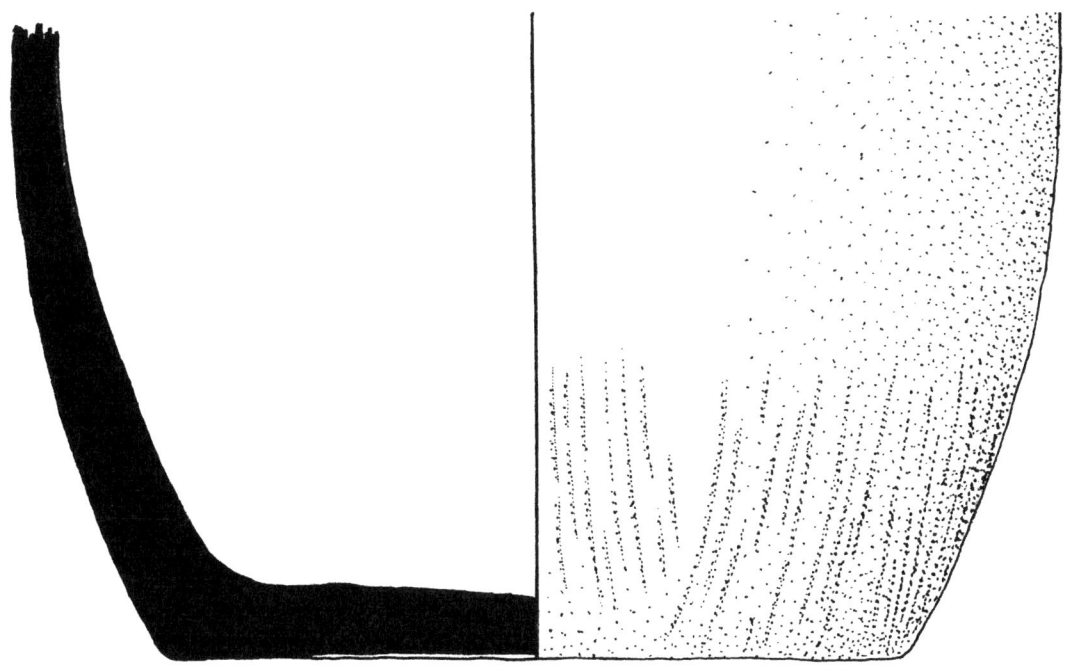

Fig. 110. Pottery base 1045.A, 1:1.

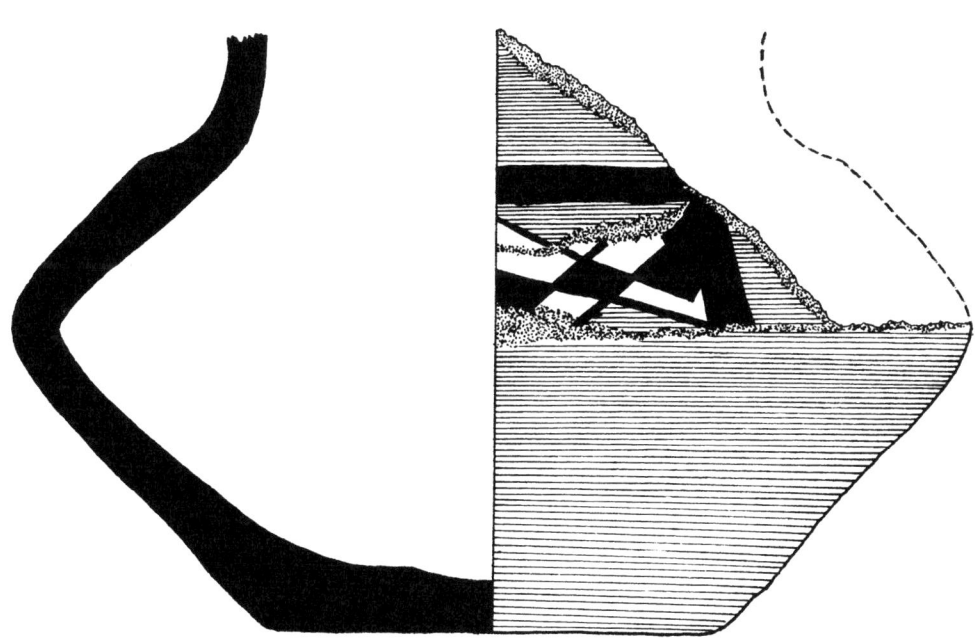

Fig. 111. Ceramic vessel with polychrome painting, horizontally hatched = red, white = cream, black = black, 1045.B, 1:1.

8. The mounds on the western mountain ridge

TOMB 1046

Location. The mound was situated at the eastern foot of the western mountain ridge at an estimated altitude of 300-310 m above sea level (figs. 112-113). It was located in the south-central part of the ridge, on a small plateau next to the talus, an area which today is adjacent to the zoo district (cf. Frifelt 1971 p. 362-363: Cairn 17).

The excavation. The tomb was excavated in 1963 under the charge of Jens Aarup Jensen. As the tomb was much more intact than in the previously excavated cases it was decided to investigate its construction in more detail. The north-eastern half of the tomb was removed in order to establish a cross section through part of the chamber and the surrounding ring wall (figs. 114-115). The section was given a slight s-curve and an inclination of c. 25 degrees to avoid collapse of the ring wall. The section was projected to a vertical plane when drawn.

Afterwards the top of the tomb was cleared to a level above the entrance passage in order to document the construction covering the entrance.

The next step was the excavation of the chamber and the entrance down to bedrock (figs. 116-117). This was done by trowel, digging in horizontal layers after the identification and removal of stones, rubble and fill in secondary locations.

Structural remains. The excavation uncovered a well preserved tomb with a chamber surrounded by a ring wall and a relatively long and narrow entrance passage towards the south (fig. 118).

The chamber had previously been entered from the top. Even though there was no evidence of stone plundering, most of the upper construction of the tomb was torn apart and an estimated third of the stone volume had been pushed down in the chamber. Also some parts of the outer ring wall face seem to have been penetrated, most likely by looters.

The chamber had a rounded to pear-shaped plan. The length in line with the axis of the entrance passage was 1.8 m and the width, measured close to the entrance, was 1.9 m. The preserved height of the wall reached a maximum of 1.9-2.0 m. As documented by the section the chamber was corbelled with a rather steep incline indicating an ogival profile, i.e. a pointed "Gothic" arch. The level floor consisted of sand above the bedrock.

The chamber wall was built of elongated stone blocks up to 0.5 m long, the longitudinal axis of these stones pointed towards the centre of the chamber.

In the sides of the entrance passage the stones were set so that their flat faces faced outwards. The entrance passage was 2.7 m long, 0.45-0.50 m wide at the base and 0.25 m at the ceiling and it had a height of 1-1.10 m. A minor extension can be observed in the floor level c. one third from the entry. The entrance passage was covered with large cap-stones, three observed in situ and at least two had slid down the side of the mound (figs. 119-120). The largest measured 1.3 × 0.4 × 0.2 m.

The entrance passage was completely filled with stones up to 0.3 m in size blocking the passage up to the top and concealing it from the outside.

The ring wall was not cleared from stone blocks tumble and rubble around its entirety but from the length of the assumed intact entrance passage and the outer wall face on both sides of it, the diameter would be about 7 m.

No finds were observed.

Fig. 112. Tomb 1046 looking N before excavation. In the horizon the white walls of the Jahili Fort in Al-Ain reflect the sun.

Fig. 113. The outline of the cairn looking W.

Fig. 114. Tomb 1046 was sectioned by removing the eastern half of the ring wall.

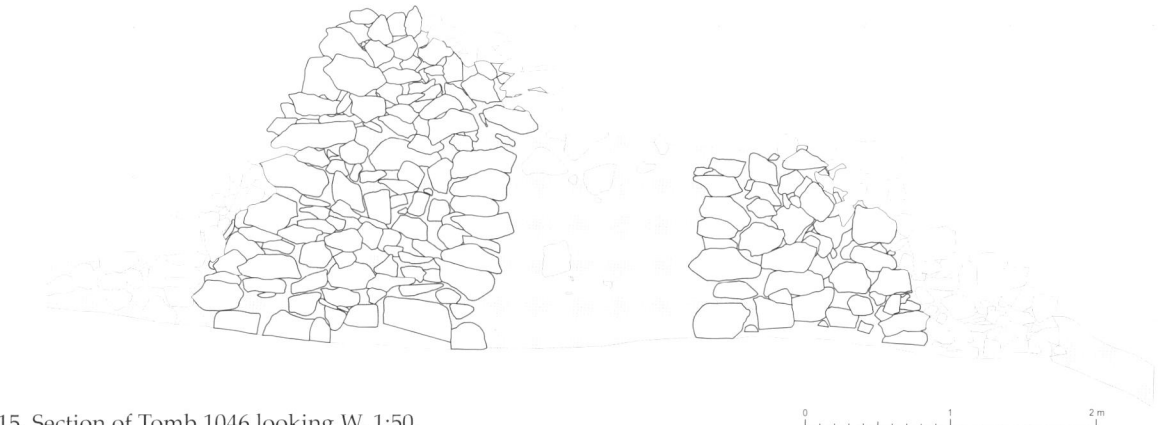

Fig. 115. Section of Tomb 1046 looking W, 1:50.

91

Fig. 116. The chamber emptied of sediments.

Fig. 117. The entrance passage viewed from outside.

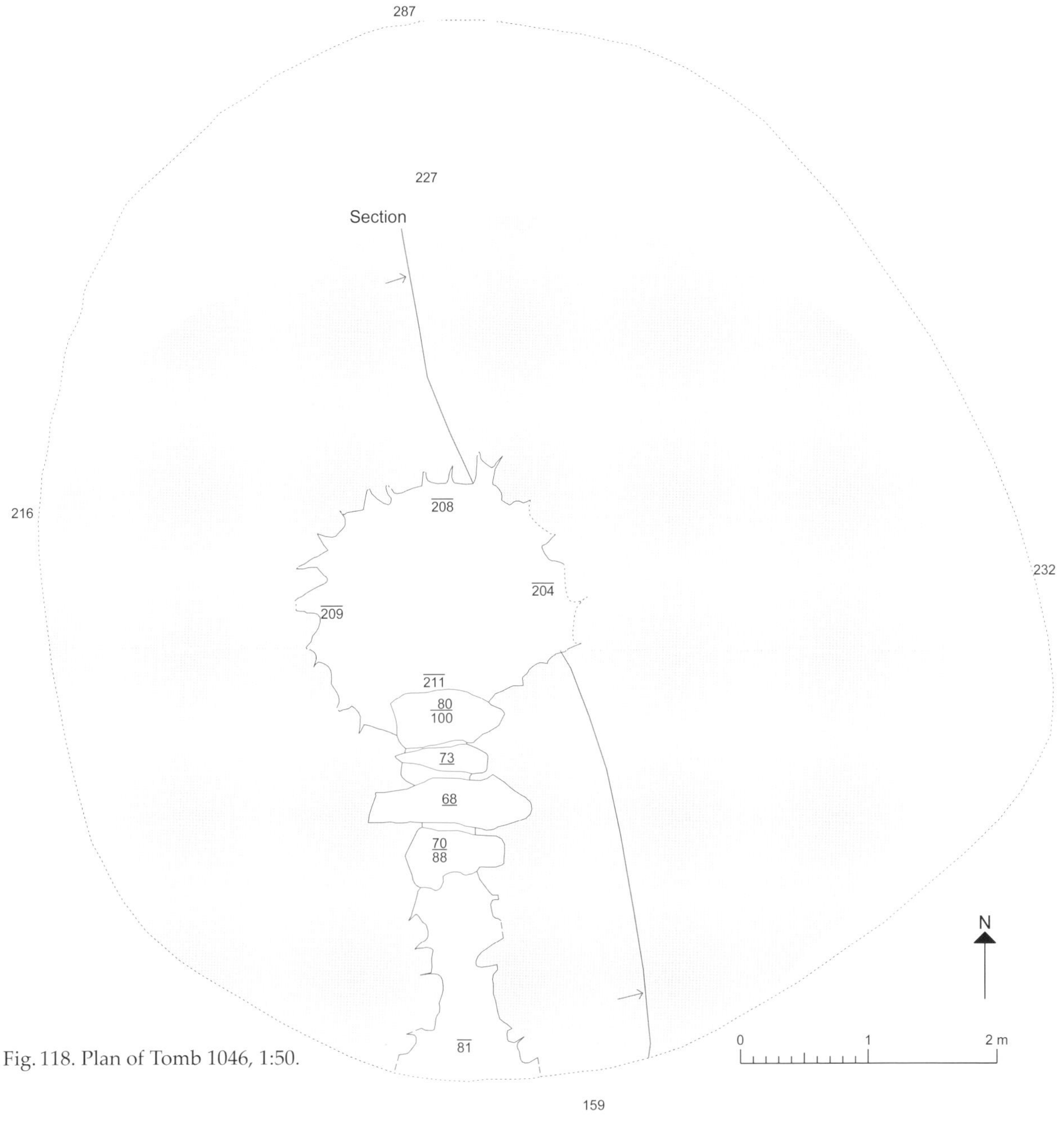

Fig. 118. Plan of Tomb 1046, 1:50.

Fig. 119. Large lintel stones cover the entrance passage, looking E.

Fig. 120. Overview of the excavated Tomb 1046.

TOMB 1047

Location. The tomb was located in the eastern foothills of the western mountain ridge, c. 1 km north of Tomb 1046 (fig. 121). It was situated among groups of mounds in the area just south of where the modern asphalt road, then a dirt track, cuts the ridge and leads westwards to Falaj Hazza. The area lies at an altitude of 280 to 290 m above sea level.

The excavation. The tomb was excavated in 1963 with Jørgen Lund leading the work. The aim was to clear and investigate the chamber floor of the almost demolished tomb. First the central area with traces of a robbing pit was cleared, and then excavation proceeded by trowel and brushes, recovering the outline of the chamber wall and the remains of the floor level.

Structural remains. The excavation identified a tomb with a central chamber and an entrance passage leading from the SSE (fig. 122). As an exception to the previously excavated tombs, the chamber's orientation was perpendicular to the axis of the entrance passage.

The chamber had an elongated oval plan with a length of 1.4 m and a width of 2.2 m. Five courses of the wall were preserved which gave a height of 0.8 to 0.5 m. The floor was disturbed, but had probably been made from sand and rubble levelled out on bedrock. The bedrock at floor level showed an inclination from west to east of c. 0.3 m. Not enough of the chamber was preserved to determine its roof construction.

The entrance passage was preserved for only 1.2 m of its length. The passage was flanked by rather large stone blocks, the largest was almost 0.6 m in length. At the entry to the chamber the passage had a width measuring 0.45 m but expanded to 0.6 m. Its height was preserved to only 0.5 m. The entrance passage had been blocked by more irregular stones up to a size of 0.2-0.3 m.

Most of the ring wall was removed by recent stone robbing. The outer diameter of the ruined wall was c. 4 m.

Finds. A few fragments of human bone were observed on the floor in the north-eastern side of the chamber.
1047.A: Human skeletal remains.

TOMB 1048

Location. The tomb was positioned in the foothills of the western ridge some meters east of Tomb 1047 (fig. 123). The altitude can be estimated to be 280-290 m above sea level (cf. Frifelt 1971 p. 381: Cairn 19).

The excavation. The tomb was excavated in 1963 headed by Jørgen Lund. It followed the procedures applied in the previous excavations of the most damaged tombs. Only the chamber area was excavated.

Structural remains. The excavation recovered the remains of a tomb with a central chamber and an entrance passage oriented towards the south (figs. 124-125).

The chamber had an oval to pear-shaped plan orientated as a continuation of the entrance passage, but a little asymmetrical in relation to the axis of the passage. In this axis the length was 1.2 m. The width could be estimated to 1.4 to 1.5 m. The walls stood only 2-3 courses or 0.5 m high having been substantially disturbed by looters and too little was preserved to determine the roof construction. The inward orientation of a few elongated large blocks, however, indicated the probability of a corbelled construction. The floor was level and to judge from a photo consisted of a compact rubble and gravel fill.

The entrance passage was not fully excavated. A lintel block at the entry to the chamber was still in place, where the height of the passage was 0.75 m and the width 0.6 m. The preserved length of the passage was c. 1.2 m.

The ring wall was badly damaged on its external side by stone removal. The preserved outer diameter was 3.5 to 4 m. It was built of irregular stone blocks in sizes up to 0.4-0.5 m.

Finds. A single carnelian bead was found approximately in the centre of the chamber.
1048.A: Spherical red carnelian bead, L 10.6 mm, D 11.6 mm, irregular polished surface (Frifelt 1991 p. 122) (fig. 126).

Fig. 121. Tomb 1047 before excavation.

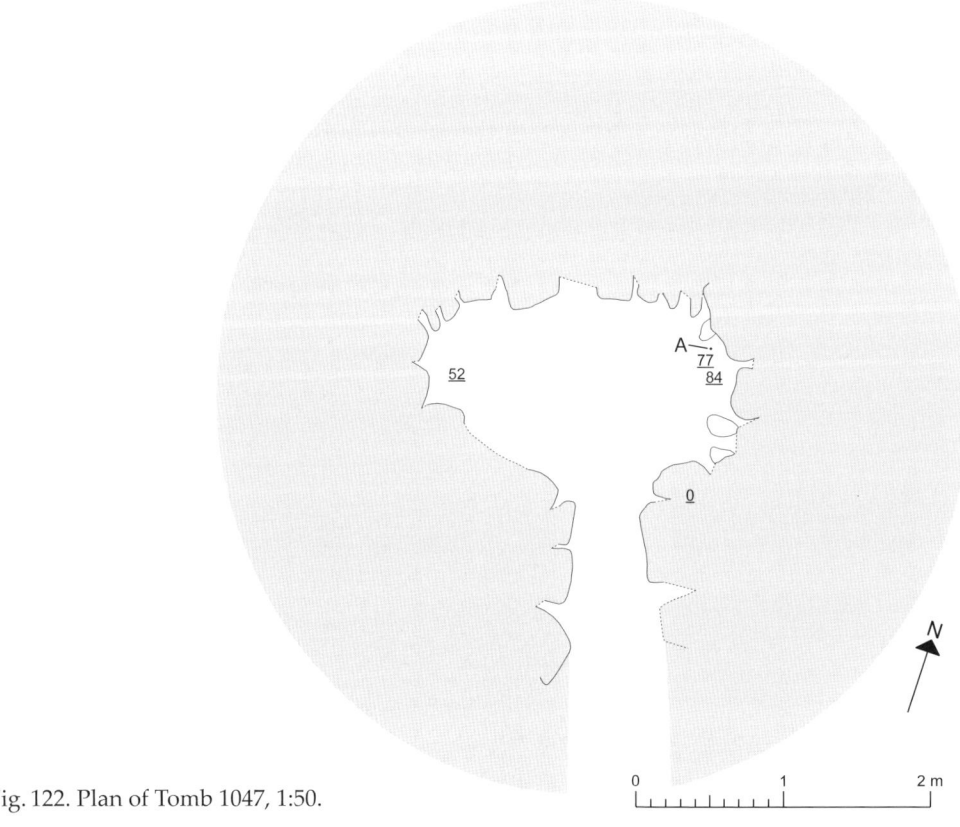

Fig. 122. Plan of Tomb 1047, 1:50.

Fig. 123. Tomb 1048 looking NE.

Fig. 124. The chamber area looking E.

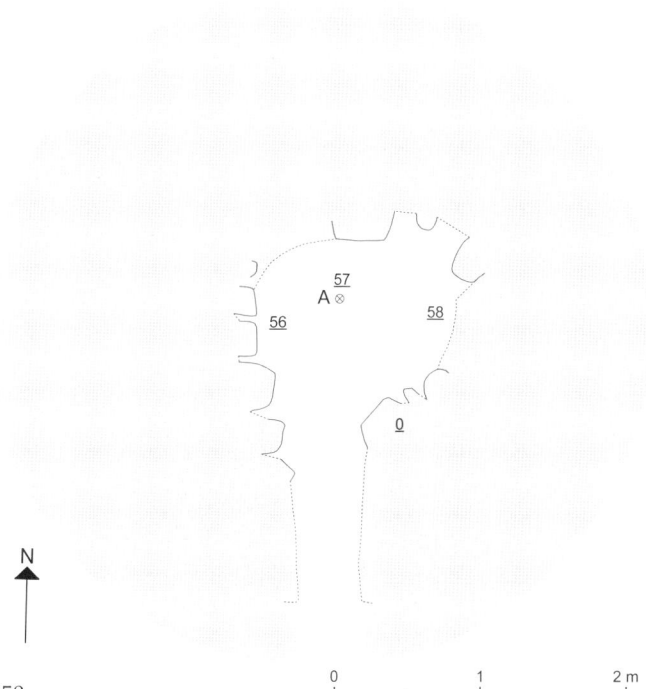

Fig. 125. Plan of Tomb 1048, 1:50.

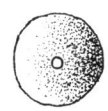

Fig. 126. Spherical carnelian bead 1048.A, 1:1.

TOMB 1049

Location. The tomb was situated between Tomb 1048 and Tomb 1052 in an area with small groups of mounds on the eastern foothills of the western mountain ridge (fig. 127). The estimated altitude was between 280 and 290 m above sea level (cf. Frifelt 1971 p. 377, 381: Cairn 20, fig. 9).

The excavation. The excavation of the tomb in 1963 was led by Vagn Kolstrup. The chamber and entrance passage were excavated whereas the outer periphery of the tomb structure was not cleared due to its damaged state.

Structural remains. The investigation uncovered a tomb with a central chamber and an entrance passage towards the south (figs. 128-129). The plan of the chamber was slightly oval, almost round, the length or depth in line with the axis of the entrance passage was 2 m and the width nearly 2.2 m. The chamber wall stood to a height of between 1.1 and 1.2 m with up to eight courses of predominantly elongated irregular blocks pointing towards the centre of the chamber. The wall indicated a rather low corbelled construction or, judging from the photographs, the stones in the wall face may, to a certain extent, have been pushed inwards as the tomb was dismantled. The southern part of the chamber was covered with parts of collapsed wall and vaulting.

The floor and lower part of the chamber consisted of a sandy to gravelly fill becoming coarser at lower levels.

The entrance passage was damaged and only preserved to a length of 0.8 m. The width was c. 0.5 m. The field report does not mention the presence of any blocking door.

The ring wall was damaged by stones having been removed from the external face. The remaining outer diameter, including disturbed material, was 6.5 m.

Finds. In the southernmost part of the chamber, just in front of the entrance passage, a human skeleton was discovered in sandy fill and at a high level almost 0.4-0.5 m above the chamber floor (figs. 130-131). The mandible, the collar bone and parts of the long bones from the arms and lower legs indicated that the body had been placed in a contracted position on the right side with the head towards the east and feet towards the west. The position of the skeleton at a high level above the chamber floor, as well as the accompanying grave goods make it clear that this is a secondary burial, much later than the construction of the tomb, dating to the Iron Age.

Close to the head two copper bowls and a softstone vessel were recovered stacked together with the softstone vessel placed below the metal bowls having 1049.D above and 1049.B on top.

At a position near the thighs or the knees was a large polished shell button and north of it a copper sword. A cobber buckle, shaped as a hook, was found to the north of the head. The finds had presumably been protected from the destruction of stone robbers by a section of wall collapse.

From the excavation photographs it appears that the sword is not in situ, but has been rearranged on a small platform of sand. The photograph shows an excavation level some 20 cm lower than the level of the skeletal and associated artefacts. Seemingly, this digging level has been extended into the burial from the centre of the chamber towards the pelvic area of the skeleton. It is most likely that the sword came from here, but was removed by some hasty work with the hoe when finding the burial at an unexpected high level.

1049.A: Belt-hook or buckle of copper/bronze with incised hatched band (fig. 132).
1049.B: Copper or bronze bowl with flat base and small spout (fig. 133).
1049.C: Bowl in light grey softstone with flat base and inwardly everted rim. Ornamented with fine incised lines forming a band of herring-bone cross-hatching below the rim, followed by acanthus-like arcs (figs. 134 and 138).
1049.D: Copper or bronze bowl with slightly thickened rim and flat base with a central concavity (fig. 135).
1049.E: Short copper sword with rim-flanged hilt to take inlay, 41.7 cm long; splayed pommel and constriction above the crescent joining the blade; inside the crescent is a raised dotted-circle ornament (figs. 136 and 138). The blade has a central thicker part which tapers out into the flat edges. The sword is seemingly worn from repeated sharpening. It is remarkable that the sword has exactly the same length as a similar sword from Jebel al-Buhais (Jasim 2012 p. 294, fig. 350).
1049.F: A large polished shell button with three drilled V-shaped holes on the interior concave side (figs. 137-138).
1049.G: Remains of human skeletal parts. The preserved parts were only slightly disarticulated.

Only limited parts of the skeleton were present. The field report does not specify the skeletal parts, so the following description is based on the field plan, in scale 1:10, and two black and white photos (figs. 129-131). Going from east to west the following skeletal remains were observed. The mandible was in "standing" or flat position next to the metal vessels. Below the jaw were observed four small bones from a hand (phalanx). Next to this was a collar bone resting on an upper arm-bone or humerus. The arms were represented by the long bones of the upper and lower arm (humerus, ulna and radius) nearly in anatomical position. Apparently, no remains of the torso and pelvic region were preserved. The only finds from the lower extremities were two long bones most likely the shin bones (tibia).

All distal and proximal parts of the large limb bones were missing, as were the majority of even the more heavy and dense bones. This might be due to several factors: Varied soil conditions, disturbances from looters and stone robbers and the excavation method. Some of the bones were still almost in anatomical position (semi-articulated) and seem not to be re-buried. The positions of the skeletal remains indicate that the body was placed with the head to the east and the legs towards the west. The position of the bones of the lower arms, lying parallel north of the upper arm bones, makes it most plausible that the body was placed on its right side. The head was close to or resting against a protruding stone in the chamber wall.

Fig. 127. Tomb 1049 looking W before excavation.

Fig. 128. Chamber with entrance looking N.

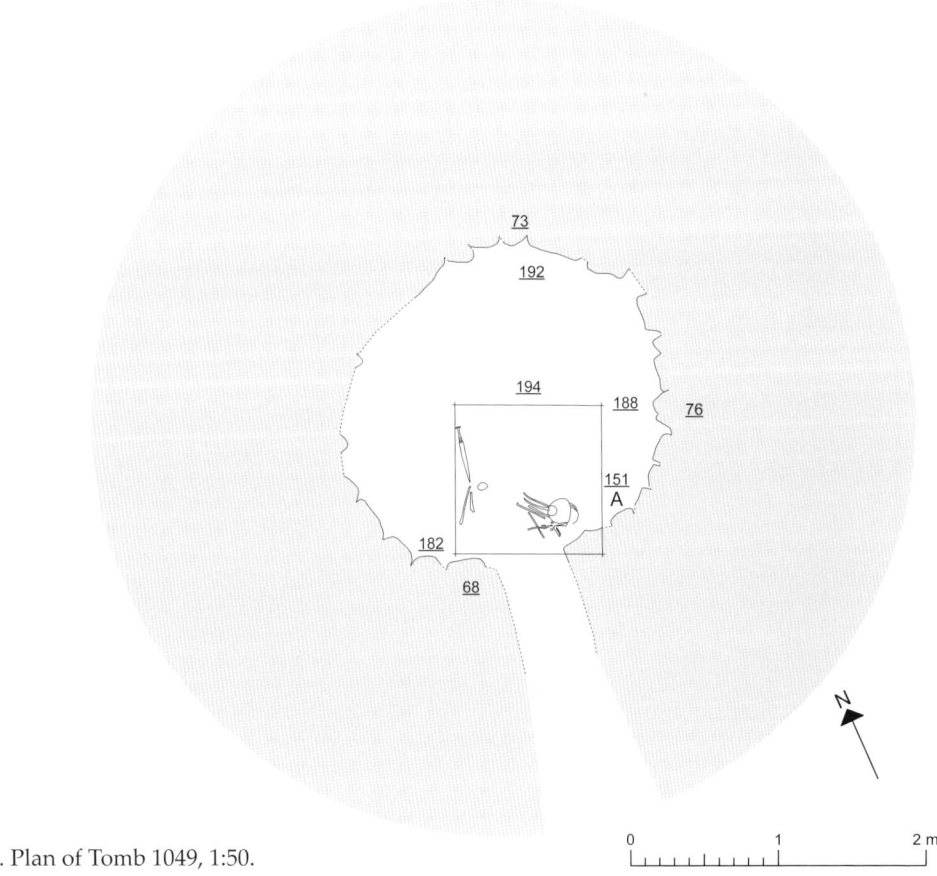

Fig. 129. Plan of Tomb 1049, 1:50.

Fig. 130. Remains of Iron Age burial looking W with bronze vessels and skeletal remains. In the background shell button and bronze sword in disturbed position.

› Fig. 131. Plan of Iron Age burial with position of body interpolated.

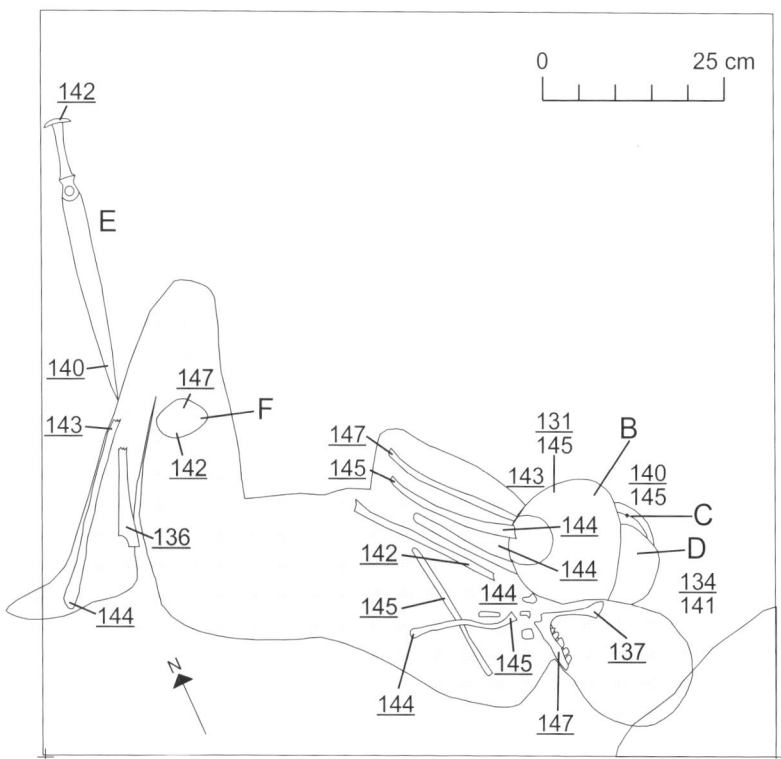

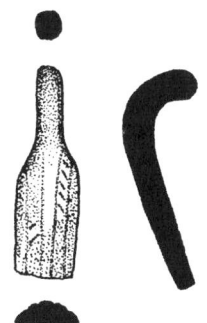

Fig. 132. Belt-hook or buckle of copper/bronze 1049.A, 1:1.

101

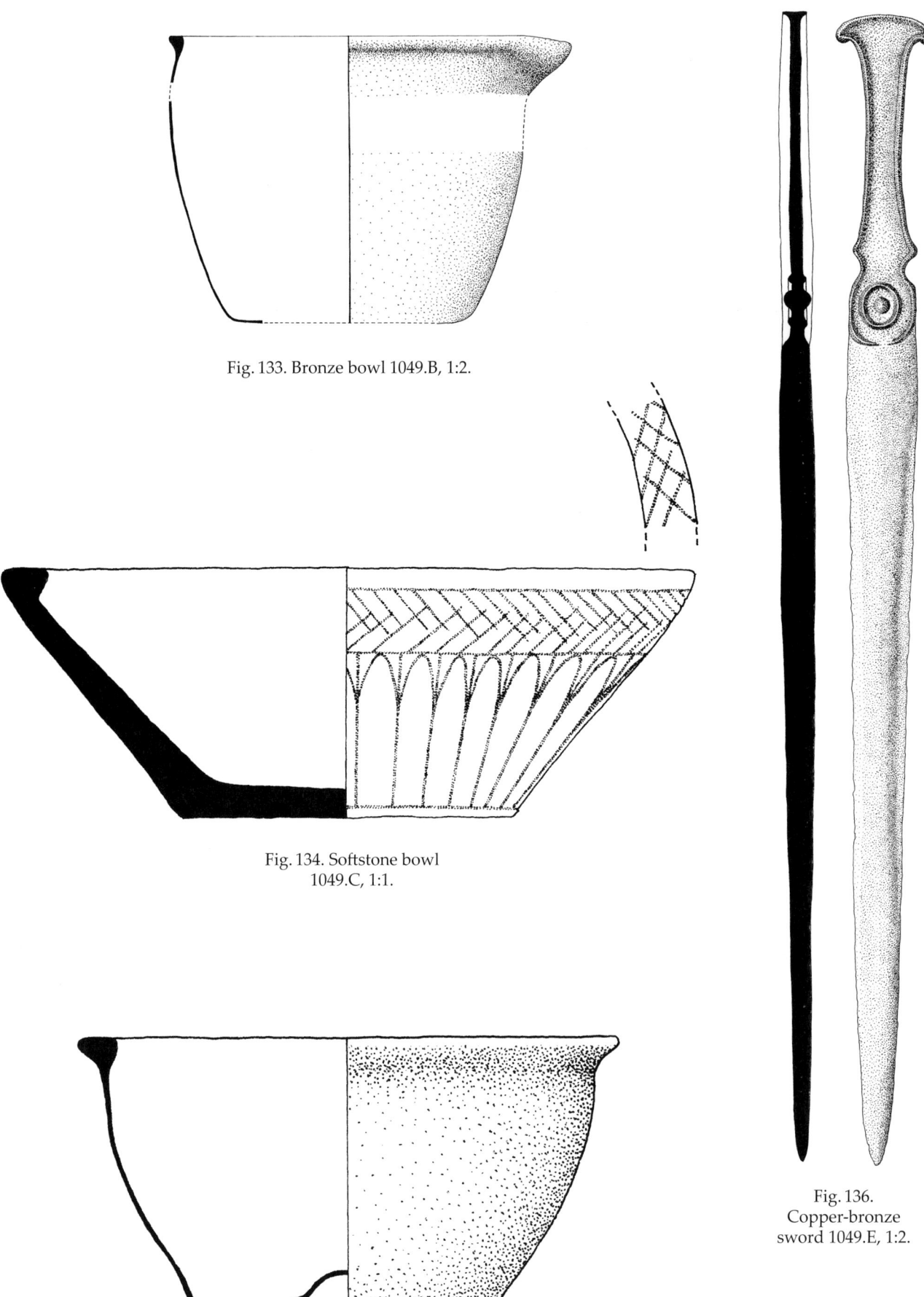

Fig. 133. Bronze bowl 1049.B, 1:2.

Fig. 134. Softstone bowl 1049.C, 1:1.

Fig. 135. Bronze bowl 1049.D, 1:1.

Fig. 136. Copper-bronze sword 1049.E, 1:2.

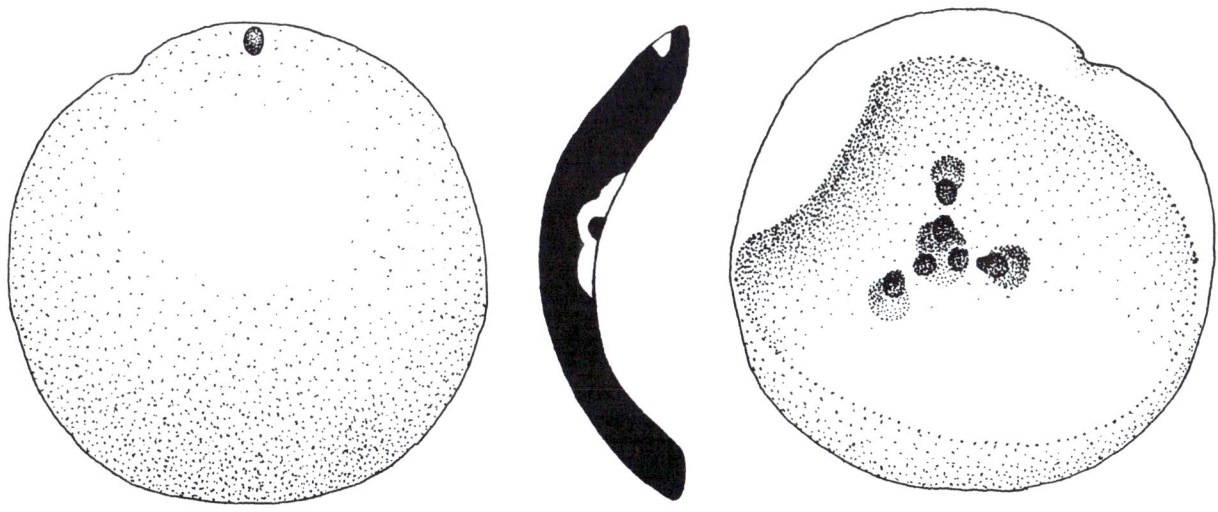

Fig. 137. Shell button 1049.F, 1:1.

Fig. 138. A selection of the burial furniture.

TOMB 1050

Location. The tomb was situated near the northernmost end of the western mountain ridge. It was positioned near other mounds on the plain at the foot of the ridge at an altitude estimated to be 270-280 m above sea level (fig. 139) (cf. Frifelt 1971 p. 382: Cairn 21).

The excavation. The tomb was excavated in 1963 with Jørgen Lund in charge. The chamber was investigated by excavating down from the hole in the top where robbers already had entered the tomb.

Structural remains. The excavation recovered the remains of a tomb with a central chamber and an entrance passage towards the southwest (figs. 140-141). The plan of the chamber was a narrow oval with a length of c. 2 m and a width of 1 m. The chamber wall was preserved to a height of 0.6-0.7 m or four stone courses. The floor consisted of a coarse, gravelly fill, probably the levelled subsoil. In the southwestern end a secondary looter's hole had been dug down to a depth of 20-25 cm below the floor. The eastern wall seemed rather straight whereas the rest had a slight incline indicating a corbelled roof.

The entrance passage was preserved to a length of 1.1 m. It had a width of 0.5 m and a preserved height at the entrance of 0.5-0.6 m. At the entry to the chamber a large stone block measuring 0.6 × 0.4 × 0.2 m acted either as a threshold or, more likely, as part of a blocking.

The outer part of the tomb, the external ring wall, was damaged and scattered after stone plundering. The present diameter was only 4 m.

The narrow plan of the chamber is rather unusual. A close parallel is seen in Cairn 4 from Tawi Silaim at the Wahiba desert in central Oman, which also had a narrow cist-like chamber with remains of a corbelled construction and an entrance. It had been secondarily used in the Iron Age, but remains of cleared out Jemdet Nasr pottery were found indicating the age of a primary burial (de Cardi et al. 1982 p. 70).

Finds. At the southwestern corner of the chamber two carnelian beads were found, one on the floor (1050.B) and the other (1050.A) in disturbed sediments in the looter's hole.
1050.A: Rounded biconical red carnelian bead, irregular polished surface, L 4.4 mm, D 5.5 mm (fig. 142).
1050.B: Disc-shaped red carnelian bead, irregular polished surface, L 2.3 mm, D 5.6 mm (fig. 143).

Fig. 139. Tomb 1050 looking N.

Fig. 140. The excavated burial chamber.

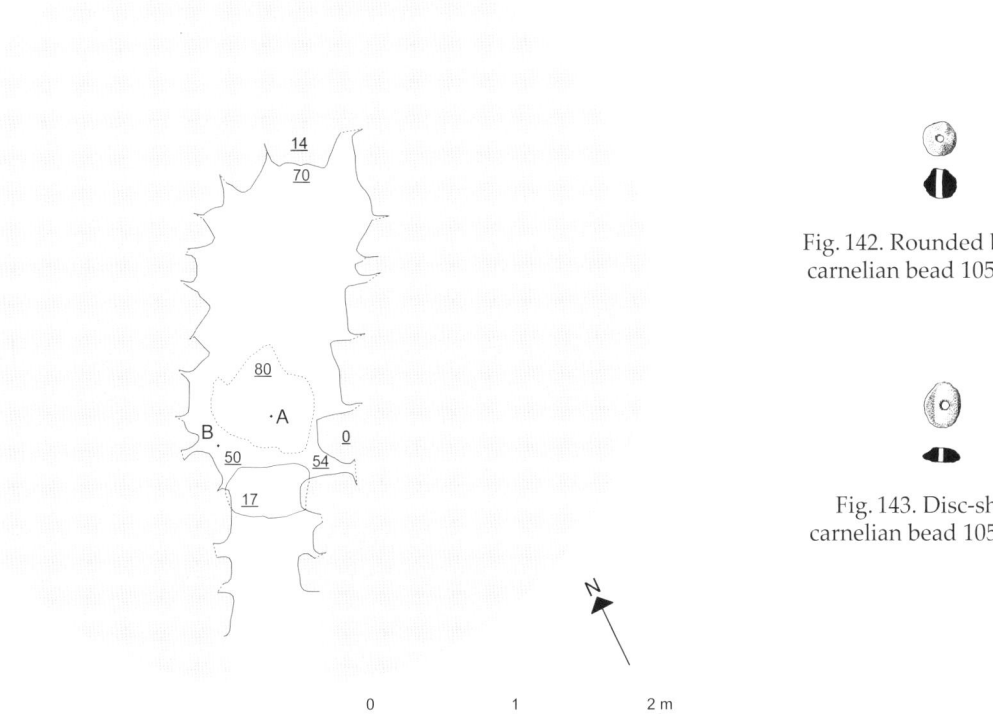

Fig. 142. Rounded biconical carnelian bead 1050.A, 1:1.

Fig. 143. Disc-shaped carnelian bead 1050.B, 1:1.

Fig. 141. Plan of Tomb 1050 with the outline of the ring wall reconstructed, 1:50. The dotted line indicate looter's hole in the floor.

TOMB 1051

Location. The tomb was situated at the eastern foot of the western ridge a few meters northeast of Tomb 1050. The altitude can be estimated to be 270-280 m above sea level. A photograph of the very scattered low mound before excavation shows a background landscape with the northern end of the eastern mountain ridge and the eastern part of Al-Ain (fig. 144). The wide sandy plain, the *hazm* or land for grazing with shrubs and trees, stretches towards the low stony escarpment where the mounds are located (cf. Frifelt 1971 p. 382: Cairn 22).

The excavation. The excavation of the tomb in 1963 was led by Jørgen Lund. Priority was given to the investigation of the chamber and entrance passage. The chamber was emptied by excavating the rubble in the "plundering hole" in the top of the mound, and then excavated gradually in horizontal layers. The outer perimeter of the tomb was not investigated due to its poor preservation.

Structural remains. The excavation recovered remains of a tomb with a central chamber and an entrance passage towards the south-east (figs. 145-146). The very large chamber had an almost circular plan measuring 2.6 m in line with the axis of the entrance passage and almost 2.8 m in width. The chamber wall was preserved with seven courses surviving and stood between 0.7 m high in the south to 1 m high in the north. Only a slight incline in the wall remnant indicated that the chamber might have had a corbelled construction. The stones used in the dry walling were of medium size, 0.2 to 0.3 m. The floor has probably been covered with flagstones as several large flat stones were observed above the base level.

The entrance passage at the mouth of the chamber had a height of 0.65 m. The preserved length was 2 m and the width tapered in from 0.6 m to 0.5 m near the entrance. A single very large block with a length of c. 0.8 m was used as part of the flanking wall in the east side of the passage. To judge from the photograph the walls were almost vertical and must have been either highly corbelled or covered with large stone blocks.

The ring wall was damaged and scattered from extensive stone quarrying, but must have been 2 to 2.5 m thick. The present diameter of the disturbed mound was c. 8 m.

Finds. A considerable number of artefacts were discovered, all found peripherally in the chamber. Their location is either a product of a burial custom where the objects were placed close to the wall or they may have been pushed aside when the burial floor was cleared for a secondary burial. In the rear of the chamber, at the northern end, three ceramic vessels were standing or lying on the floor close to the chamber wall (fig. 147), indicating several interments on the primary level. East of the entrance were a large quantity of faience and heated steatite beads and some beads of carnelian. On the western side four carnelian beads were recovered. A fragment of a sea shell was found in the disturbed fill at a higher level. On a protruding wall stone, 10 cm above the floor level, lay a copper or bronze arrowhead of Late Bronze Age date and therefore indicating a secondary burial. No skeletal material was observed apart from bone splinters.

1051.A: Biconical ceramic vessel of Jemdet Nasr type, well made, thin walled, in fine orange ware with a creamy slip (fig. 148).
1051.B: Biconical ceramic vessel of Jemdet Nasr type, in buff sand-tempered ware, partly discoloured by fire; faint traces of plum-red paint on the rim (fig. 149).
1051.C: Biconical ceramic vessel with marked, grooved shoulder of Jemdet Nasr type, in reddish-brown sand-tempered ware with faint traces of plum-red paint on shoulder and base (fig. 150).
1051.D. Tanged, leaf-shaped arrowhead of copper, 5.1 cm long (fig. 151).
1051.E: A large cluster, 375-390, of beads (fig. 152); 240-255 cylindrical of greenish faience, L 2.2-6.5 mm, D 2.5-5.1 mm (figs. 153-154); 6 double segmented, cylindrical of greenish faience, L 6-10.3 mm, D 4.2-4.9 mm (figs. 155-156); 120 cylindrical of heated steatite, L 2-4.1 mm, D 2.5-3.7 mm (figs. 157-158); 7 biconical of heated steatite, L 1.5-3 mm, D 2.2-3.8 mm (figs. 159-160); and 2 red carnelian ring-shaped beads, L 2.1-3 mm, D 4.2-6.2 mm (figs. 152).
1051.F: Two large (L 2.7-3.1 mm, D 5.8 mm) (fig. 161) and two small (L 1.4-2 mm, D 4.2-4.4 mm) (fig. 162), ring-shaped, red carnelian beads.
1051.G: Rim sherd, maybe from vessel 1051.C, found in secondary position.
1051.H: Fragment of cockle shell (fig. 163).

Fig. 144. Tomb 1051 looking NE. In the distant background Al-Ain can be seen.

Fig. 145. The chamber and entrance passage looking NW.

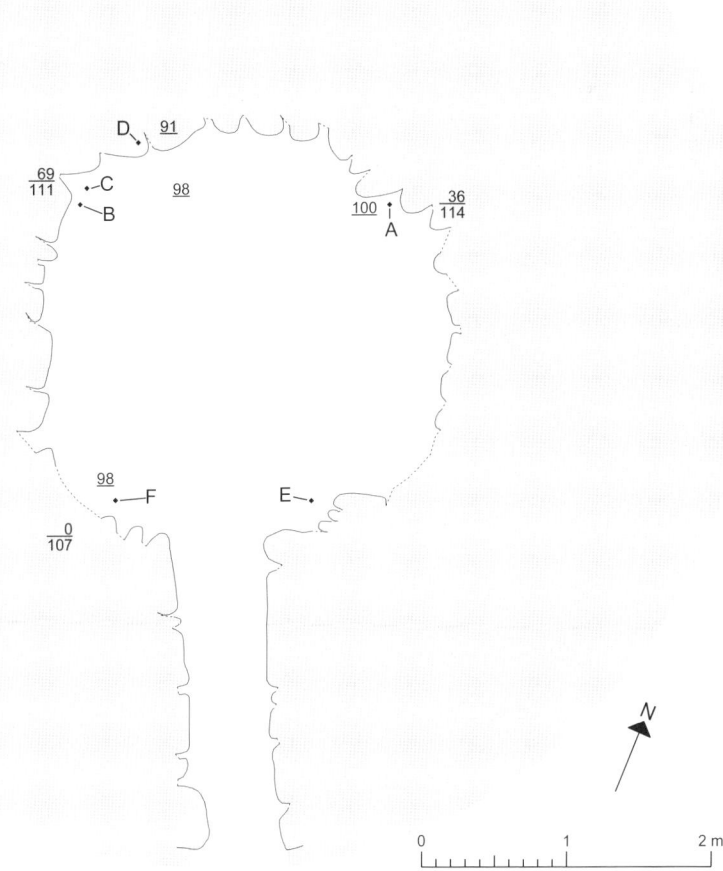

Fig. 146. Plan of Tomb 1051, the estimated outline of the ring wall is indicated, 1:50.

Fig. 147. Two ceramic vessels in situ close to the wall in the north-western side of the chamber.

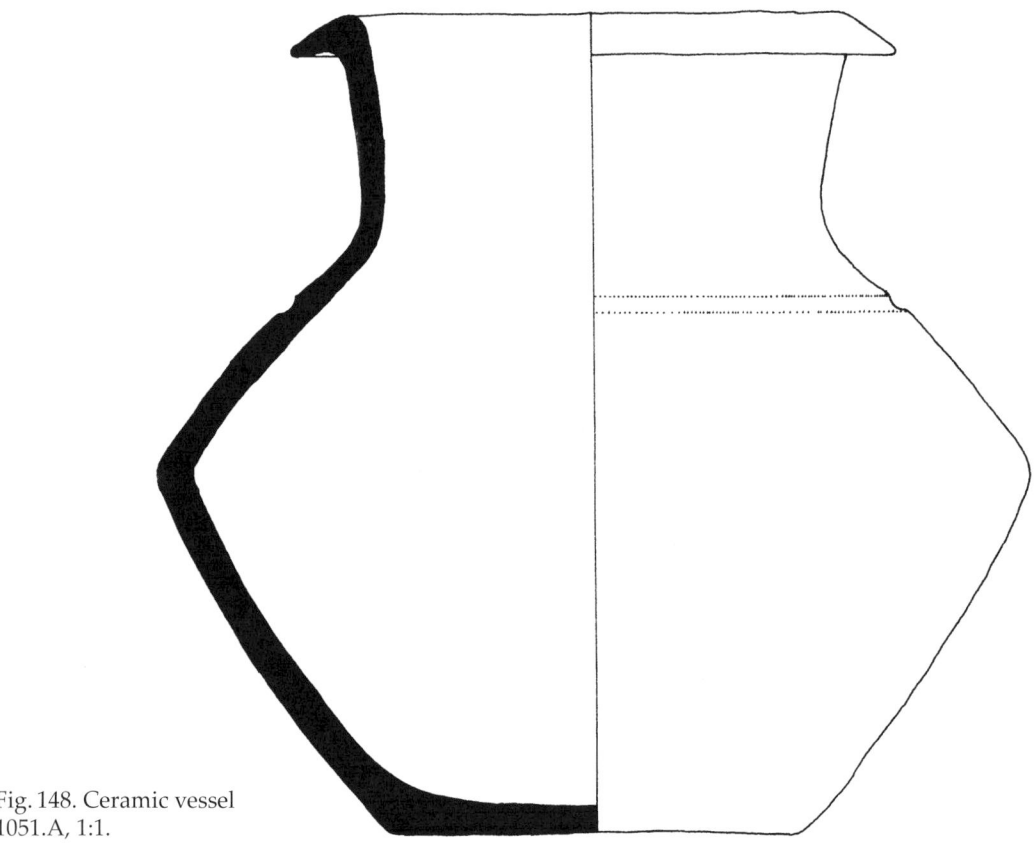

Fig. 148. Ceramic vessel 1051.A, 1:1.

Fig. 149. Ceramic vessel 1051.B, 1:1.

Fig. 150. Ceramic vessel 1051.C, 1:2.

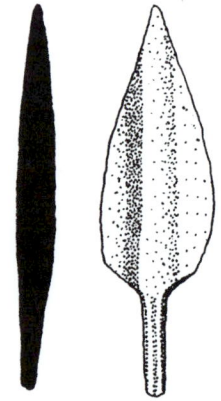

Fig. 151. Copper arrowhead
1051.D, 1:1.

Fig. 152. Beads from Tomb 1051.

Fig. 153. Light greenish cylindrical faience bead 1051.E, 1:1.

Fig. 154. Light greenish, cylindrical faience bead 1051.E, 1:1.

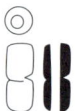

Fig. 155. Light greenish, double-segmented faience bead 1051.E, 1:1.

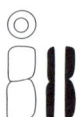

Fig. 156. Light greenish, double-segmented faience bead 1051.E, 1:1.

Fig. 157. Cylindrical bead in heated steatite 1051.E, 1:1.

Fig. 158. Cylindrical bead in heated steatite 1051.E, 1:1.

Fig. 159. Biconical bead in heated steatite 1051.E, 1:1.

Fig. 160. Biconical bead in heated steatite 1051.E, 1:1.

Fig. 161. Ring-shaped carnelian bead 1051.F, 1:1.

Fig. 162. Ring-shaped carnelian bead 1051.F, 1:1.

Fig. 163. Shell fragment 1051.H, 1:1.

TOMB 1052

Location. The tomb was situated within a group of mounds which includes the previously described Tombs 1047-49 situated on the foothills of the western mountain ridge. The altitude is estimated to be between 280 and 290 m above sea level. The tomb was placed on a natural hillock (cf. Frifelt 1971 p. 382: Cairn 23).

The excavation. The excavation in 1963 was led by Vagn Kolstrup. The burial chamber and entrance was excavated commencing from the plundering hole on top of the scattered structure. The outer periphery was not investigated in any detail.

Structural remains. The excavation revealed the remains of a tomb with a central chamber and entrance passage pointing towards the SSE (figs. 164-165).

The chamber had an oval, slightly asymmetrical plan with a length of 2 m in line with the axis of the entrance and a width of 1.9 m. The chamber wall was preserved to a height of c. 1.3 m with seven courses remaining. The stones were up to 0.4 m in size, rather irregular and with the longest axis pointing towards the centre of the chamber. This together with the incline of the wall indicated a corbelled roof construction. The floor consisted of sand and gravel.

The entrance passage could be traced for 1.8 m and had a width of c. 0.5 m. The flanking walls had six remaining courses and a height of around 1 m. Two flagstones were observed roofing the inner part of the passage (fig. 166). The largest stone measured 0.9 × 0.35 × 0.1 m. They were both from slate-like greenish sandstone or a cherty (dolomite) limestone, quite different from the usual local whitish-grey limestone. The source of this particular type of stone was located during the 1971 campaign as an exposure of stratified, shale-like hard limestone in outcrops in the western mountain ridge.

The entrance passage was partially blocked with stones to a height of 0.5 to 0.6 m. The entrance had not survived stone quarrying, so it is not known whether the entrance was completely sealed.

The ring wall was destroyed from the outside. The outer diameter of the remains was c. 5.5 m, but it must have been somewhat larger on the basis of the intact tomb.

Finds. The chamber contained two ceramic vessels lying on the floor to the south (1052.A) and to the north (1052.B) and probably corresponding to two interments. The latter was next to a large copper blade and two copper pins. Also next to the vessel some human cranial fragments were observed as were scattered bone splinters in upper deposits.

Fig. 164. Tomb 1052 during excavation looking N. Note the large flagstone used as lintel in the interior entrance passage.

1052.A: Ceramic vessel with rim and neck of Jemdet Nasr type, but with a globular body, in reddish brown sand-tempered ware (fig. 167).

1052.B: Biconical ceramic vessel of Jemdet Nasr type of very careful manufacture in fine beige ware with incised line on the shoulder; probably flat base, though too badly broken to decide, with diameter about 4 cm (fig. 168).

1052.C: Copper pin with square section, 12.1 cm long (fig. 169).

1052.D: Copper pin with square section, 11.4 cm long (fig. 170).

1052.E: Copper blade with slight midrib and two rivet-holes, 21.7 cm long (fig. 171).

1052.F: Human skeletal remains.

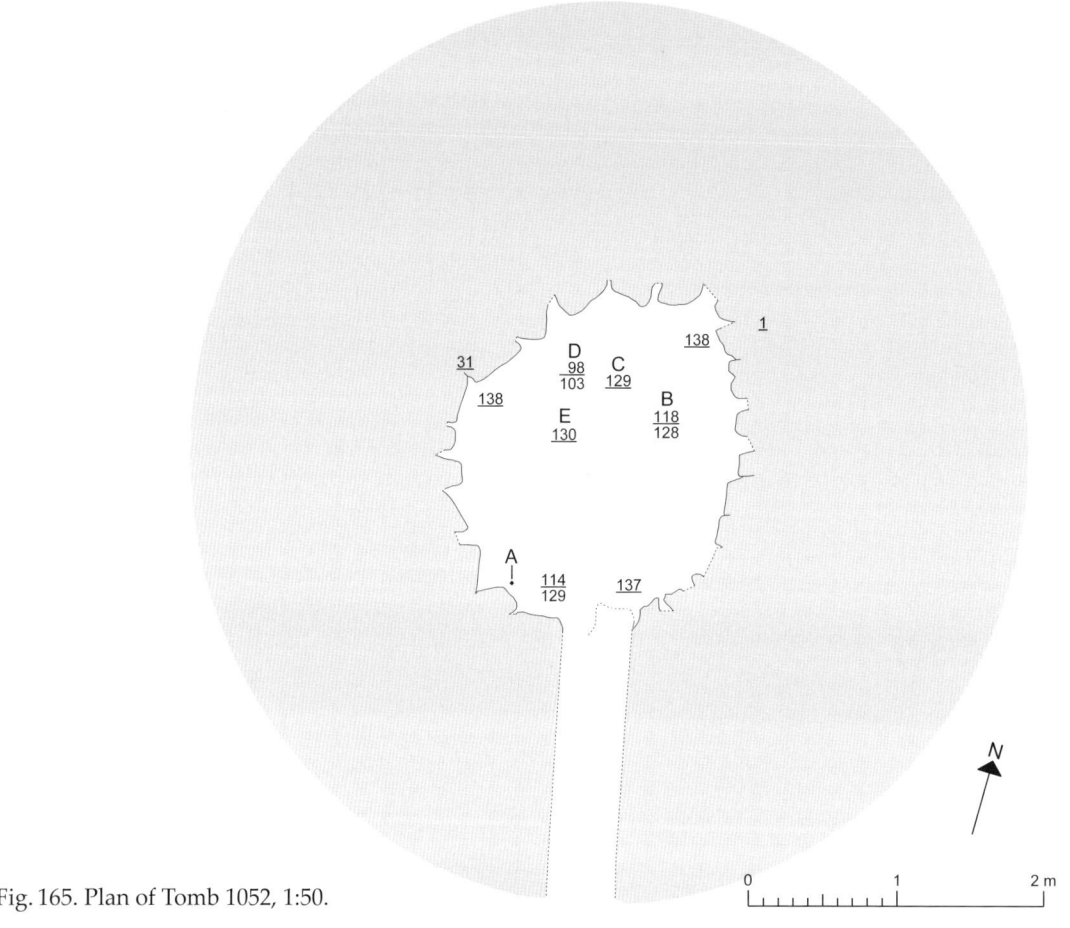

Fig. 165. Plan of Tomb 1052, 1:50.

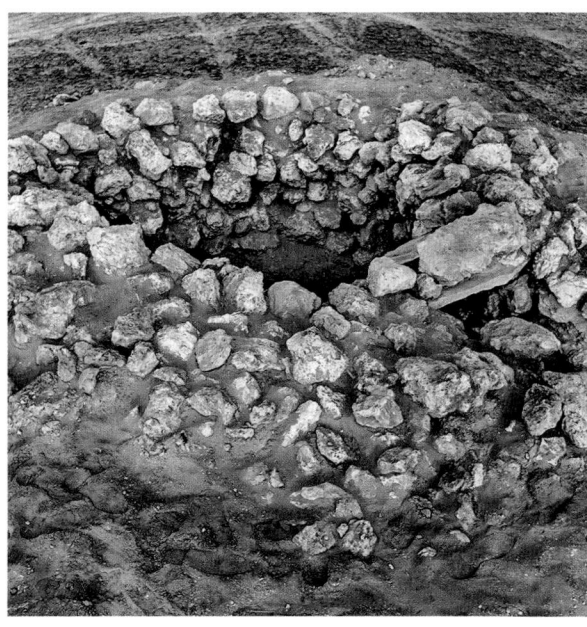

Fig. 166. Tomb 1052 looking NE.

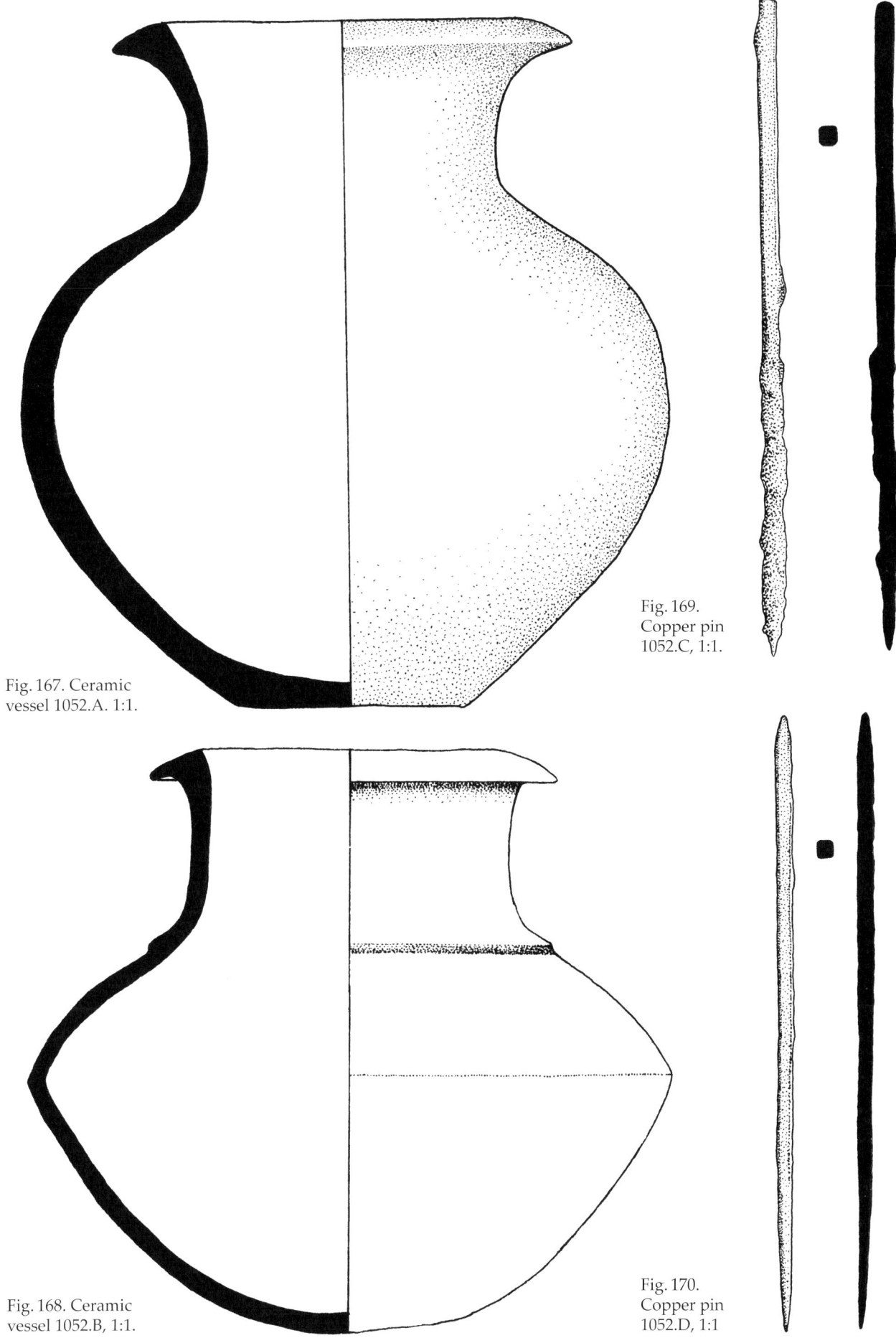

Fig. 167. Ceramic vessel 1052.A. 1:1.

Fig. 169. Copper pin 1052.C, 1:1.

Fig. 168. Ceramic vessel 1052.B, 1:1.

Fig. 170. Copper pin 1052.D, 1:1

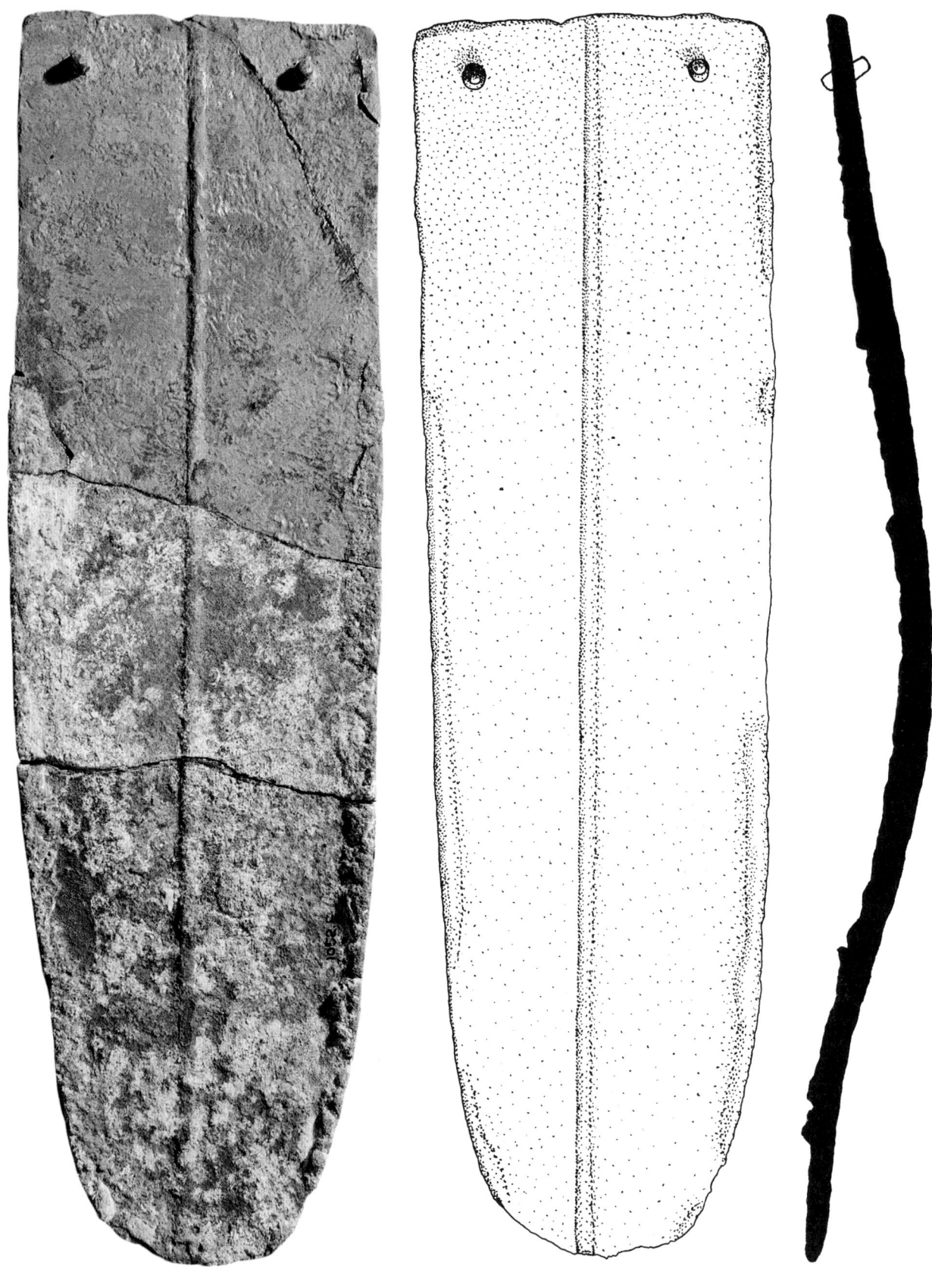

Fig. 171. Copper blade 1052.E, 1:1.

TOMB 1053

Location. The tomb was situated at the northernmost end of the western mountain ridge (fig. 172). It was positioned to the west of Tombs 1050 and 1051 on sloping terrain at the foot of the ridge. The altitude is estimated to be around 280 m above sea level (cf. Frifelt 1971 p. 382: Cairn 24).

The excavation. The investigation in 1963 was led by Vagn Kolstrup. It revealed a double structure with two adjacent tombs under the same mound of disturbed stones. Only the chamber areas were closer examined. The excavation started from clearing the top of the western part of the mound, which had a fresh plundering hole and from there expanded into what proved to be a separate eastern chamber.

Structural remains, the primary tomb. The investigation uncovered the remains of a tomb with a central oval to rounded chamber that falls within the design of the Hafit type tombs (figs. 173-174). The length was c. 2.2 m and the width had been somewhere between 1.6-1.9 m. The east wall had fallen in or was damaged from the east. The chamber was preserved to nearly a metre in height with seven courses of stones. The stones in the chamber wall were of medium size, elongated and around 0.3 to 0.4 m in size. They were rather carefully stacked with an inwards incline and their longest axis pointing towards the centre of the chamber, giving an appearance of the lower part of a corbelled vault. The floor consisted of sand and gravel. An entrance passage was not noticed.

The outer remains of the mound had a preserved diameter estimated to be 6-7 m.

No finds were observed in the chamber.

Structural remains, the secondary tomb. The remains indicated a cist-like, oblong chamber oriented ENE (figs. 173-175). The estimated length was 2.3-2.4 m and the width c. 0.9 m. The structure was strongly damaged by stone quarrying, and the wall only preserved with three courses to a height of 0.5 to 0.7 m. The stones were rather randomly stacked or maybe disturbed. The wall was too low to indicate any corbelled construction.

This chamber seems to be of a different construction resembling some of the Wadi Suq as well as some large Iron Age cists (Vogt 1994). The excavator expressed doubt in the field notes whether the eastern chamber had an entrance. On the field plan a hypothetical entrance towards the southeast is indicated as two short hatched lines, but it is also plausible to consider this area as a disturbance from stone robbing or looting.

Finds. 1053.A: Fragments of two limb bones were found close to the southern chamber wall of the secondary tomb.

Fig. 172. Tomb 1053 before excavation.

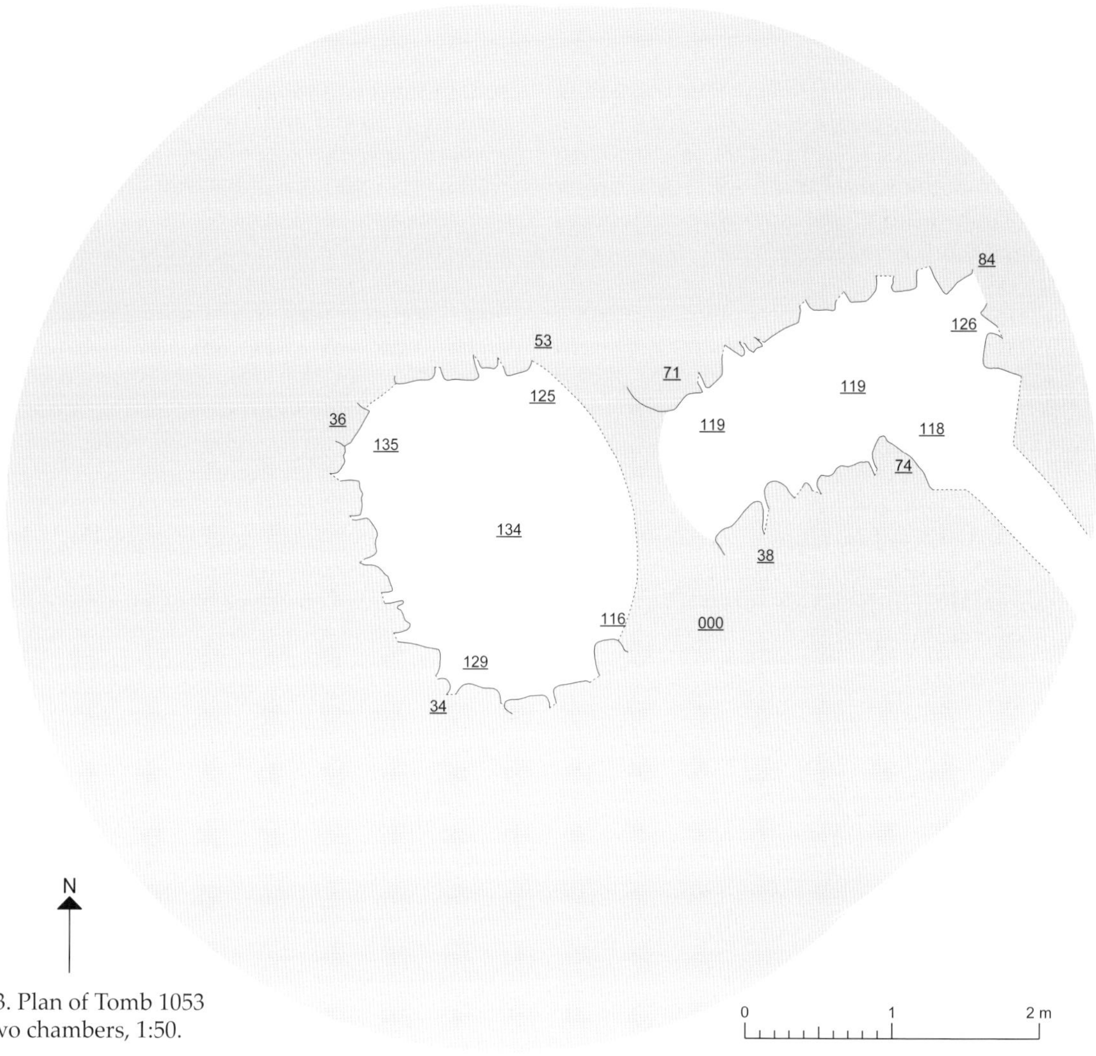

Fig. 173. Plan of Tomb 1053 with two chambers, 1:50.

Fig. 174. In the foreground the secondary chamber; in the background the primary Hafit type tomb.

Fig. 175. The secondary tomb viewed from NNW.

TOMB 1054

Location. The tomb was positioned in a small side valley around ten meters up from the foot of the western mountain ridge (fig. 176). The tomb was part of a group of other mounds 80-100 m west of Tomb 1053 and 2-2.2 km south of the north end of the ridge at an estimated altitude of 290 m above sea level.

The excavation. Vagn Kolstrup was in charge of the excavation which took place in 1963. The tomb was placed on a hillock, which made the mound appear larger. Larger stones from the passage were protruding from the surface of the mound. The mound had a plundering hole in the centre. The excavation commenced from this location by identifying the outline of the chamber wall and the entrance passage, which were thereafter emptied by digging horizontal layers by hoe and trowel. The periphery of the tomb structure was not investigated.

Structural remains. A tomb with a central chamber and an entrance passage towards the south was identified (figs. 177-178). The chamber had a rounded rectangular plan twisted a little towards the east from the axis of entrance. It was c. 1.8 m long and 1.5 m wide. The chamber wall was only preserved to a height of 0.5 to 0.6 m with four courses still remaining. The dry walling consisted of densely stacked elongated blocks up to 0.4 m in size. Only their orientation toward the centre of the chamber indicated a corbelled construction since the incline of the wall was very limited. The floor consisted of a sand fill levelled on the bedrock.

The entrance was 0.4 m wide at the chamber. It was preserved to a length of 1.2 m. The ring wall was damaged and scattered by stone quarrying or looting. The outer diameter of the ruined tomb was 6 m.

Finds. The finds consisted of a few bone fragments.

Fig. 176. Tomb 1054 before excavation looking N.

Fig. 177. The excavated tomb viewed looking N.

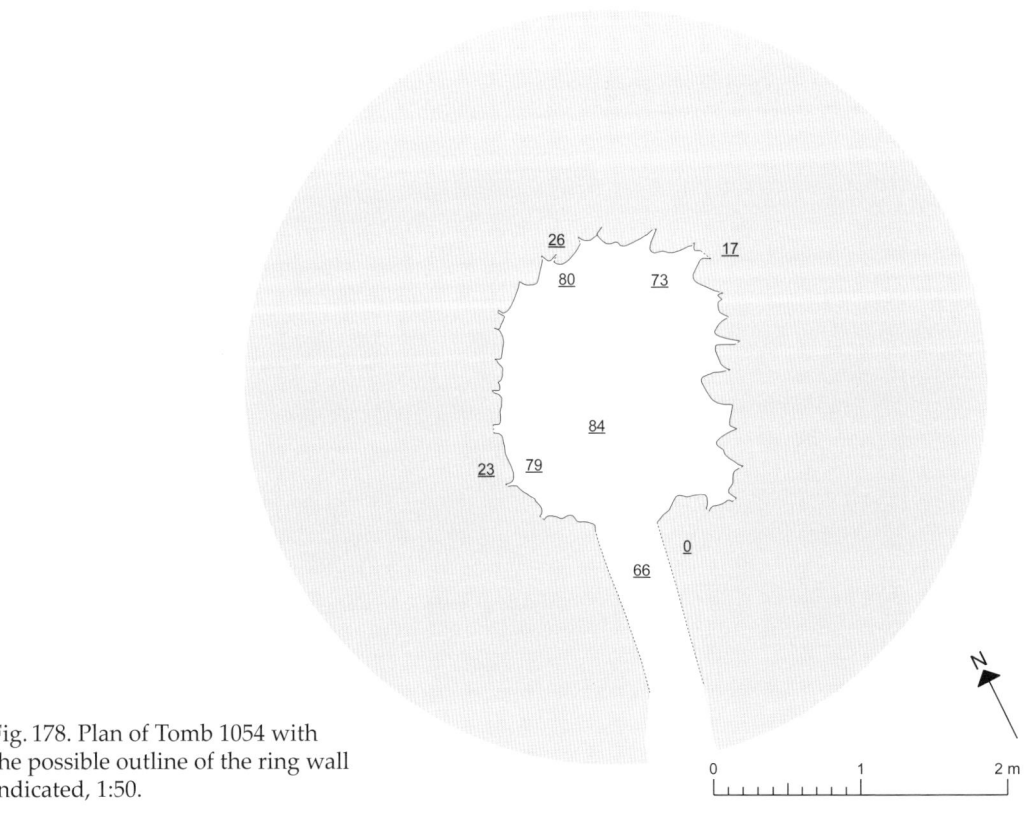

Fig. 178. Plan of Tomb 1054 with the possible outline of the ring wall indicated, 1:50.

TOMB 1055.B

During the 1971 campaign in the Hafit area, an almost completely demolished tomb was discovered on the western mountain ridge. The tomb was located in a transverse valley about 150 m east of Tomb 1310 at an approximate altitude of 290-300 m above sea level. The damage done by stone plundering offered no chance of any excavation results with respect to the tomb structure. The area was carefully searched and fragments of pottery were collected.

Finds. 1055.B: Rounded biconical ceramic vessel of Jemdet Nasr type in brown micaceous ware, greyish-yellow slip (fig. 179).

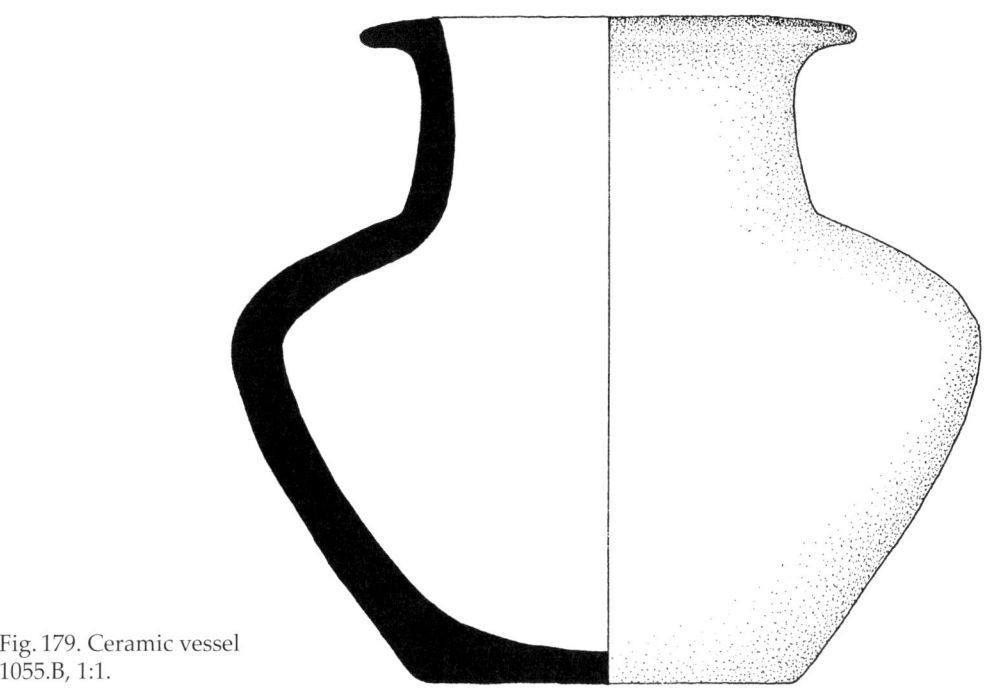

Fig. 179. Ceramic vessel 1055.B, 1:1.

TOMB 1055.D

A demolished tomb situated c. 100 m east of Tomb 1310. Part of a ceramic vessel was collected in 1971 after searching the area.

Finds. 1055.D: Lower part of rounded biconical ceramic vessel with carinated shoulder of Jemdet Nasr type in brown micaceous ware with greyish-yellow slip and purple-red paint (fig. 180).

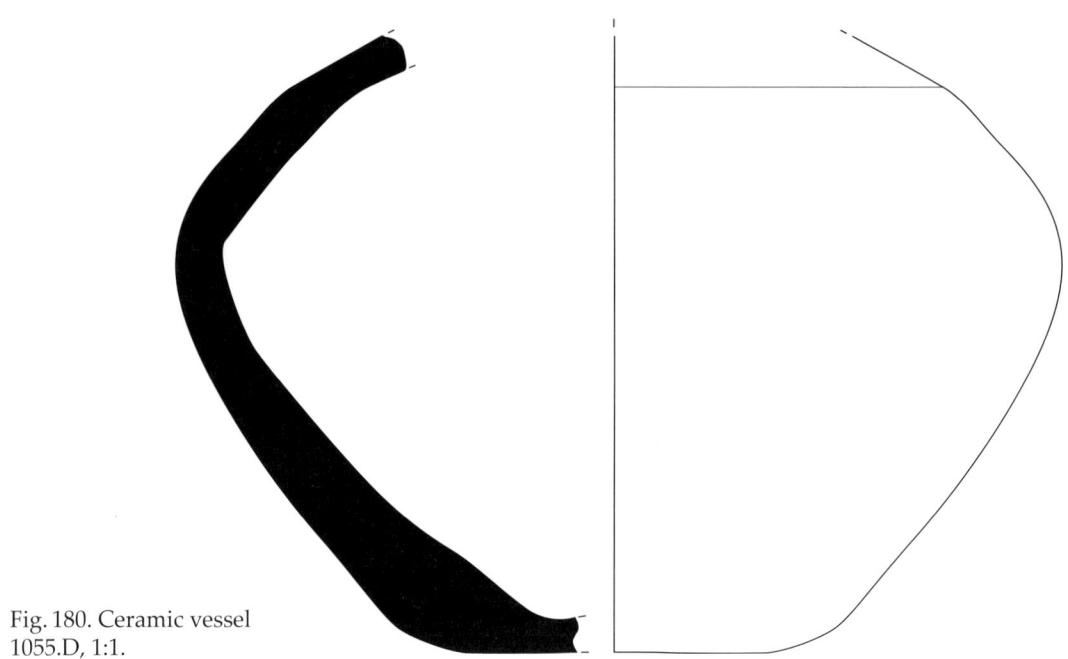

Fig. 180. Ceramic vessel 1055.D, 1:1.

TOMB 1055.L

A demolished tomb situated c. 170 m east of Tomb 1314. A few beads were found on the surface.

Finds. 1055.L: Three green glazed cylindrical faience beads, two of which were double segmented, with a length of 7.2-7.8 mm, and a diameter of 4 mm (fig. 181), and five square beads of heated steatite, drilled through opposing corners, 6-6.6 × 6.1-6.5 × 2.3-3.6 mm (fig. 182).

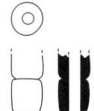

Fig. 181. Double segmented cylindrical faience bead 1055.L, 1:1.

Fig. 182. Square bead in heated steatite 1055.L, 1:1.

TOMB 1300

Location. The tomb was situated in the northernmost end of the western ridge on the slopes of the fifth peak from the north at an altitude estimated to be 290 m above sea level (figs. 183). The mound lay on a low hillock on the eastern side of a natural pass approximately 30 m above the valley to the east. The position was close to the dirt track that ran through the pass. A small shack was located on the opposite side of the pass and was used by foreign labourers quarrying stone from the tombs to be used for cement production in kilns about one kilometer away. The pass had numerous small tracks on the lower slopes from herders driving their animals through for generations.

The excavation. The tomb was excavated in 1971 by the whole team as a test case. The structural remains were manually uncovered by removing loose soil, rubble and disturbed stones. The most destroyed southern half was cleared until the level of the lowest course in the ring wall, and the bedrock around was cleared. The chamber area was carefully excavated in horizontal layers until the bedrock was reached.

Structural remains. The grave appeared as a low mound due to extensive digging and stone removal. During the excavation remains of a central chamber could be identified, but traces of an entrance passage were not found (fig. 184).

The width of the oval chamber was c. 1.6 m. The length could not be determined with certainty, but probably not more than a couple of meters. The northern part of the chamber was preserved to 3-4 courses and a height of just 0.3 to 0.5 m above the bedrock. Several elongated, up to 0.5-0.6 m long blocks were placed pointing toward the centre of the chamber, an orientation often seen in corbelled construction.

Remains of a pavement made from thin stone slabs, 0.2 to 0.3 m long, were found in the northern end of the chamber (fig. 185). The slabs most likely came from layers of sandstone or limestone observed at the foot of the mountain ridge. The pavement was laid on a levelled layer of sand resting on the bedrock. From 0.1 m under the slabs some bone fragments were observed indicating that the pavement was from a secondary burial level (assuming that the splinters are from human bones). Under the floor pavement and sand as well as under the ring wall itself a charred zone was observed indicating a fire, the heat of which had caused a reddening of the limestone.

The southern part of the chamber and the possible entrance area were too demolished to be identified.

The outline of the tomb was only partially preserved. Remains of concentric stone lines from a ring wall could be identified on the western side. The building material was irregular, but more or less flat stones of varied sizes, from 0.2 to 0.4 m, were used. The diameter of the ruined ring wall was c. 4 m, but must have been somewhat larger.

Finds. A number of small beads were found scattered in the mixed deposits above the floor along the northern side of the chamber. In the mixed deposits across the entire structure small bone fragments were observed.

Fig. 183. Tomb 1300 looking E.

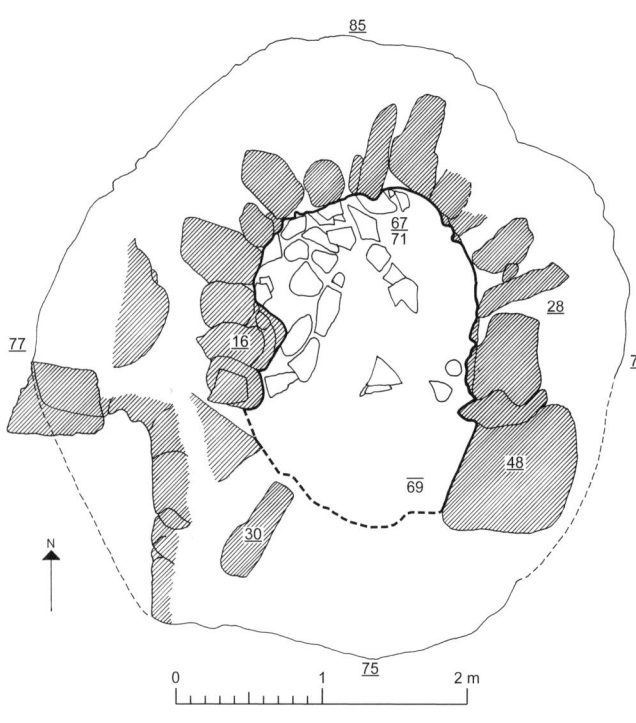

Fig. 184. Plan of Tomb 1300, 1:50.

1300.A: 19 beads; 11 green glazed, cylindrical faience, L 2.8-3.9 mm, D 2.7-4 mm (fig. 186); 5 cylindrical, heated steatite, L 3.2-4.3 mm, D 3-3.3 mm (fig. 187); 1 cylindrical, red stone (possibly radiolarite), L 1.8 mm, D 2.6 mm, perforated from two sides with clear rotational marks (fig. 188); 2 disc-shaped, green, translucent rock crystal, L 1.2-1.3 mm, D 3 mm (fig. 189).
1300.B: Fragments of shell.
1300.C: Splinters of human bone.
1300.D: Charcoal sample collected from underneath the ring wall and bottom flagstone pavement.

Some additional finds were registered during the field work in spring 1971 through Mr. Taisir Kayed of the Department of Information & Tourism. The finds had been received from Sheikh Ahmad bin Hamad (Head of the Ministry of Information) and were said to have been collected from the vicinity of Tomb 1300 or from the tomb itself by workmen quarrying stone from tombs for cement manufacture.
1055.E: Copper vessel (fig. 190).
1055.F: Upper part of ceramic vessel with rim-neck-shoulder of Jemdet Nasr type but with a tall body in red-brown, micaceous ware with greyish-yellow slip (fig. 191).
1055.G: Large sherd from a softstone vessel with a fish-like ornament.
1055.H: Rim sherd from ceramic bowl, of reddish-brown micaceous ware with greyish-yellow slip.
1055.I: Small fragments of long bones, probably human.

Fig. 185. Fine flagstones at the chamber floor.

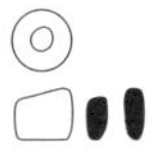

Fig. 186. Green faience bead 1300.A, 1:1.

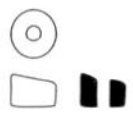

Fig. 188. Red stone bead 1300.A, 1:1.

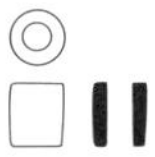

Fig. 187. Bead of heated steatite 1300.A, 1:1.

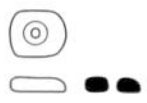

Fig. 189. Green rock crystal bead 1300.A, 1:1.

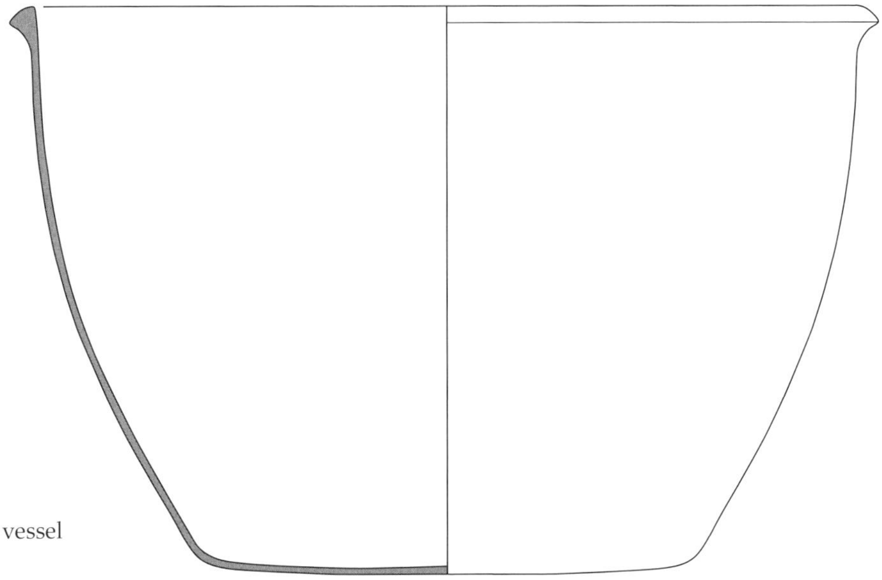

Fig. 190. Copper vessel 1055.E, 1:1.

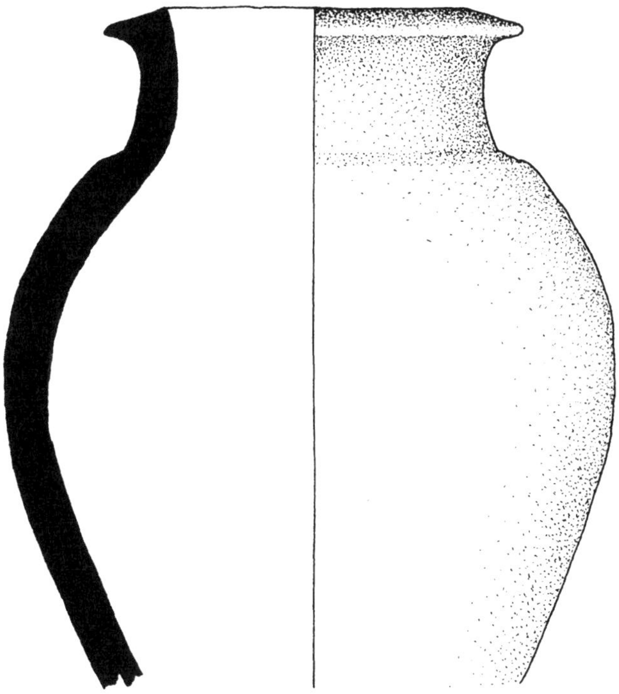

Fig. 191. Ceramic vessel 1055.F, 1:1.

TOMB 1301

Location. The grave was discovered some 15 m west of Tomb 1300 on a steep rock slope facing north. The grave was positioned 3 m below the top of the slope and placed against a 1 m tall vertical cliff.

The excavation. The disturbed grave was discovered by N.A. Boas in 1971 who noticed some stone blocks that resembled remains of a wall on the side of the mountain ridge. When taking a closer look a few human bones, primarily the posterior side of the cranium with the characteristic occipital bone were spotted lying amongst the stone and rubble. The cranium and other skeletal remains were uncovered, cleaned and photographed (fig. 192).

Structural remains. The skeletal remains had been positioned behind a semicircular stone structure built on a narrow shelf in front of and probably leaning against the rock wall. A few irregular blocks of this wall still remained on the eastern side of the skeletal remains. The structure was estimated to be 1.5 m wide and 1 m deep. This was the first time such a rock shelter type tomb was excavated. Similar tombs have later been investigated around Jebel al-Buhais (Jasim 2012 p. 293).

Finds. A cranium lay face down with disarticulated extremities on either side of it, but at a higher level. The limbs are represented by parts of a femur, tibia, fibula and some scattered bones from the feet. It appears that burial took place after the bones had become disarticulated. East of the cranium, separated by a distance of 0.15 m, a perforated shell button was found in mixed sediments.

1301.A: A conical shell button with three V-shaped perforations (fig. 193).
1301.B: Skeletal remains.

Fig. 192. Dislocated skeletal material in Tomb 1301; remains of the north sealing wall can be seen in the left side of the photo.

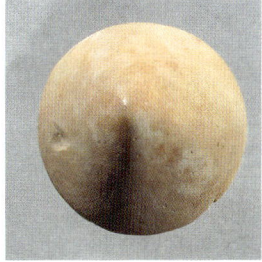 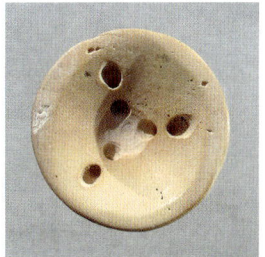

Fig. 193. Shell button 1301.A, 1:1.

TOMB 1302

Location. The tomb was located on the south side of a transverse valley with a dirt track cutting the western mountain ridge. Its altitude was close to 330 m above sea level. The mound lay between Tombs 1301 and 1303. Coming through the pass the rather intact tomb could be seen high up at the end of a steep mountain side where it was placed on a small peak (figs. 194-196).

The excavation. The investigation took place in 1971 and was carried out by N.A. Boas, Michael Beck and Karen Frifelt. It commenced from the plundering hole on top of the mound. The chamber was excavated in horizontal layers by scraping carefully with a hoe, removing fallen stones and then later on digging with trowels. Most of the outer structure was cleared with the exception of the southern part where the outer face of the ring wall had collapsed.

Structural remains. The excavation revealed a well preserved tomb with a central chamber (fig. 197). The chamber had an oval- to pear-shaped plan, c. 2 m long in a northeastern to southwestern direction and 1.8 m wide. The chamber wall was made from densely stacked stones up to a size of c. 0.4 m. It was preserved to a height of 1.8 to 2 m above bedrock. The incline of the wall was about 0.4 m indicating that a relatively high corbelled vault had covered the chamber.

The upper sediments consisted of rather loose sand and scattered stone blocks. In the lowest 0.3 m the fill was consistently harder along the eastern and northern side. In the more loose sediment towards the south numerous rodent holes as well as rodent bones were found together with scats from bird of prey. Additionally, some possible egg shells were encountered. At the base of the chamber a partial pavement of hand sized, irregular stones were found on a level sand layer (fig. 198). Towards the southwest the floor consisted of bedrock over an area measuring c. 0.4 × 0.5 m.

The entrance passage was probably overlooked during the excavation. In some of the later excavations carefully sealed entrance passages were found where, even from the inside of the chamber wall, it was difficult to spot the secondary blocking because the stones blocking the entrance passage were carefully wedged in line with the chamber wall. It is likely that the south wall is actually blocking and hiding the entrance to the chamber.

The ring wall with the base and outer wall face was preserved in some parts (fig. 199). The northeastern quarter had slid downwards towards the steep slope just below, but for the rest of the tomb the outer line of at least the lower stone courses was in place. Concentric rows of stone could be observed in the ring wall construction. On the south side a concentric wall part could be observed until half a meter above the outer baseline. The diameter was around 6 m.

Finds. Badly preserved skeletal remains were found in the northeastern part of the chamber and cranial parts of three individuals could be identified. The skeletal material was observed from about 0.5 m above the chamber floor until the level of the floor.

1302.A: Skeletal remains from 3 individuals.
1302.B: Fragments from shells or eggs.

Fig. 194. Tomb 1302 looking S.

Fig. 195. Tomb 1302, looking NW, with sand dunes and palaeo-soil, spring 1971. The area is today part of suburban Al-Ain town, the zoo-district and Falaj Hazza.

Fig. 196. Tomb 1302 before excavation.

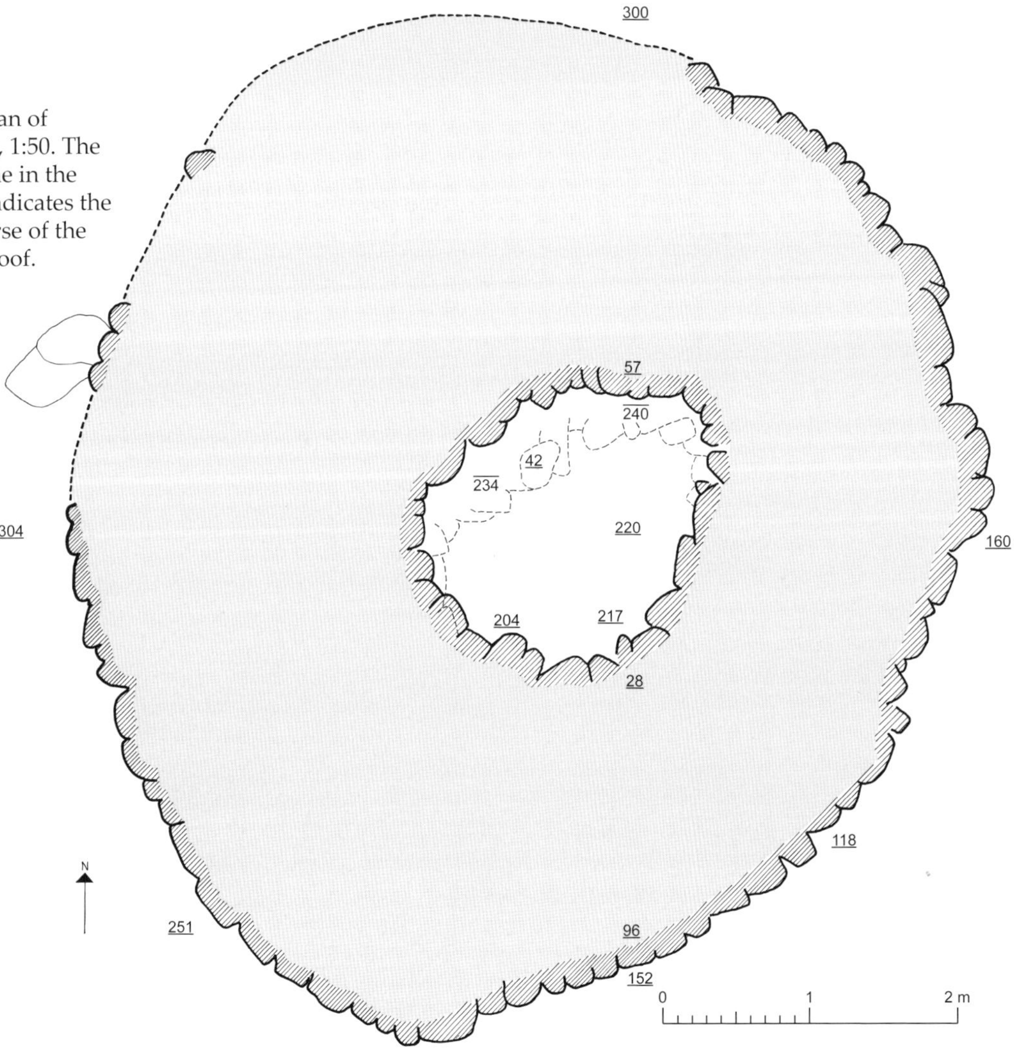

Fig. 197. Plan of Tomb 1302, 1:50. The hatched line in the chamber indicates the upper course of the corbelled roof.

Fig. 198. The floor level in the chamber.

Fig. 199. The outer ring wall cleared of loose blocks and rubble.

TOMB 1303

Location. Tomb 1303 was positioned at the western mountain ridge c. 100 m WSW of Tomb 1302 and south of the same pass as described above (figs. 200-201). The altitude is estimated to be 300 m above sea level and around 30 m above the desert surface to the west. Tomb 1303 was placed on a northward side ridge with a small sloping plateau large enough for a small mound.

The excavation. Steen Andersen and Bo Madsen were in charge of the investigation which took place in 1971. The excavation commenced from a depression in the top of the stone mound. After identifying the chamber wall, the chamber was gradually excavated in horizontal layers. The eastern part of the mound periphery was uncovered by clearing loose stone and rubble.

Structural remains. The excavation uncovered a tomb consisting of a ring wall with a central chamber (figs. 202-203). The large chamber had a rounded rectangular plan with the long axis oriented towards the southeast, the length was 2.8 m and the width 2.2 m.

The chamber wall was difficult to locate in the upper part of the chamber as some of the dry walling had slid into the chamber, probably in relation to the interment of the uppermost burial. The space for excavation was very limited as it was important to proceed gradually to avoid stone blocks or wall parts from falling down. Some large, more flat blocks had slid down from the roof construction into the upper chamber.

Between 1 and 1.3 m of the chamber wall was preserved and consisted of medium elongated blocks up to a size of 0.4 m, densely stacked with the longest axis towards the centre of the chamber. An incline of more than 0.3 m indicated a corbelled construction. The sediments in the chamber were mixed with sand and stones. The floor consisted of uneven bedrock which was higher at the north side by almost 0.2 m.

An entrance passage was not identified, but most likely would have pointed towards the southeast with a length of c. 1.7 m.

The outer ring wall was preserved to a height of 1 to 1.5 m. On the eastern side the wall face still stood up to 0.6-0.8 m and was only slightly inclined inwards. The outer diameter would have been around 6 m.

Finds. In a high position in the southeastern part of the chamber, 0.8 to 1 m above the floor, a relatively well preserved skeleton, 1303.A, was recovered lying in a flexed position (figs. 204-205). The body was placed on the right side with the head towards the north. The arms were flexed, but with the right lifted towards the head with the hand in front of the head. The long bones, humerus and femur etc., indicate by length and their robustness a rather large and sturdy individual. The cranium is also relatively large. From the long bones including the clavicle the height can be calculated to about 1.73-1.74 m. On the back of the head a round hole was observed. It could not be determined whether this was a *post mortem* damage from a fallen stone or a lesion from an injury. Some of the teeth have been identified as belonging to a young adult, age around 20 years (Højgaard 1980a, 1980b, Højgaard 1985).

Fig. 200. Tomb 1303 guarding the western end of the mountain pass, looking NNE.

Above the right hand and in front of the cranium a badly preserved iron object was found. Some concretions of rust were initially seen above a cylinder standing vertically besides some dots of copper. At the feet of the body another badly preserved iron object with some traces of copper adhering was found. The cylinder can be interpreted as a socket or ferule from a spear or lance head. The vertical position may have been caused by a down fallen stone. The copper may be remnants of shaft rivets.

The upper burial was placed on such a high level that there would have been no access from a possible entrance passage. The very disturbed nature of the deposits in the south-east part of the chamber additionally suggests that this late interment was done by breaking through the top of an already ancient corbelled tomb.

The sediments directly below the skeleton contained no finds. About 0.5 to 0.6 m deeper, above the bedrock floor, some very fragmented human bones were found along the western chamber wall, probably representing a primary burial. In the northernmost corner was a small ceramic vessel. The vessel lay as sherds within an area of c. 0.25 m. The upper part with the rim was found on a stone in a secondary position 0.2-0.3 m above the bedrock (fig. 206).

1303.A, B: Skeletal fragments.
1303.C: Biconical ceramic vessel with faint marked shoulder of Jemdet Nasr type in brown, micaceous sand-tempered ware with black design on red slip. The vessel has subsided somewhat while drying before being fired (fig. 207).
1303.D, E: Iron cylinder, c. 8 cm long and c. 3.5 cm in diameter (fig. 208), with traces of copper or copper alloy. Spear socket or ferrule?

Fig. 201. Tomb 1303 before excavation looking WNW.

Fig. 202. The disturbed chamber during excavation.

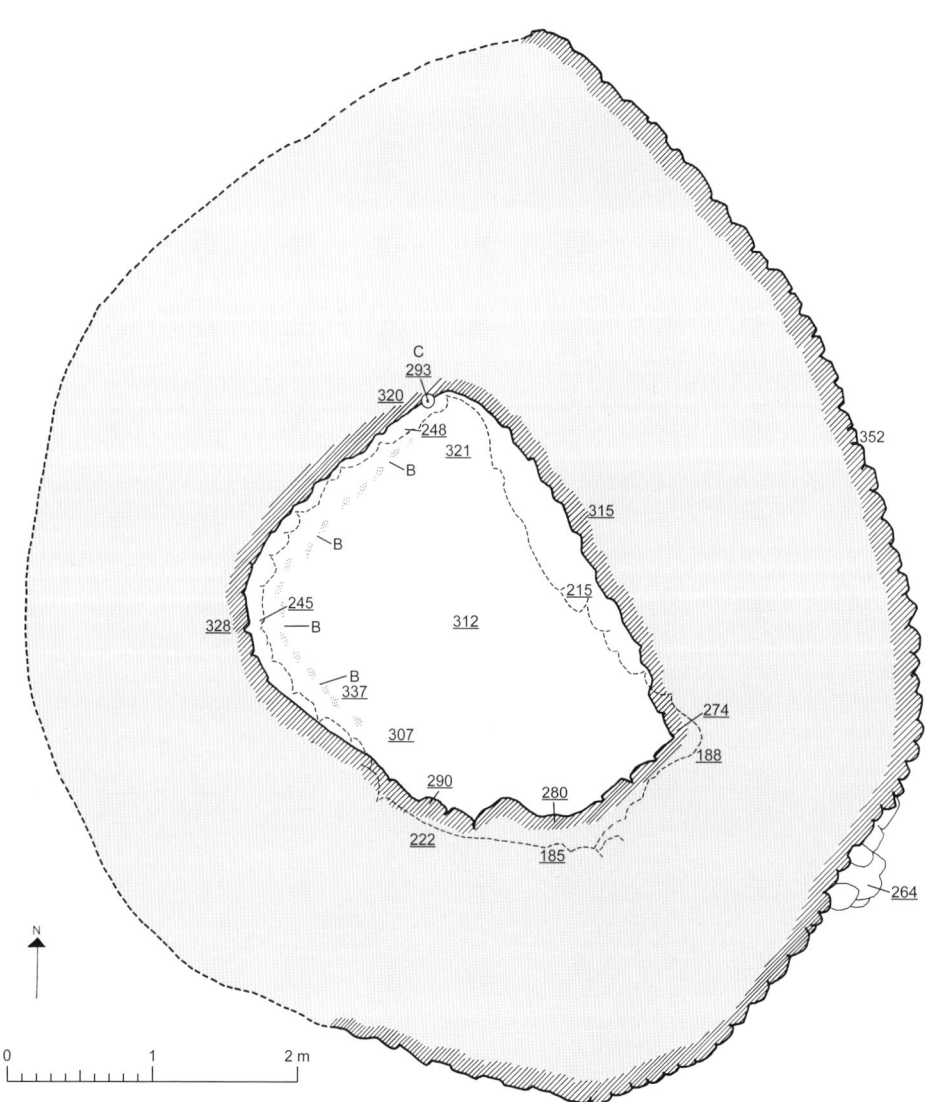
Fig. 203. Plan of Tomb 1303, 1:50. The hatched line in the chamber indicates the upper course of the corbelled roof.

Fig. 204. Iron Age burial in the upper level of the chamber.

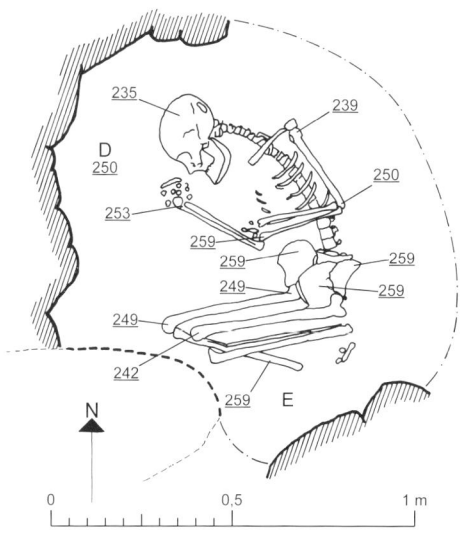

Fig. 205. Plan of the skeleton, 1:20.

Fig. 206. The upper part of vessel 1303.C.

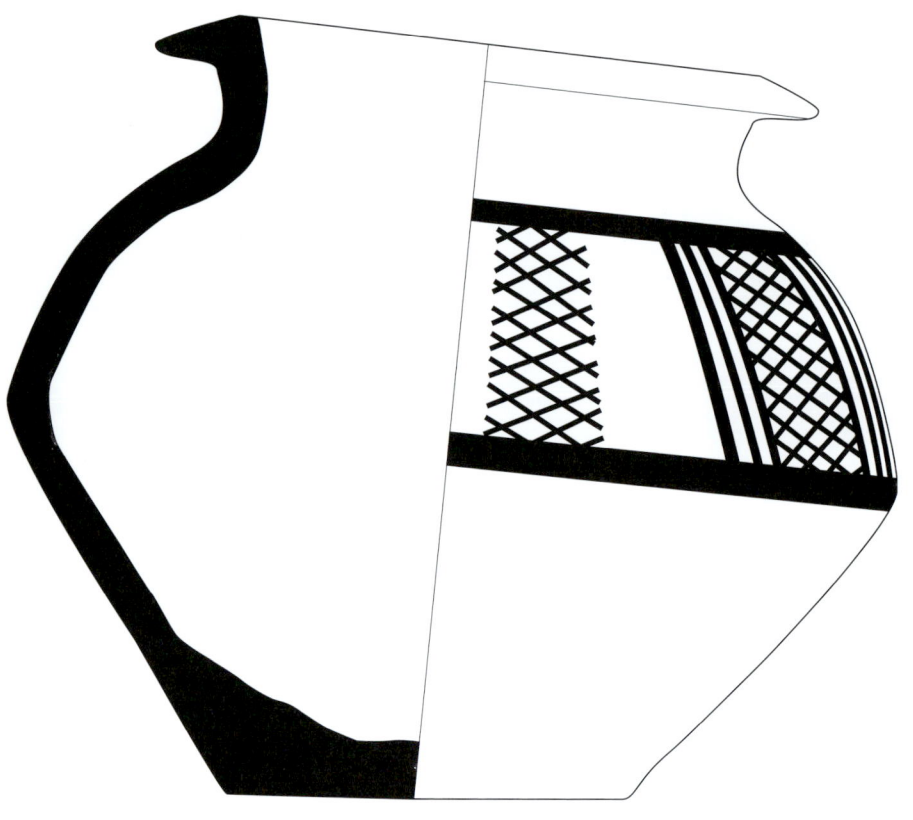

Fig. 207. Ceramic vessel 1303.C with polychrome painting, 1:1.
The shape of the vessel was distorted before firing.

Fig. 208. Iron cylinder 1303.D, 1:2.

134

TOMB 1304

Location. The tomb was found c. 3.5 km south of the northern point of the western mountain ridge just north of the westward track that crosses out to the desert through a gap in the ridge (figs. 209-210). In 1971 this track, "the Zoo Road", led to the Al-Ain Zoo which had been established a few years before. Today there is a roundabout where the modern road leads to the Falaj Hazza and Zoo districts of southwestern Al-Ain. The tomb was situated at an altitude of c. 295 m above sea level.

The excavation. The tomb was excavated in 1971 by Michael Beck and N.A. Boas. The top of the low mound was cleared revealing an outline of a low chamber which was excavated in horizontal layers until bedrock was reached. The surrounding construction was additionally uncovered.

Structural remains. The investigation identified a new type of grave with a narrow cist-like stone setting, but it had been heavily damaged by stone removal. It had a rectangular slightly rounded plan and was 2 m long and 0.8 m wide, with a slight bend in the middle (figs. 211-212). The chamber wall was 0.65 m tall in the best preserved southern part. The wall was built using medium-sized rather uneven (eroded) stone blocks up to 0.5 m long with five to six courses with a relatively even wall face with (to judge from the photographs) an inward incline.

The floor consisted of sand and rubble levelled out on the bedrock. One large stone block in the southern end had slid downwards from its original position as part of the roof construction. It indicated a roof made from slightly inclining walls with large cap-stones on top. The surrounding mound built of stone and rubble was oval and had an average diameter of c. 3 m.

A possible similar structure may be seen in the secondary chamber of Tomb 1053. There is also a resemblance to the early oblong graves of Wadi Suq and early Iron Age type (Vogt 1985 taf. 100-103, Vogt 1994). These graves are, however, in many instances sunk into the subsoil.

Finds. The only finds consisted of some scattered bone fragments in the southern end of the tomb which included some pieces of human teeth.

1304.A: Skeletal fragments.

Fig. 209. Tomb 1304 looking NNE.

Fig. 210. Tomb 1304 after excavation, looking NE.

Fig. 211. The elongated cist viewed looking S.

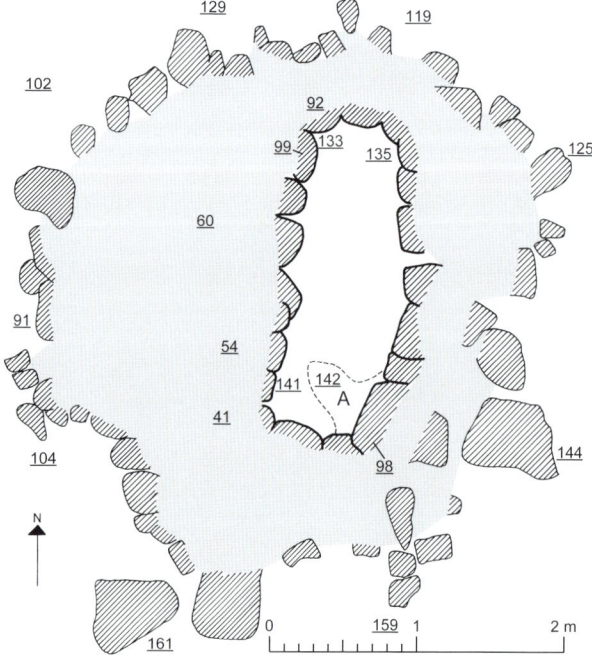

Fig. 212. Plan of Tomb 1304, 1:50.

TOMB 1305

Location. The tomb was situated at the western ridge c. 400 m west of Tomb 1304 on a westward ridge at an altitude of around 295 m above sea level (fig. 213). It lies on the north side of a pass leading to the western desert plains. The tomb was placed on a small hillock giving it a more impressive appearance.

The excavation. The tomb was excavated in 1971 by Michael Beck, N.A. Boas and Karen Frifelt. The outline of the chamber was located by clearing the plundering hole in the upper part of the mound. The chamber and entrance passage were excavated in horizontal layers. The outer perimeter of the mound was not uncovered.

Structural remains. The excavation revealed a ring wall, a small central chamber and an entrance passage towards the WSW (fig. 214). The chamber had an oval to pear-shaped plan, 1.7 m in length along the same axis as the entrance passage and 1.4 m wide. The chamber wall was preserved to a height of 0.8 m and consisted of six to seven courses of medium sized stones densely stacked with their longitudinal axis directed towards the chamber. In the dry walling the stones tended to have their flattest side facing upwards. The wall had a slight inward incline. Most likely the tomb had a corbelled roof.

The floor of the north-eastern part of the chamber was covered with small flagstones (fig. 215). These stones were 25-30 cm long and 5-8 cm thick and placed on a levelled sand layer. The remaining portion of the floor consisted of bedrock.

The entrance was preserved to a length of 1.6 m. It was 0.5 m wide at the chamber and expanded gradually outwards to 0.7 m. It was preserved to a height of 0.5 m with four to five stone courses of flat blocks. Some of these were relatively large, up to 0.6 × 0.4 m. Some remaining blocks at the entry marked a possible blocking from outside. The floor consisted of the bedrock which declined in height by 0.25 m towards the chamber. Between the passage and the chamber a step had been pecked in the hard limestone (fig. 216).

The ring wall including many stones in secondary position had a diameter of c. 5.2 m and stood from 1.3 to 1.6 m above the surrounding rock. It seemed the ring wall was built on a very uneven surface which decreased in height in all directions from the centre of the chamber, with exception of the area in front of the entrance passage which, as mentioned, lay somewhat higher.

Finds. The few finds were scattered and in secondary positions including fragments of (probably human) bones and a few beads. The only exception was a copper rivet found in the eastern side of the chamber in loose sand on the stone pavement which may derive from a primary burial. Outside the chamber in what seemed to be deposits cleared from the chamber itself, was found a large copper pin.

Fig. 213. Tomb 1305 looking NNW. Buildings in the background are the Al-Ain Zoo.

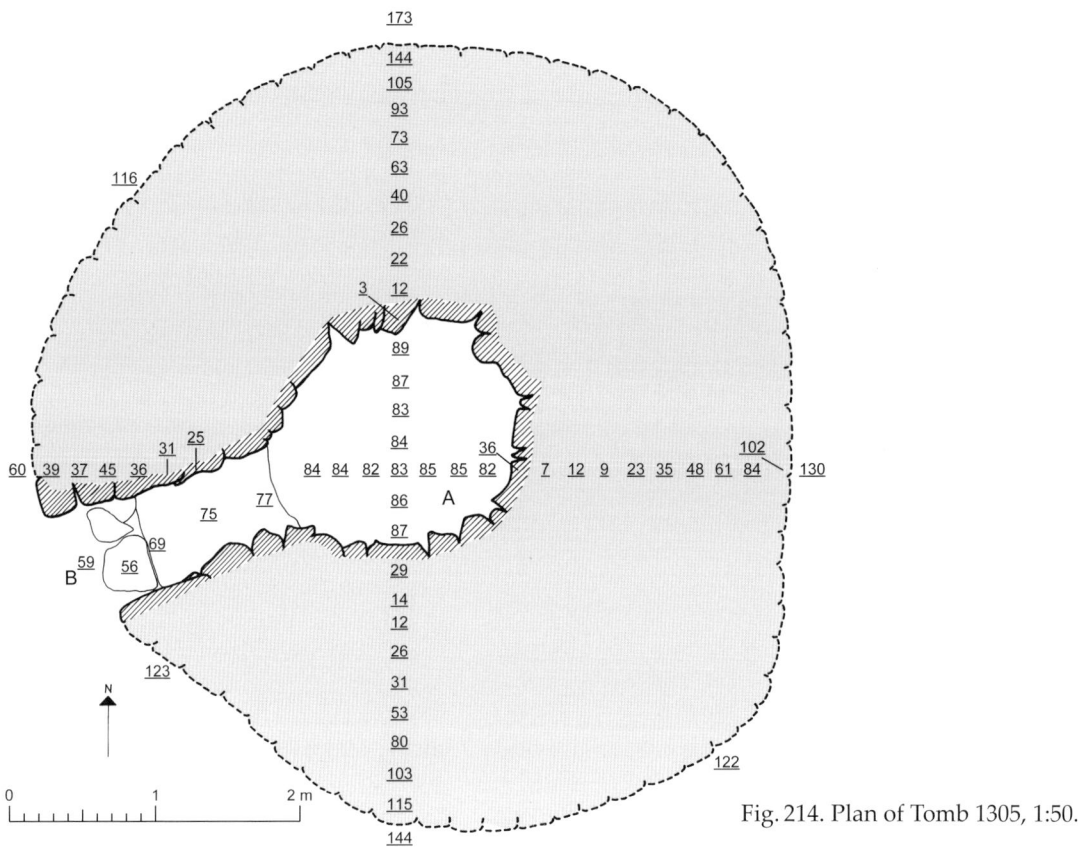

Fig. 214. Plan of Tomb 1305, 1:50.

1305.A: Copper rivet, 4 cm long, 0.5 cm in diameter, with a flat head, 0.8 cm in diameter, in both ends (fig. 217).

1305.B: Copper pin, 11.3 cm long, with round section and a flat hammered part near one end (fig. 218).

1305.C: Ring-shaped, white-surfaced red carnelian bead with irregular polished surface, L 2.5 mm, D 5.1 mm (fig. 219).

1305.D: Green glazed, cylindrical, faience bead, L c. 3 mm, D c. 2 mm.

1305.E: Spherical red carnelian bead with irregular polished surface, L 7 mm, D 7.6 mm (fig. 220).

1305.F: Skeletal fragments.

Fig. 215. The excavated chamber floor.

Fig. 216. A step between the entrance passage and the chamber.

Fig. 217. Copper rivet 1305.A, 1:1.

Fig. 218. Copper pin 1305.B, 1:1.

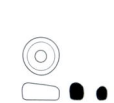

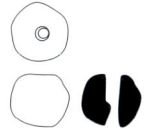

Fig. 219. Carnelian bead 1305.C, 1:1.

Fig. 220. Carnelian bead 1305.E, 1:1.

TOMB 1306

Location. The tomb was situated at the western mountain ridge c. 50 m east of Tomb 1305 at a relatively high altitude, estimated to be c. 330 m above sea level. It was placed on a sharp ridge sloping down towards the southwest and rising to a peak of c. 380 m above sea level (fig. 221). Several disturbed cairn burials lay along the ridge.

The excavation. Tomb 1306 was excavated by Bo Madsen and Steen Andersen in 1971. The tomb lay on a sharp and tilted part of the crest with a considerable westward slope and a magnificent view of the western desert. This location left nearly no room outside the tomb and made the excavators feel like working in a tilted bird's nest. First, the northeast quadrant was cleared and uncovered down to the lowest course of the ring wall in order to compare the sections. Then the northwest quadrant was excavated to establish a cross section cutting through the middle of the chamber. Following these stages, the southern part of the chamber was investigated from the inside, and finally the southern part of the periphery of the ring wall was examined.

Structural remains. The tomb was chosen for excavation because of its high and rather inaccessible position which, it was hoped, would have deterred grave robbers. It seemed relatively intact, but excavation soon revealed that it was more destroyed than expected. Part of the outer ring wall had collapsed, and the southern part of the top of the cairn had caved in from previous intrusions into the chamber.

The investigation identified a tomb with a ring wall and a central chamber from which an entrance passage led out to the south (fig. 222). The chamber was relatively large, with a triangular to pear-shaped plan. It measured 2 m north-south and 2.2 m east-west. The chamber wall was preserved to a height of c. 1.3 m and still had eight or nine courses standing (fig. 223). Some of the blocks in the dry walling were quite large, being more than 0.6 m long. They were elongated or flat on the upside face and oriented with their long axis towards the centre of the chamber. The wall had an incline which showed that the chamber had been corbelled. The chamber contained varied deposits of sand and stone. The upper deposits were dominated by collapsed material from the roof and walls.

Two floor levels were identified. An upper level of regular stone slabs was placed horizontally 0.2 to 0.4 m above bedrock (figs. 224-225). The lower level consisted of more homogeneous sand with some scattered smaller stones. The hard limestone bedrock was irregular, with some large slabs protruding at an angle into the chamber floor. The bedrock sloped considerably downwards towards the southwest. The incline was c. 0.4 m from one end of the chamber to the other. Probably the lower mixed sediments, mainly sand, had constituted a levelling deposit placed on the sloped bedrock.

The entrance passage was not excavated, but entered the southern side of the chamber and was carefully blocked from outside, as seen in a photograph (fig. 223). At the chamber wall the passage was c. 0.5 m wide, A-shaped and more than 0.7 m high. The upper part was disturbed by a large intrusion from above, which had removed the roof. A large flat roof stone lay overturned amongst rubble and other disturbed stone blocks from the covering. The entrance to the passage was not located in the southern ring wall face.

The ring wall had an outer diameter of c. 5 m with an oval outline following the different levels of the bedrock surface (fig. 225). The ring wall was erected on an area with nearly 1 m difference in level. On the north-western side some very heavy blocks, measuring up to 0.8 × 0.6 × 0.5 m, had been placed as foundation under the outer ring wall (fig. 226). The remains of the stone mound had a height of c. 1.8 m.

The ring wall was 1.4 to 1.6 m wide and made from densely stacked and interlocking stones of very different shapes and sizes, but with the largest placed on the outer face and in the chamber wall. While examining the ring wall in the sectioned part of the tomb it was observed that a layer of small stones and rubble (5-10 cm long) had been used as a levelling stratum in between the stone courses (fig. 227). Looking closer at the wall faces, it is evident that small stones and even large gravel had been used as shims in between the stones. This has ensured both stability and provided better friction at many points in the dry walling.

Finds. From the upper level, above the layer of stone slabs, came a few fragments of human bones. This high level corresponds to the middle of the entrance passage which suggests that this level would not have been accessible through the passage, but rather through a hole in the corbelled roof from the southern side above the entrance passage.

The skeletal remains at the lower, primary level were also badly preserved and disarticulated, probably from two or more interments (fig. 222). To the north were parts of a cranium and some long bones as well as a femur (fig. 228); to the south were fragments of cranium and long bones.

1306.A, B, C: Skeletal fragments.

Fig. 221. Tomb 1306, built on the end of a narrow mountain crest.

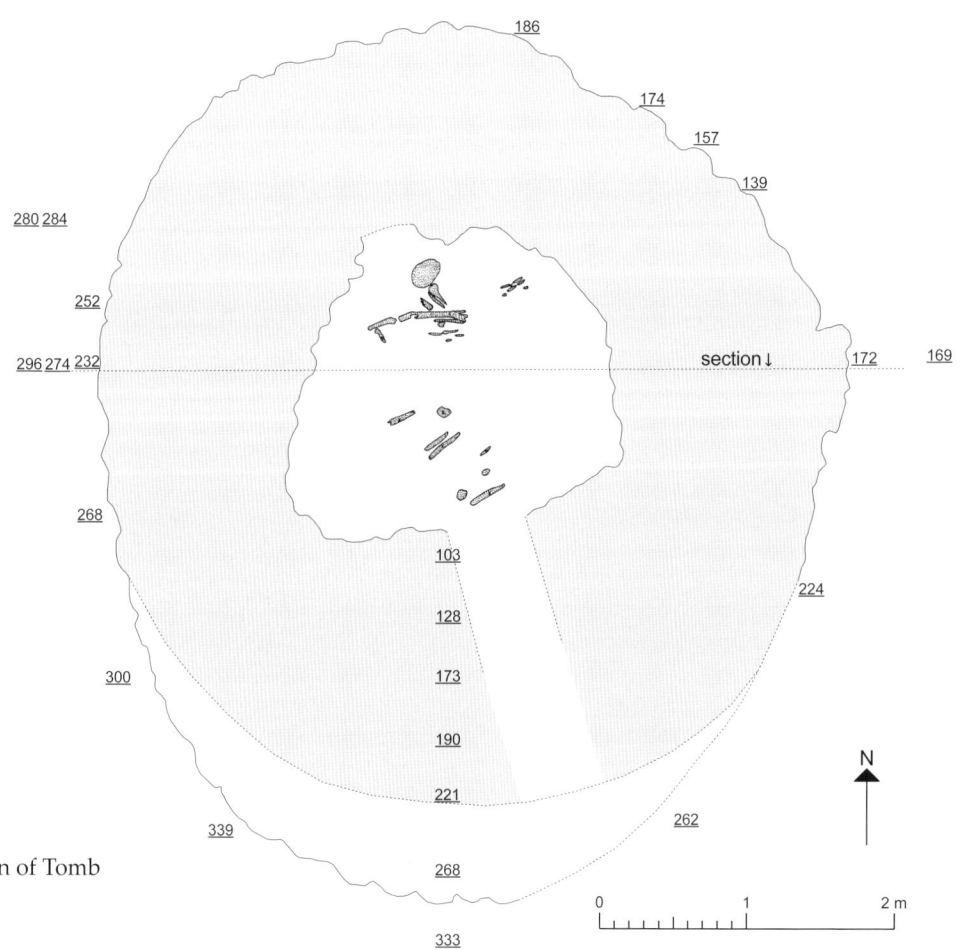

Fig. 222. Plan of Tomb 1306, 1:50.

140

Fig. 223. Remains of the corbelled chamber, looking S.

Fig. 224. A section through the middle of the tomb looking S.

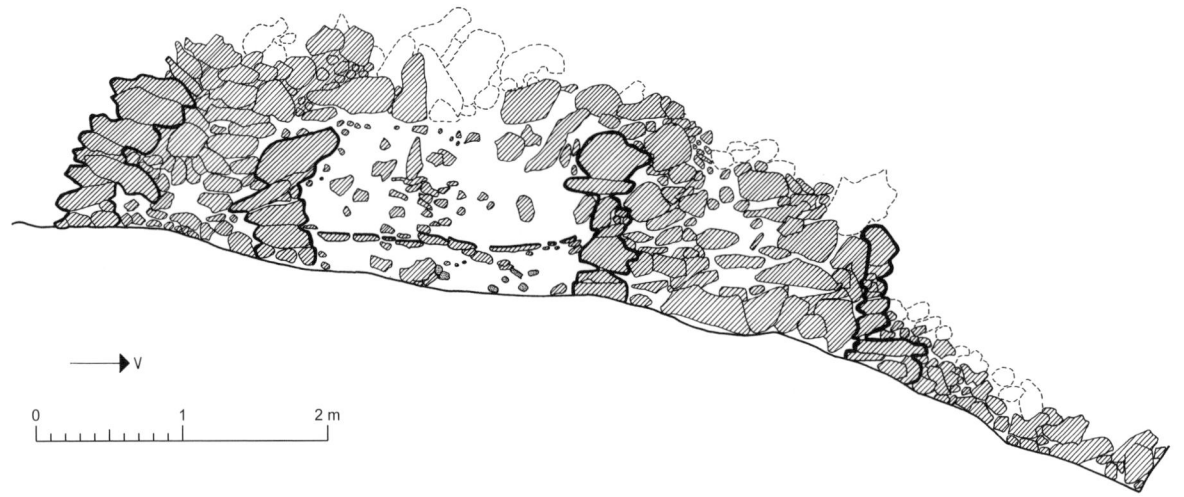

Fig. 225. Northward section through Tomb 1306, 1:50.

Fig. 226. Heavy foundation blocks on the NW side.

Fig. 227. The ring wall with levelling material in between the larger blocks.

Fig. 228. Skeletal remains on the floor of the grave.

TOMB 1307

Location. The tomb was located at the western mountain ridge c. 100 m south of the gap connected to the "Zoo Road". South of the track the limestone outcrops rise to 350 m above sea level. On the northward slopes, which lead down towards the road, numerous miniature rock shelters can be seen in locations where the hard surface crust has been undercut by erosion (fig. 229). In some cases, the shelf below the overhang had been used for burials by building a semi-circular stone wall in front of the overhang (cf. Tomb 1301 above). Tomb 1307 lay an estimated 20 m from the top of the slope with remains of some other structures close by to the west. The tombs are difficult to identify from a distance as their stone walls blended in with the loose stones and erosion rubble on the mountain side.

The excavation. The tomb was excavated in 1971 by Michael Beck, N.A. Boas and Karen Frifelt. The small chamber was entered from the western side where an opening, c. 1.5 m wide and 0.5 m high, was cleared initially. The deposits from the top consisted of material eroded from the limestone surface and some scattered hand-size stones. The deposits were excavated in horizontal layers.

Structural remains. The structure consisted of a slightly curved stone wall 3 m long, 1.2 m wide and c. 1 m high, stacked in front of the cavity in the mountainside and with a slight inward incline. A stabilizing extension or buttress had been made a meter down slope on which the construction was firmly based (fig. 230).

The frontal wall together with the cavity gave the chamber a D-shape. The wall survived to just a height of 0.2 m below the overhanging rock. On the western side there were traces of a foxhole giving access to the cavity on top of the archaeological deposits, leaving only 0.15 m to the ceiling of the overhang.

The wall was built with local stones of 0.2 to 0.4 m in size. Towards the grave chamber the stones were elongated and flat. The interments were placed on erosion material where the volume of the cavity gave most space.

Finds. The rock shelter tomb contained skeletal remains from two interments. Above was a partially preserved skeleton with the head towards the west (1307.A). The interment just below consisted of a better preserved and fully articulated skeleton 1307.B with the head orientated to the east and an iron sword alongside the body.

1307.A: Fragments of a disarticulated skeleton badly preserved and disturbed probably by animals using the grave cavity (fig. 231). The body was placed close to the stone wall. In the east was an area with scattered foot bones including the toes and the middle of the foot (phalanges, metatarsals and some unidentified bones). Further to the west some long bones lay semi-articulated, the shin bones (tibia, fibula) and thigh bones (femura). Next to the wall and further to the west were scattered fragments of the pelvis, mandible and unidentified fragments possibly from the cranium.

1307.B: Just under 1307.A a much better preserved and articulated skeleton was recovered (figs. 232-233). The body was placed in a contracted position with the legs lifted to the height of the lower chest, the arms were bent and the hands placed in front of the head. The measurements taken on the long bones from the precise field plan indicate a height in the range of 1.6-1.62 m.

1307.C: Brown organic material, fruit or kernel? Found west of the upper skeleton 1307.A (maybe from animal activity?).

1307.D: Grey-brown matter under and around cranium from 1307.B, observed in an area of c. 0.25 × 0.25 m.

1307.E: Remains/impressions of textile in metal salts on and below iron sword 1307.G, stretching from 0.2 m below the end of the grip and down the length of the blade, 1-2 mm thick and 3-4 cm wide.

1307.F: Grey matter scattered under and around the feet of the skeleton.

1307.G1: Long sword in the form of fragments of iron corrosion and metal salt with no true metal preserved. The sword lay along the back of skeleton 1307.B (figs. 232-233). The hilt was placed close to the head of the deceased. The blade was straight and probably double-edged. It had a length of 0.8 m including a tang or grip measuring c. 10 cm. The width of the blade was c. 4 cm. The sword had evidently been in a scabbard, probably wooden, as indicated by a bronze chape found at the tip. Impressions of fabric were observed in the rust and metal salts around it.

1307.G2: C. 10 cm from the tip of the sword was a lump of 3-4 completely rusted elongated objects about 7 cm long (figs. 234-237), possibly arrowheads.

1307.H: Square sword chape of bronze made from rather thick sheet metal, which has been bent and soldered into an ovate shape (figs. 233, 238-239). It was decorated with horizontal lines and fixed to the scabbard by two bronze rivets. Its outer measurements are 5.2 cm in width, 1.8 cm in height and 0.9 cm in thickness. The rivets are 1.4 cm long and their heads measure 0.5 cm in diameter. They are slightly deformed by hammering.

Fig. 229. Tomb 1307 among other rock shelter tombs on a north facing slope.

Fig. 230. Tomb 1307 before excavation of the interior.

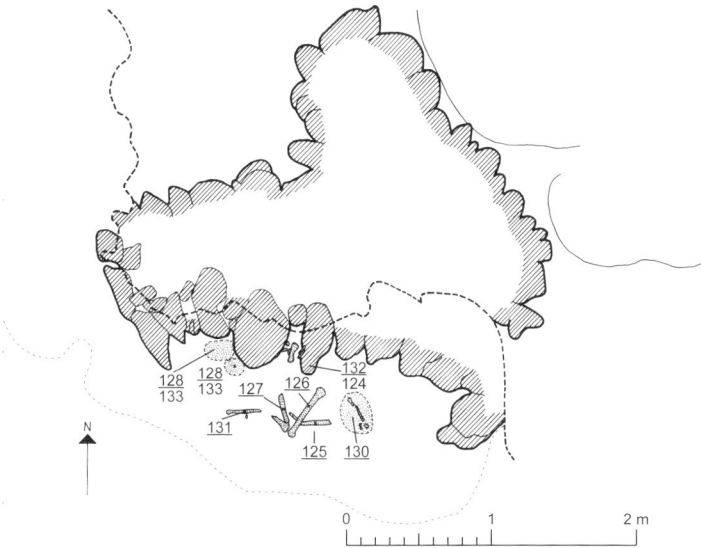

Fig. 231. Plan of Tomb 1307 with upper skeleton 1307.A, 1:50. The thin hatched line indicates the foot of the rock face; the bold hatched line indicates its upper edge.

Fig. 232. Lower skeleton 1307.B with iron long sword 1307.G1.

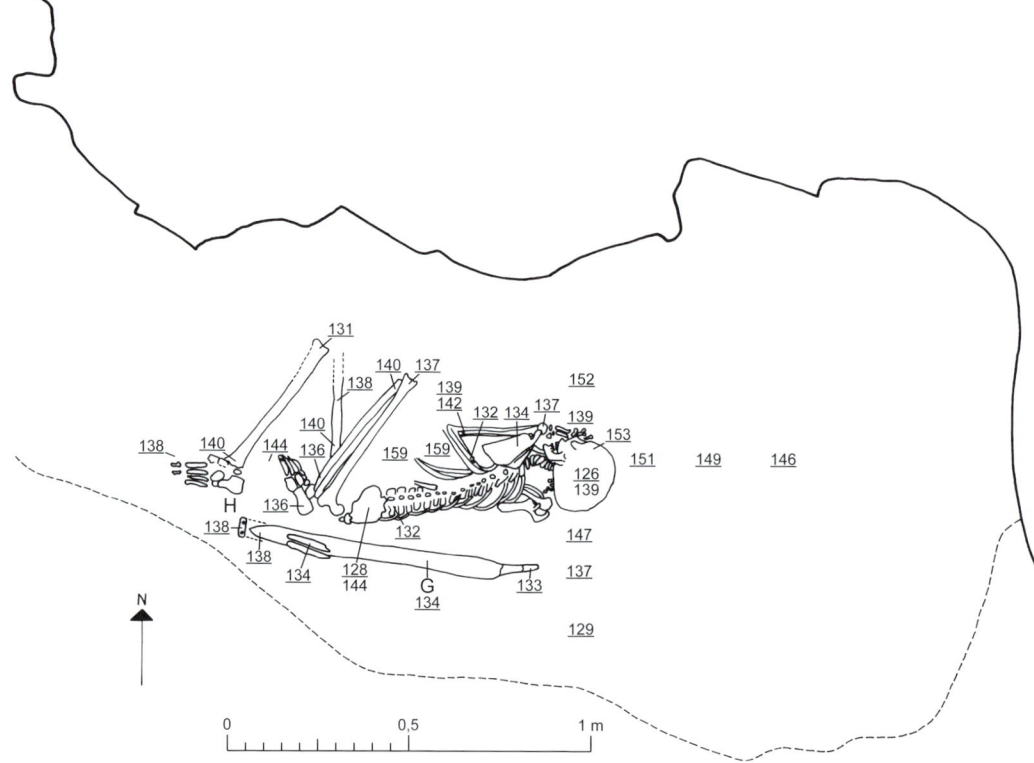

Fig. 233. Plan of lower skeleton 1307.B with iron long sword, bronze chape and possible arrows, 1:20. The thin hatched line indicates the foot of the rock face; the bold line indicates its upper edge.

Fig. 234. Iron fragment 1307.G2, 1:1.

Fig. 235. Iron fragment 1307.G2, 1:1.

Fig. 236. Iron fragment 1307.G2, 1:1.

Fig. 237. Iron fragment 1307.G, 1:1.

Fig. 238. Close-up of bronze chape and iron sword. Note the symmetrical tip of the blade.

Fig. 239. Bronze chape 1307.H, 1:1.

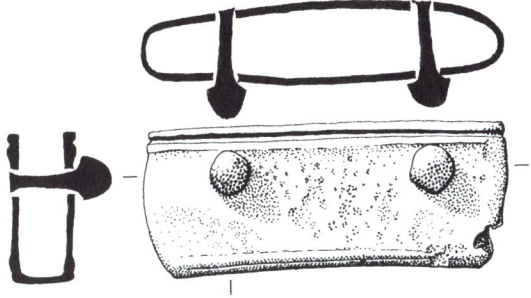

TOMB 1308

Location. The structure was located 50 m west of Tomb 1307. It was situated below a group of 8-10 small assumed rock shelter tombs built as walls hiding a small cave or overhang. The small grave field lies near the top of the mountain ridge at an altitude of estimated 320-330 m above sea level.

The excavation. The structure appeared to be a grave very similar to Tomb 1307. It was excavated by N.A. Boas in 1971. The sediments that remained in the damaged tomb were excavated by scraping in thin horizontal layers until bedrock was reached. Sediments that had been thrown out and down slope of the tomb during the assumed plundering of the structure were carefully searched as well.

Structural remains. The structure had a semi-circular plan, with the rock-face forming the southern side of the chamber and a curved stone built wall delimiting the rest of the chamber (figs. 240-241). The chamber measured lengthwise 2.3 m east-west and had a width of 1.4-1.3 m. The structure was severely damaged on its eastern side where the wall had been dismantled down to bedrock. The wall was 1 m wide and made from stone blocks up to a size of 0.4-0.5 m. Its inner face was almost vertical from bedrock to the ceiling of the rock overhang. The rock-face had a slight outward incline. The chamber floor consisted of bedrock and a levelling layer of sand and rubble. The chamber was quite large and spacious compared to the previously investigated rock shelter tombs.

Finds. Only splinters and fragments of bone were found in the chamber as well as outside, below the tomb downslope of the rock shelter.

1308.A: Bones from at least two domestic dromedary individuals (Camelus dromedarius), both sub-adult (cf. Uerpmann & Uerpmann below p. 243). Burials with camel are known from Bahrain (Bibby 1954 p. 140), Bat in Oman (Frifelt 1985 p. 102), and in the UAE, Ed Dur (Haerinck 2001 p. 44) and Jebel al-Buhais, Tomb 12 radiocarbon dated to 600 AD (Jasim 2012 p. 55-63), often buried in stone-lined pits. The graves are primarily dated to Iron Age/late pre-Islamic time (Daems and De Waele 2010). The remaining bones, from cattle, sheep/goat, donkey, gazelle, oryx and dog (cf. Uerpmann & Uerpmann below p. 245), may have been transported to the site by wild animals, dog/wolf, using the tomb as a lair.

Fig. 240. The rock shelter tomb 1308 looking W.

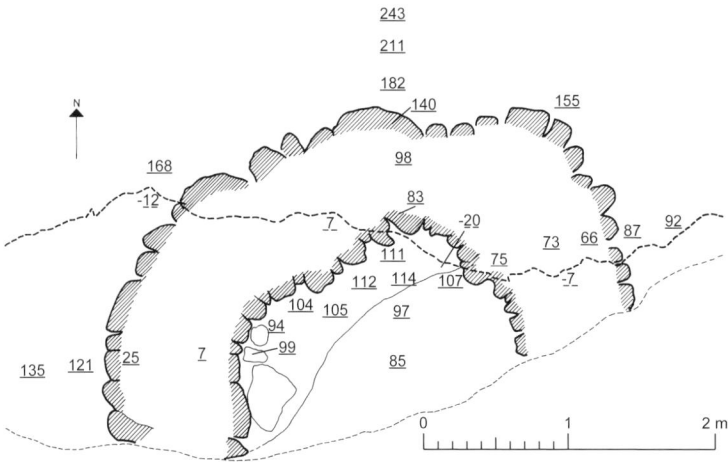

Fig. 241. Plan of Tomb 1308, 1:50. The thin hatched line indicates the foot of the rock face; the bold hatched line indicates its upper edge.

TOMB 1309

Location. The tomb was located on the eastern side of the western mountain ridge about 1 km south of the "Zoo Road". It was situated on the northern side of a narrow pass with a track leading east-west (figs. 242-243). The altitude was estimated to be 290-300 m above sea level. The tomb was placed on a small crest where the pass opened towards the east and the foothills and slopes leading into the valley. This adjacent part of the valley was a terrain with many hillocks and a large group of tombs, which were encountered here already during the archaeological survey in 1962 and of which eight tombs, 1047 to 1054, were investigated the following year.

The excavation. The tomb was excavated in 1971 by N.A. Boas, who was in charge of the field report, assisted by Bo Madsen, Steen Andersen and Karen Frifelt. The excavation commenced from the top of the mound through an old intrusive hole.

The chamber and entrance passage were emptied by digging thin horizontal layers and using brushes as more and more skeletal material occurred. The outer face of the ring wall was cleared and identified towards the southwest.

Structural remains. A central grave chamber surrounded by a ring wall and an entrance passage towards the SSE was uncovered (fig. 244). The chamber was oval to pear-shaped and measured c. 2.6 m in line with the axis of the entrance passage. It was 2.4 m wide. The chamber and ring wall were preserved to a height of 1.8 m on the eastern side of the chamber, and even though the structure had suffered from stone plundering, a substantial part of the chamber was preserved. The cross-section shows the incline of the chamber wall to a height of 1.6 m (fig. 252) and judging from the proportions, the full height of the corbelled chamber must have been between 2.2 and 2.4 m. The chamber wall was constructed as dry-stone walling with the stones protruding inwards with their pointed ends directed towards the centre of the chamber and with the flattest side facing upwards.

The chamber was filled with sand and scattered stones. The sediment was relatively cemented in the upper part. The "burial layer" started c. 1.4 m down and had a thickness of c. 0.3 m. The chamber floor was almost level with an irregular pavement of small stones (less than 0.1 m across) with rubble and gravel making up a surface for the interments (fig. 245).

Seen from the chamber, the entrance was very carefully blocked, the blocking stones being closely aligned with the chamber wall face. The entrance passage measured 2.8 m in length and was funnel-shaped. The width, measured at floor level and nearest the chamber, was 0.5 m and at the exterior end it was extraordinarily wide, namely 1 m. The upper part had been destroyed. Only one stone from the roof remained and this was not found in its original position. The height of the passage had been 0.8 to 1.0 m. The bedrock floor inclined c. 0.2 m downwards to the entrance.

The ring wall was damaged by stone plundering on all sides. The outer diameter of the mound before excavation was around 10 m, but had originally, to judge from the still standing wall faces, been around 8 m. The ring wall was massive with a thickness varying from 2.8 to 2.9 m.

Some of the excavation photographs show the southern half of Tomb 1309 after cleaning off the disturbed stone blocks and rubble (fig. 246). The stone plundering had left only 3-4 courses of the outer wall face to the south and torn open the upper parts of the chamber and the entrance, thereby revealing some construction details. The largest blocks in the construction were used in the interior wall faces of the chamber and entrance, with blocks up to 0.5-0.6 m of which most had an elongated shape. The interior of the ring wall consisted of circular lines of interlocking smaller stones which appeared to have been laid down in a step like fashion indicating the method by which the ring wall could have been made in stages (cf. fig. 394).

Finds. Skeletal remains from five or six individuals were uncovered: 1309.A, 1309.B, 1309.C, 1309.D, 1309.E and 1309.I. The bones and the artefacts lay in a c. 0.3 m thick zone consisting of sand with a few scattered small stones and skeletal parts in different stages of fragmentation. The grave goods consisted of beads found with 1309.B and 1309.E, and two ceramic vessels, which were found on either side of the entrance (figs. 247). The two pots probably represent grave goods intended for two separate burials as they were placed some distance apart. The stratigraphic position is in level with the uppermost skeletal parts which have suffered some disturbance and dislocation so no further relation can be postulated.

1309.F: 16 green glazed, cylindrical faience beads, L 3.6-5.6 mm, D 3.5-4.5 mm and 1 green glazed, segmented cylindrical faience bead, L 6.8 mm, D 4.2 mm. Around 10 of these beads were found lying in a row, at cranium 1309.B.

1309.G: Ceramic vessel, ovoid with pointed base of Jemdet Nasr type, in brown ware (fig. 248).

1309.H: Biconical ceramic vessel with faint marked shoulder of Jemdet Nasr type, in yellow-brown, sand-tempered ware with traces of red paint (fig. 249).

1309.J: 3 green glazed, cylindrical faience beads, L c. 4 mm, D c. 4 mm, above cranium 1309.B.

1309.K: 1 green glazed, cylindrical faience bead, L 5.4 mm, D 3.9 mm, in the SE side of the chamber at the mandible 1309.E.

1309.N: Charcoal pieces found just above the skeletons in the northern part of the chamber.

The skeletal remains were represented by both nearly complete and fragmented bones, as well as articulated and disarticulated parts of moderate preservation (figs. 250-252). The bones were mapped at a scale of 1:10, and the major skeletal features were levelled. The individual bone aggregations are listed below.

1309.A: The partially articulated skeleton of an adult individual lying on its right side in a contracted position with the head towards the south and its feet towards the north. Only limited parts of the skeleton are present with parts of the upper legs (femora), the pelvis and lower back still conjoined. Limited parts of the upper left arm (humerus) were recovered. Cranial parts were lying disturbed and south of their expected position and two unidentified bones were found west of the body.

1309.B: Aggregation of skeletal parts lying in front of the entrance. Cranium and a possible tibia are lying close together with some unidentifiable tubular bones. A second tibia together with bones from part of the foot (tarsus, calcaneus and phalanges) appear articulated and lay a little apart to the northeast. Another unidentified long bone was found to the southwest.

1309.C: A few skeletal parts were situated in the northern end of the chamber and in the same level as A. They consisted of the pelvic bone, presumably the left side, and some parts of unidentified long bones.

Fig. 242. Tomb 1309 looking E.

1309.M were remains of the dentition probably belonging to skeleton C.

1309.E: The badly preserved skeleton of an adult located in the eastern side of the chamber. The body had been placed in a contracted position on the right side with the head towards the north and the feet towards the south. It was positioned under 1309.B. The individual is represented by a mandible, the lower part of the upper arm (left humerus), parts of the spine (undetermined vertebrae) and some ribs, both articulated and disarticulated. From the lower limbs remain one thigh bone (femur) and the lower ends of both shin bones (tibiae and fibulae) together with parts of the feet (tarsus, calcaneus, tarsals).

1309.D: Skeletal parts from one individual. The body had been placed in a contracted position lying on its right side, with the head towards the west and the feet towards the east. The head was placed almost in the centre of the chamber, just above the hand bones. The interment is positioned east of 1309.A and at a level 8 to 10 cm deeper. The skeleton was represented by articulated or semi-articulated parts with the cranium, a fragment of mandible and some cervical vertebrae, but no remains of the central torso were present. An aggregation consisting of fragments from the pelvic bones and the legs (femur, tibia and fragments of tibia) was found articulated. The teeth indicate an adult person with traces of caries (Højgaard 1985).

1309.I: A complete articulated skeleton was resting on the western part of the chamber pavement 5 to 10 cm above bedrock. It was positioned under individuals 1303.A and 1303.C. The body was placed on its right side in a contracted position with the head to the south and the feet to the north. The arms were raised in front of the chest; the upper spine was markedly curved forward. The cranium was still in position and had been pushed slightly downwards to the shoulders lying with the calotte upwards. It was very flattened by compression from the above sediments and the traffic related to later interments. During the recovery "seven to eight heavy lesions on the skull" were noted by the excavator N.A. Boas. The skull was subsequently examined by Judith Littleton after the major fragments of the calotte had been somewhat refitted at the Smithsonian Institution (Littleton and Frifelt 2006). The cranial remains consist of the upper cranium with neither the basis cranium nor the lower facial bones. The age determination was based on the status of the suture closures and indicated a possible young adult (Littleton and Frifelt 2006 p. 140). The morphology of the brow and cheek bone pointed to both female and male traits. The skull being extremely thin and gracile made Littleton suggest that it represented a possible female.

The post-cranial skeleton was apparently not examined by Littleton. It can be added that the skeleton was photographed and mapped in considerable detail in the field. The sub-cranial skeleton points more to a male gender for the individual. The long bone-measures taken on the field drawing indicate a rather tall individual being in the range of 1.75-1.77 m. This falls above the average height of males from a sample of 18 males from three Umm an-Nar tombs (Kunter 1991) where the heights ranged from 1.64 to 1.73 m. In a more local Umm an-Nar context, namely the skeletal material from Hili North, Tomb A, a large chambered tomb from the heyday of this culture, the average male height was around 1.78 m and around 1.70 m for females. The sample consists of 31 articulated skeletons. For the final part of the culture represented by Hili Tomb N, the heights were c. 1.71 m and 1.64 for males and females respectively (McSweeney et al. 2008).

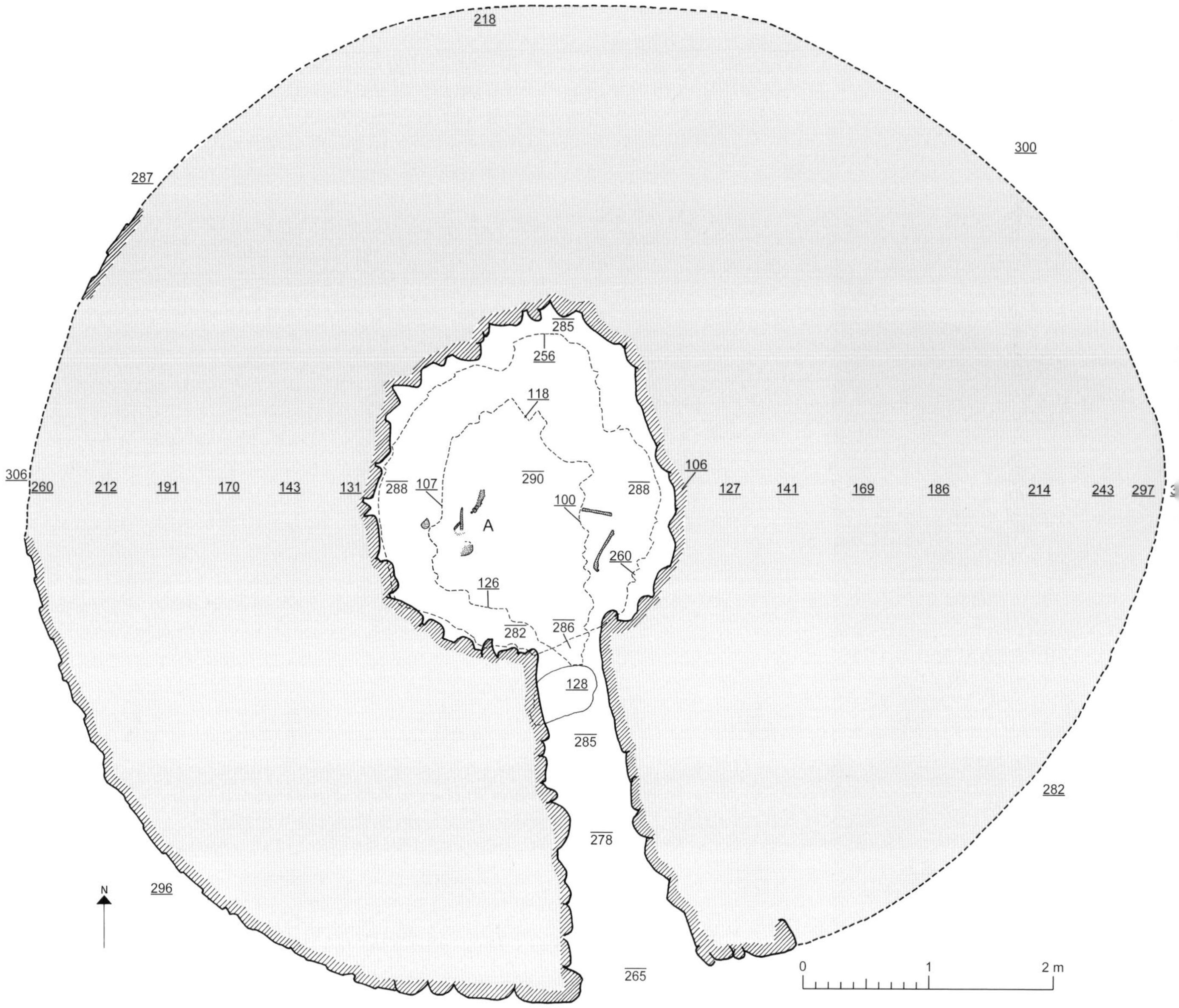

Fig. 244. Plan of Tomb 1309, 1:50. The hatched line in level 100 to 126 indicates the upper course of the corbelled roof. The hatched line in level 256 to 260 indicates the level and area where the first skeletal remains appear.

◀ Fig. 243. Tomb 1309 before excavation.

Fig. 245. The floor level of the chamber.

Fig. 246. Tomb 1309 after excavation. The ring wall exposes stages of overlapping circular stone courses.

Fig. 247. The burial level with two ceramic vessels and skeletal remains looking S.

Fig. 248. Ceramic vessel 1309.G, 1:1.

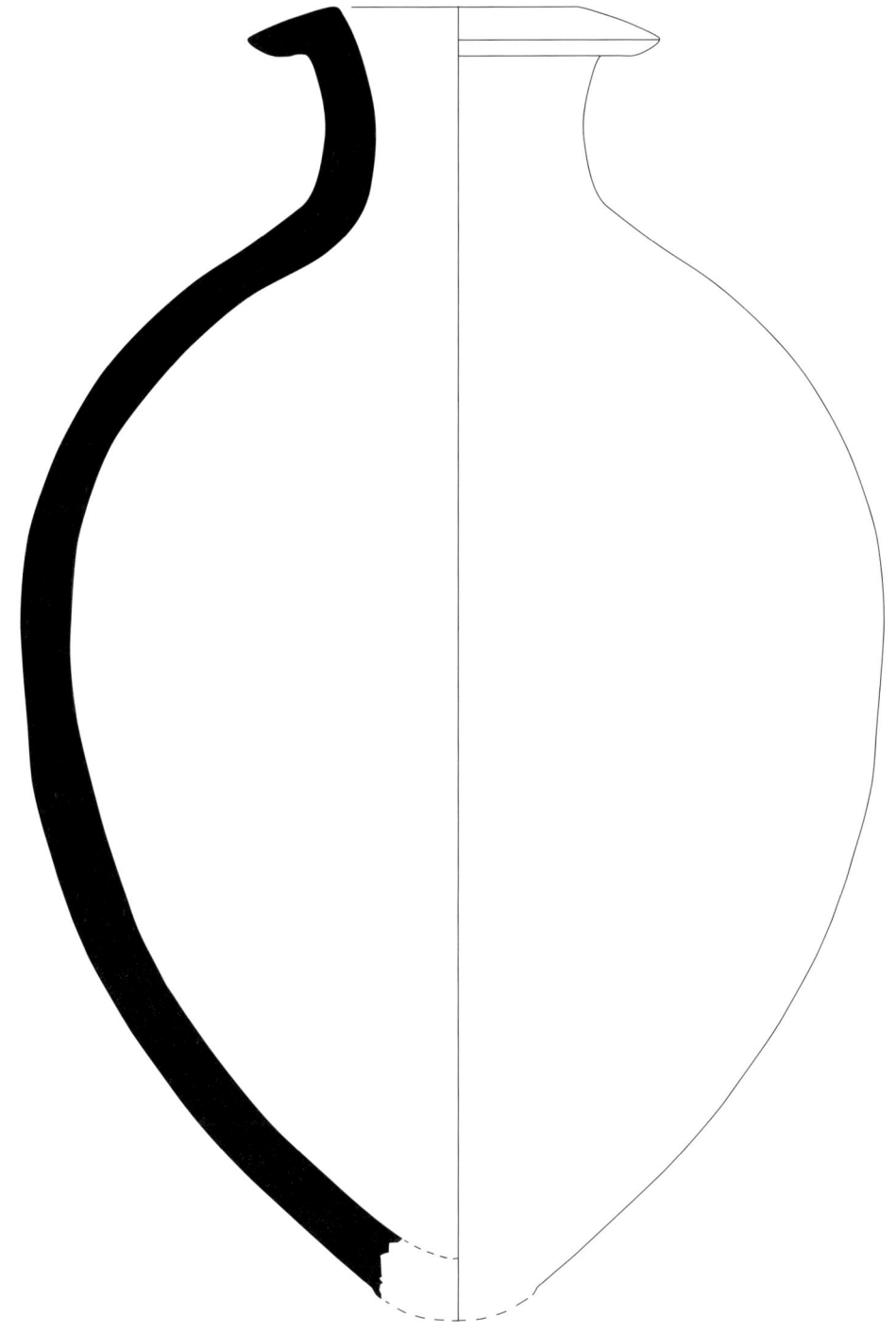

155

Fig. 249. Ceramic vessel 1309.H, 1:1.

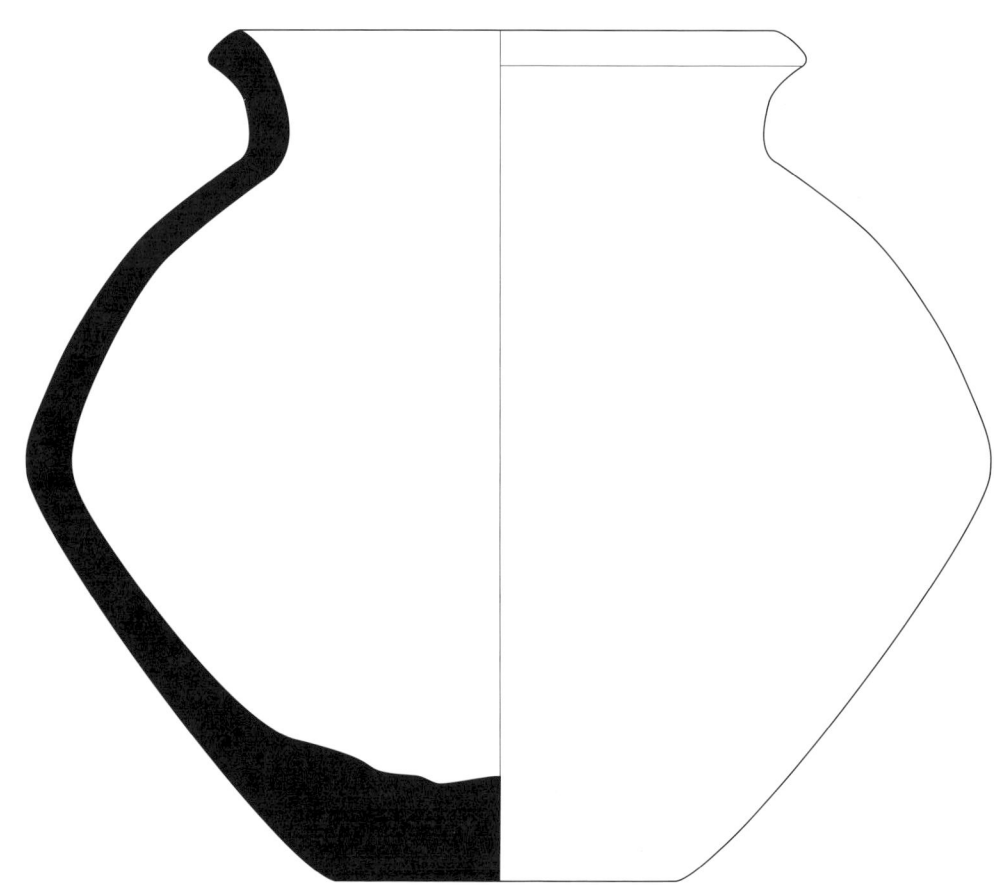

156

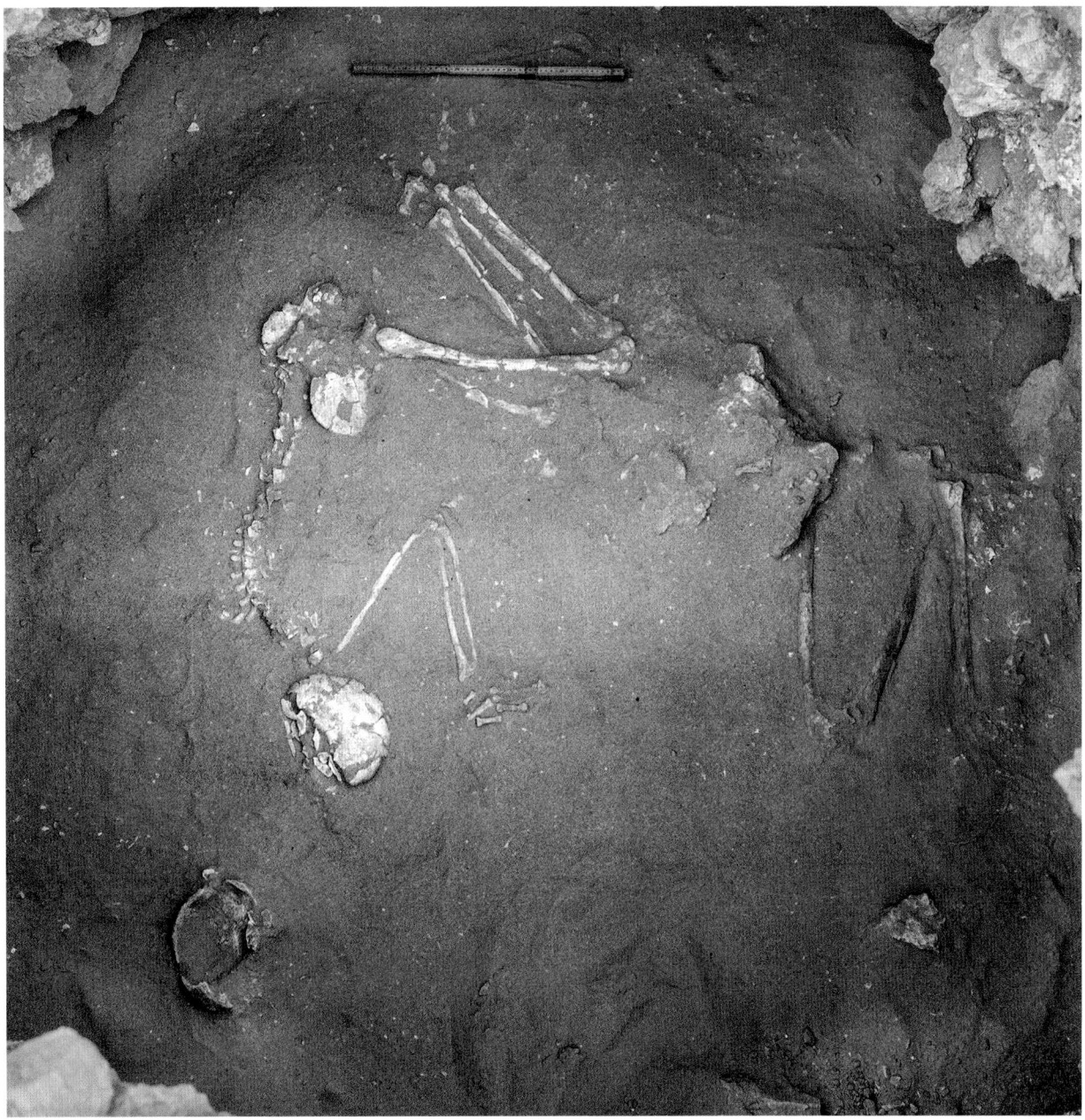

Fig. 250. The burial level in the second stage of excavation.

The calotte exposed nine oval lesions measuring 2.1 to 3.2 cm in length which Judith Littleton identified as traces of trepanation. According to the signs of healing in the bone structure on some of the lesions the operations had been carried out over an extended time period.

A dental investigation of 1309.I revealed that some teeth suffered from moderate caries (Højgaard 1985).

The placement of the dead in this chamber does not indicate any preferred orientation. The most significant shared element of the burial practice is the contracted position and the fact that the deceased were placed on their right side.

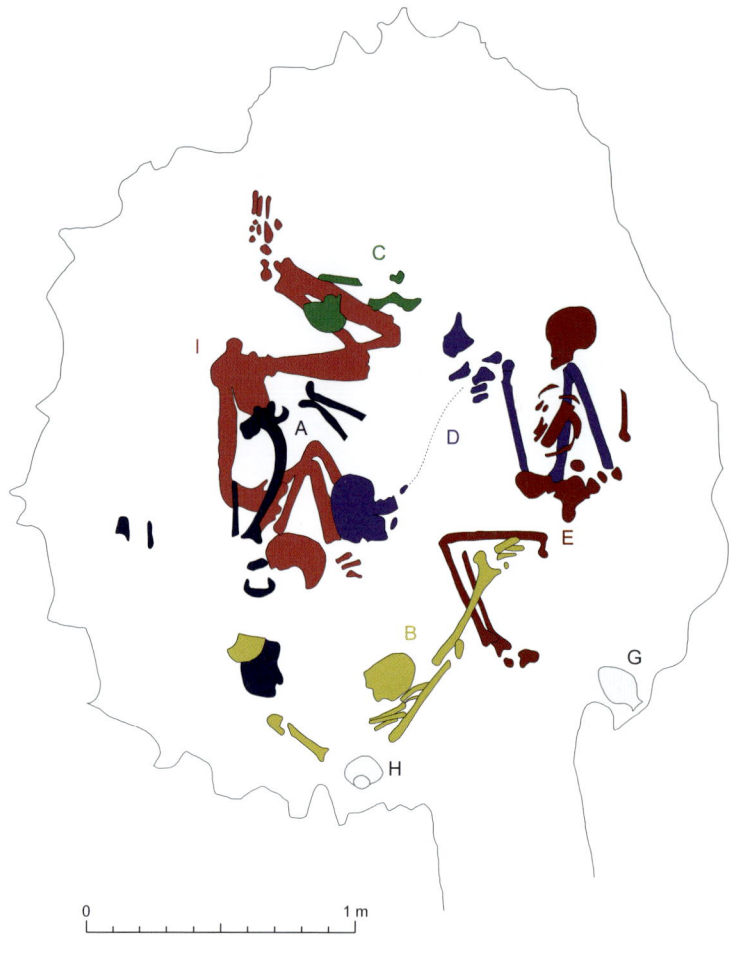

Fig. 251. Plan with skeletal assemblages and pottery in Tomb 1309

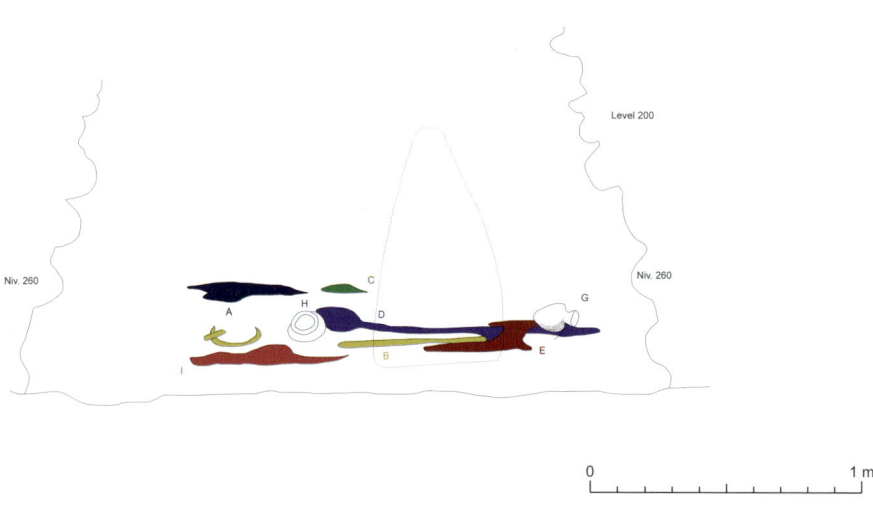

Fig. 252. Vertical positions of skeletal assemblages and pottery, and section through the chamber walls of Tomb 1309.

TOMB 1310

Location. The tomb was situated at the western foothills of the western mountain ridge c. 220 m south of the "Zoo Road" (fig. 253). The tomb and the neighbouring Tomb 1311 were found close together at the western end of a low pass cutting east-west through the mountain ridge. The altitude can be estimated to be c. 290-295 m above sea level.

Discovery and rescue. While excavating tombs and reconnoitring the hills in 1971 the team became aware that stone quarried from tombs in the vicinity was being used for cement manufacture. One labourer was engaged in removing stones from the ring wall of a tomb (Tomb 1311) south of the "Zoo Road". The hard work was done by hand and with the aid of a heavy iron pick. The stone blocks were being tilted out from the construction and were prepared to be rolled downwards to a spot where they would be loaded on to a lorry. Next to the partially intact tomb was the base of another almost destroyed structure, Tomb 1310, which had already had all stones feasible for cement manufacture removed. When explained to the man that he was tearing a human grave apart, he stopped work.

The scattered soil in the remains of the chamber contained several fine beads and most of a painted Jemdet Nasr vessel. It was, therefore, decided to excavate the tomb in order to save the remaining finds and document their context. The structure was excavated by Michael Bech with Bo Madsen participating in the first part of the excavation. The ring wall was almost removed by the stone quarrying leaving only the base of the chamber for excavation. The last preserved sediments above the chamber pavement were excavated horizontally and sieved.

Structural remains. The excavation recovered a tomb with the remains of a ring wall and a central chamber, but no traces of the entrance passage (fig. 254). Only part of the floor of the chamber and some scattered stones from the surrounding ring wall were preserved.

The chamber area was identified by the extension of a flat stone pavement and a scatter of artefacts just outside. The inner line of the chamber wall was indicated just by the impressions of stones in the subsoil, primarily consisting of erosion material on which the tomb had been constructed. The estimated extension of the chamber was around 2 m east-west and 1.6 m north-south. The stone quarrying had left an untouched portion of the lower chamber sediment resting above the pavement. It had a thickness of 0.3-0.4 m above the subsoil. The sediment consisted of compacted sand mixed with some hand-size

Fig. 253. Tomb 1310 situated at the valley floor between Tomb 1312 in the front, and Tomb 1311 in the distance. Bo Madsen to the right.

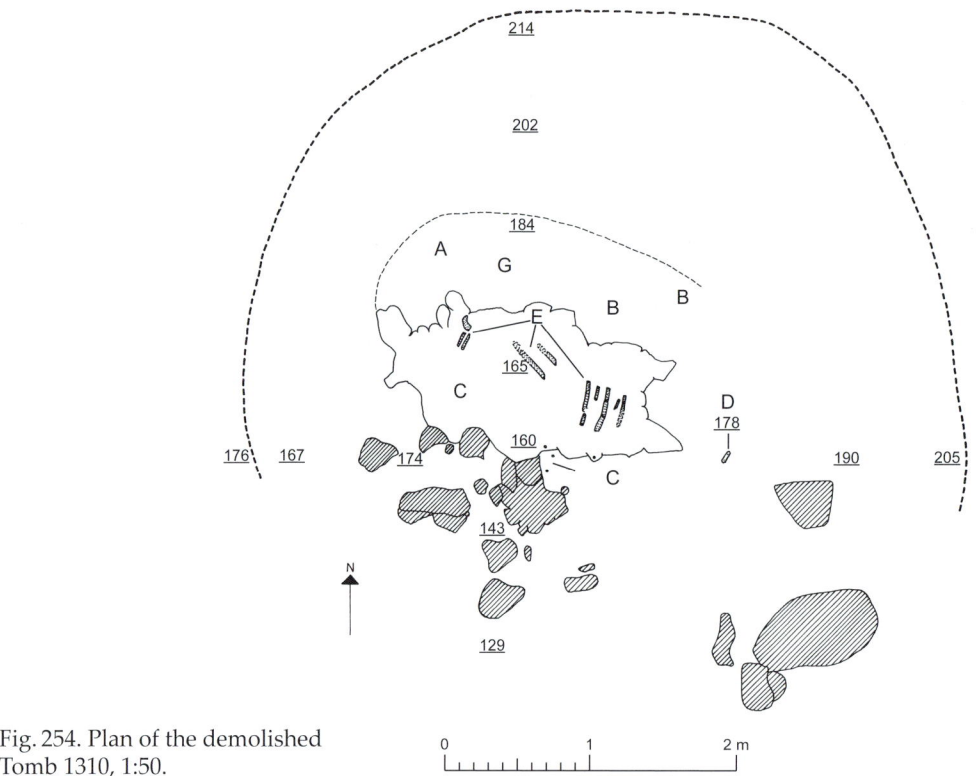

Fig. 254. Plan of the demolished Tomb 1310, 1:50.

Fig. 255. Ceramic vessel, polychrome painted, dotted = red, white = cream, black = black, 1310A, 1:1.

stones. The pavement was made of 0.1-0.2 m wide irregular stones of which some were relatively flat on the upper side.

Only few stones remained from the ring wall on the southern side of the chamber. However, impressions in the subsoil from the outer stone line at the base of the ring wall, observed in the northern side, indicated a thickness of between 1 and 1.6 m.

Finds. Human bone fragments and splinters lay scattered on the stone pavement and all over the chamber area. On the pavement were some parts of badly preserved and unidentified long bones. In the mixed soil there were also fragments of dentition and a cranium.

Two ceramic vessels were recovered, with 1310.A in the north-western part of the chamber area and 1310.B in the north-eastern part. Whether they represent one or two interments cannot be determined due to the lack of skeletal evidence.

A rectangular plaque, 1310.D, made from mother-of-pearl was found in a disturbed position on the eastern edge of the chamber zone.

The most predominant finds were beads. 72 beads of faience and heated steatite were found by sieving, besides one carnelian bead and two of shell. Only 4 of these beads were found in contact with the floor pavement, the rest were found in disturbed soil.

1310.A: Biconical ceramic vessel with a faint shoulder ridge of Jemdet Nasr type in brown, micaceous sand-tempered ware, polychrome painted (fig. 255).

1310.B: Biconical ceramic vessel with a faint marked shoulder of Jemdet Nasr type in brown micaceous sand-tempered ware with traces of red slip (fig. 256).

1310.D: Rectangular plaque of mother-of-pearl with a hole in each end (fig. 257).

1310.C: 75 beads: c. 32 green glazed cylindrical faience beads, L 2-3.7 mm, D 3-4.4 mm (figs. 258-259); c. 10 cylindrical beads in heated steatite, L 2.4-4.1 mm, D 3-3.7 mm (fig. 260); 1 biconical red carnelian bead, L 6.1 mm, D 6.1 mm (figs. 258 and 261); 2 shell beads from *Engina mendicaria*, perforated laterally (fig. 258); and 30 square beads from heated steatite, 5.8-7.5 × 5.8-7.3 × 2.3-3.4 mm, drilled through opposing corners (figs. 262-264).

1310.E: Human long bones and bone fragments.

1310.F: Skeletal fragments.

1310.G: Fragments of dention.

1310.H: Fragments of egg-like shells (from snakes or reptiles?)

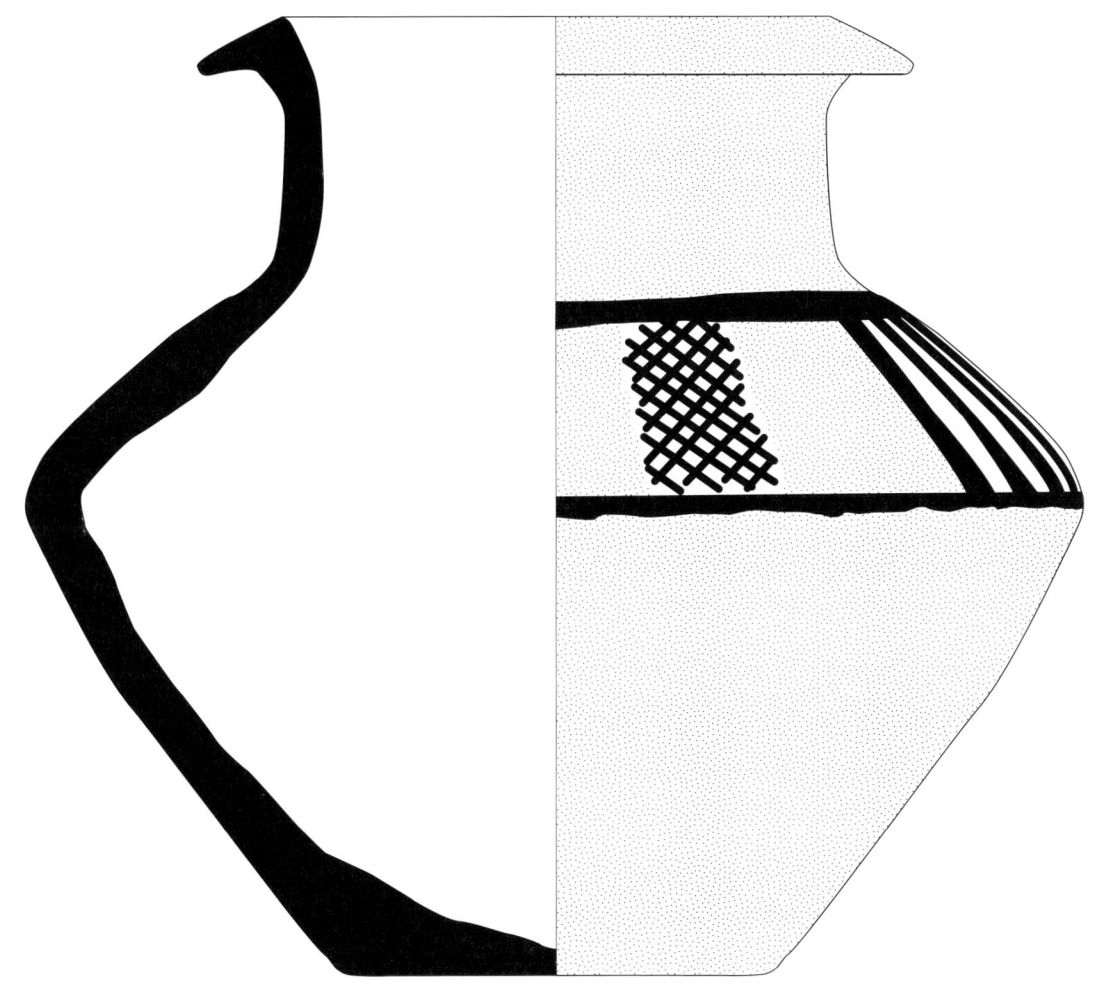

Fig. 256. Ceramic vessel 1310.B, 1:1.

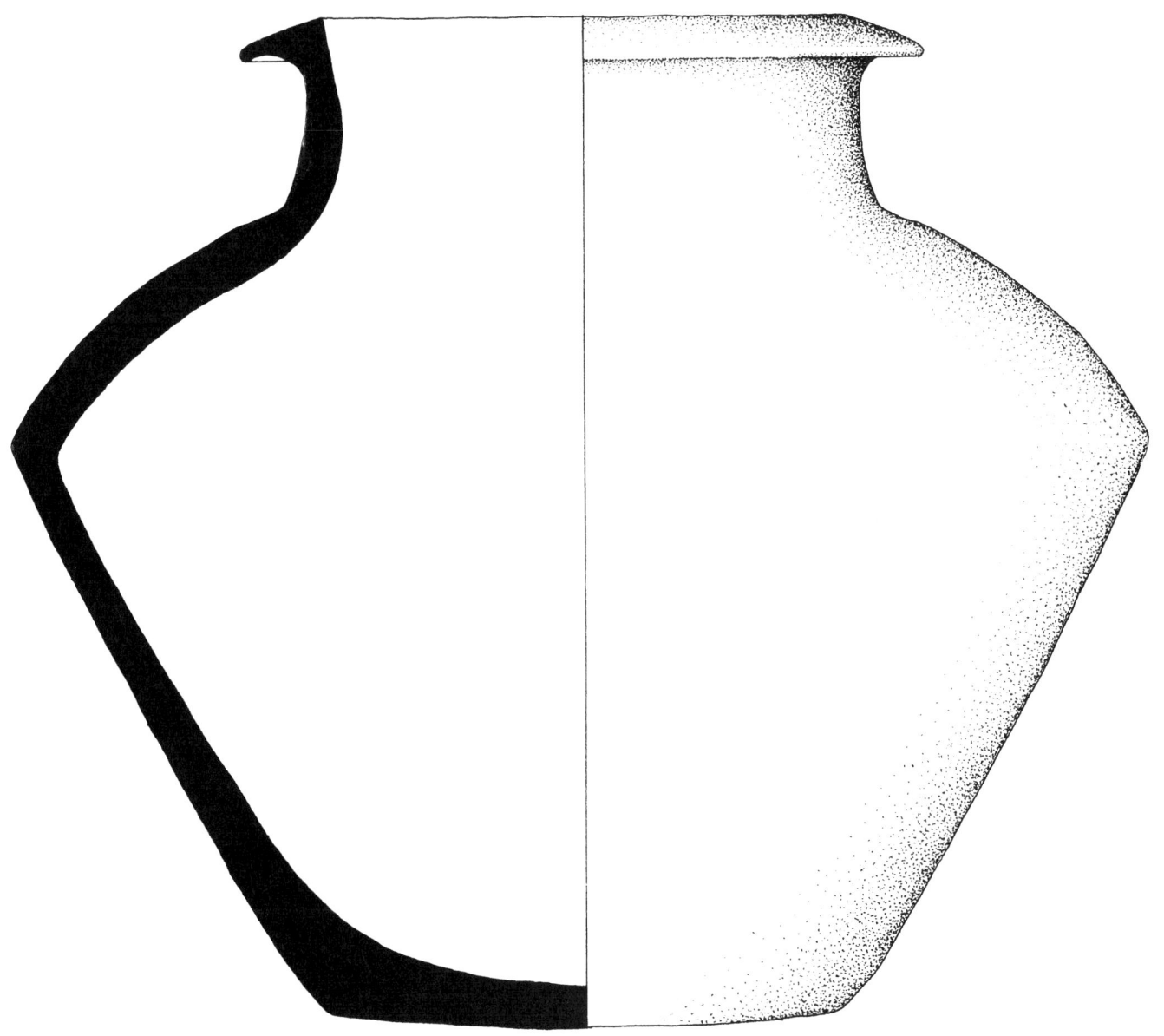

Fig. 257. A pendant or plaque from mother-of-pearl 1310.D, 1:1.

Fig. 262. Square beads in heated steatite 1310.C, 2:1.

Fig. 258. Selection of beads found by sieving of disturbed sediments in Tomb 1310, 2:1. Faience beads, beads from *Engina mendicaria* and a carnelian bead, 1310.C, 2:1.

Fig. 259. Cylindrical bead in greenish faience 1310.C, 1:1.

Fig. 260. Heated steatite bead 1310.C, 1:1.

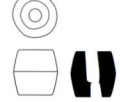

Fig. 261. Carnelian bead 1310.C, 1:1.

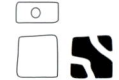

Fig. 263. Square bead in heated steatite 1310.C, 1:1.

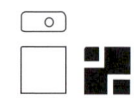

Fig. 264. Square bead in heated steatite 1310.C, 1:1.

TOMB 1311

Location. The tomb was positioned only 20-25 m WNW of Tomb 1310 and at the same altitude at the base of the low pass (figs. 253 and 265).

The excavation. The still monumental tomb had been quarried for stones with a cut in the southeast side. It was excavated in 1971 by Michael Beck, Steen Andersen and Karen Frifelt as it was feared that stone robbers would soon return. The mound also had traces of a more ancient penetration from the top into the chamber area. The original shape was diffuse since many stones had fallen beyond and around the outer ring wall obscuring its original form. The recent damage had cut across the outer entrance passage which was thus easily identified. The tomb was excavated from the top going downwards in the chamber and entrance in horizontal layers.

Structural remains. The investigation identified the lower half of a central chamber with a surrounding ring wall and an entrance passage toward the south (figs. 266-267). The chamber was almost round with a diameter of 2.4 m. The chamber wall was preserved to a height of 1.5 m on the western side with 7 to 9 courses surviving. It was constructed of densely stacked elongated or flat stone blocks. The wall face had a gradual incline of c. 0.6 m indicating a corbelled construction which, with the diameter in mind, probably reached a height in the range of 2.2 to 2.5 m.

The lower half of the chamber, which was preserved, was filled with fine sand and increasing inclusions of charcoal particles at lower levels. About 30 cm above the floor a circular zone, c. 0.60 m in diameter, of charcoal particles indicated the presence of a fireplace (1311.K) and was evidently the origin of the charcoal spread above. On the western side it was bordered by four stones and to the east three similar stones may have formed part of the fireplace. Some scattered finds, amongst them a glass bead, indicated that the feature belonged to very late activities in the chamber. Skeletal remains were found on the floor pavement at a deeper level.

The chamber floor consisted of an irregular pavement of hand-sized stones placed on a subsoil of sediments eroded from the mountain side. The natural surface had a slight incline from north to south across the chamber and through the entrance of c. 0.3 m.

The entrance passage had a length of 2.5 m and a width of 0.5 m at the chamber but widening to 0.6 m at the outer edge of the tomb. The height was preserved to c. 0.8 m, but must have been somewhat higher. The covering stone blocks had been removed.

The ring wall was recovered on both the east and the west side. It had a diameter of around 8 m and the wall face had been torn down to a height of 0.5 to c. 1 m.

Finds. At the secondary fireplace, 1311.K, a glass bead 1311.A was found as were a thick copper nail, 1311.B, and a small bent copper rod, 1311.C. The glass

Fig. 265. Tomb 1311 before excavation looking NW. In the southeastern side stone plundering has been commenced.

Fig. 266. The chamber during excavation viewed looking S.

bead was found east of the feature and both metal objects inside the stone-lining.

Skeletal remains appeared at a lower level (fig. 268). There were traces of three individuals all with the head towards the south and placed on the same level. No stratigraphic relationships were indicated by placement of the burials. The skeletal parts were semi-articulated and badly preserved. The cranial parts indicate the minimum number of individuals. Only individual 1311.I in the western side appears articulated with spine, cranium and traces of ribs in almost anatomical order. At the same level a small ceramic vessel was found (fig. 269). It stood by the north wall towards the back of the chamber at the assumed position of the feet of the skeleton.

1311.A: Brown barrel-shaped glass bead, L 6.9 mm, D 7 mm.

1311.B: Copper nail with small flat head, 2.5 cm long, 0.3 cm thick (fig. 270).

1311.C: Part of bent copper rod, 1.5 × 0.9 cm (fig. 271).

1311.D: Rounded biconical ceramic vessel of Jemdet Nasr type in red-brown sand-tempered ware, with broken rim and a row of 11 holes around the base of the neck and at least 4 holes on the neck (fig. 272).

1311.E: Charcoal sample from 1311.K.

1311.F: Samples of roots found at the level of the skeletal remains on their northern side.

1311.G: Skeletal fragments. The aggregation is interpreted as the remains of one individual consisting of the skull (calotte parts), fragments of teeth and some fragments of disarticulated long bones, among them probably part of an upper arm (humerus) to judge from the field drawing. The teeth indicate a young adult (Højgaard 1985).

1311.H: Skeletal remains consisting of parts of an upper skull and two teeth. To the northeast lay remains of disarticulated, badly preserved and indeterminable long bones. Their association with the cranium is uncertain.

1311.I: Skeletal fragments. The outline of the skull, parts of the mandible, the spine, part of a shoulder (scapula) and ribs could be identified together with fragments of the pelvis still in anatomical order. Disarticulated long bones from the lower arms (?) were found by the cranium. An unidentified long bone was positioned along the spine. The position of the cranium and the curve of the spine indicate that the body had been placed on its right side.

1311.K: A circular concentration of charcoal particles and a rounded angular stone setting. The charcoal zone measured c. 0.6 m across, the stone-lining measured 1.4 × 0.4 m.

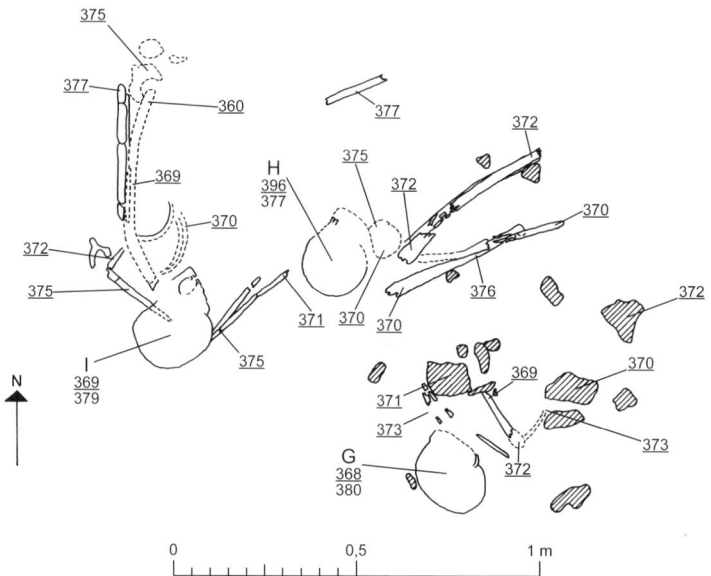

Fig. 268. Skeletal remains from three individuals, 1:20.

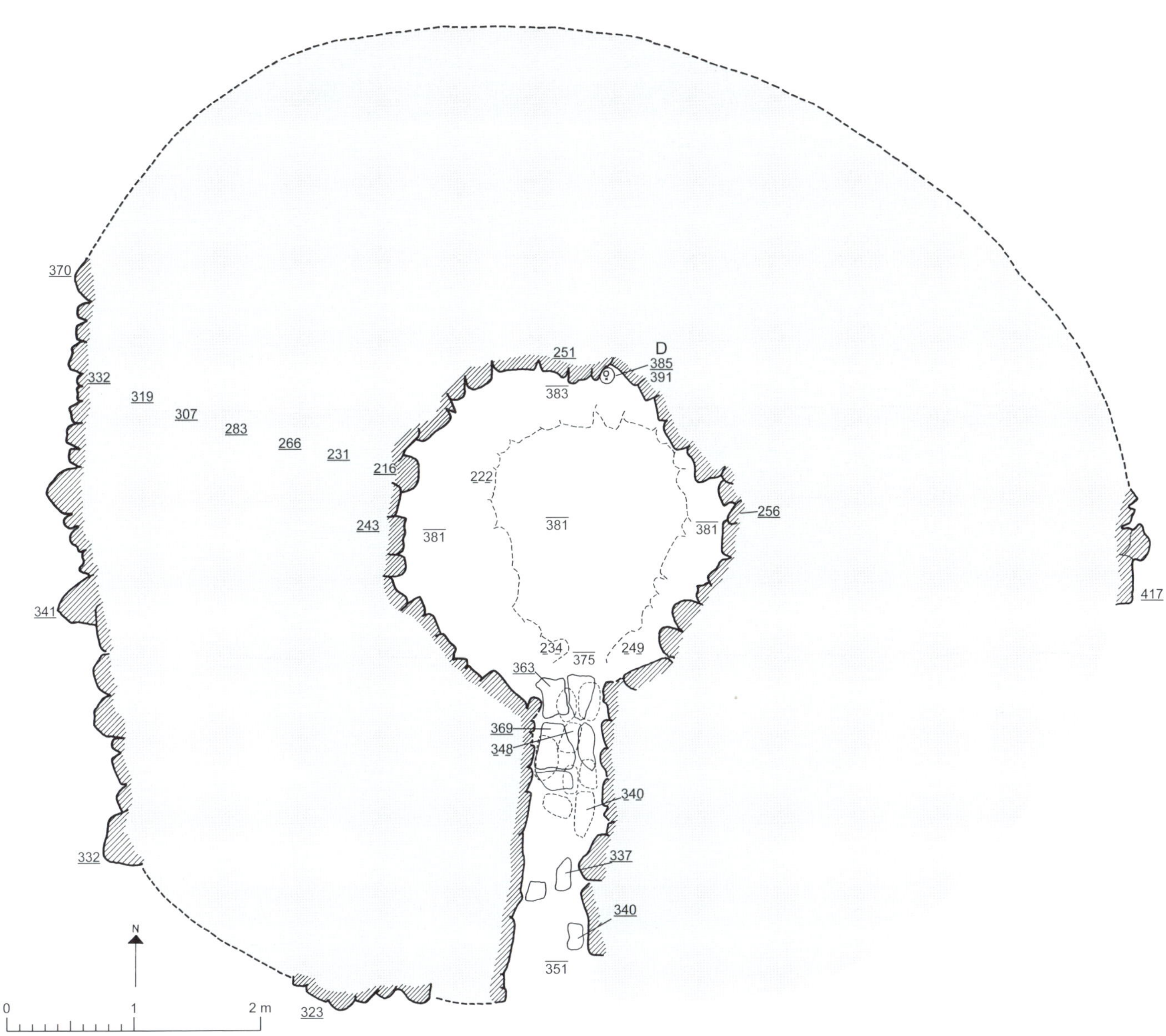

Fig. 267. Plan of Tomb 1311, 1:50. The hatched line in the chamber indicates the upper course of the corbelled roof.

Fig. 269. Ceramic vessel 1311.D in situ.

167

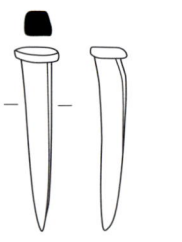

Fig. 270. Copper nail 1311.B, 1:1.

Fig. 271. Bent copper rod 1311.C, 1:1.

Fig. 272. Ceramic vessel 1311.D, 1:1.

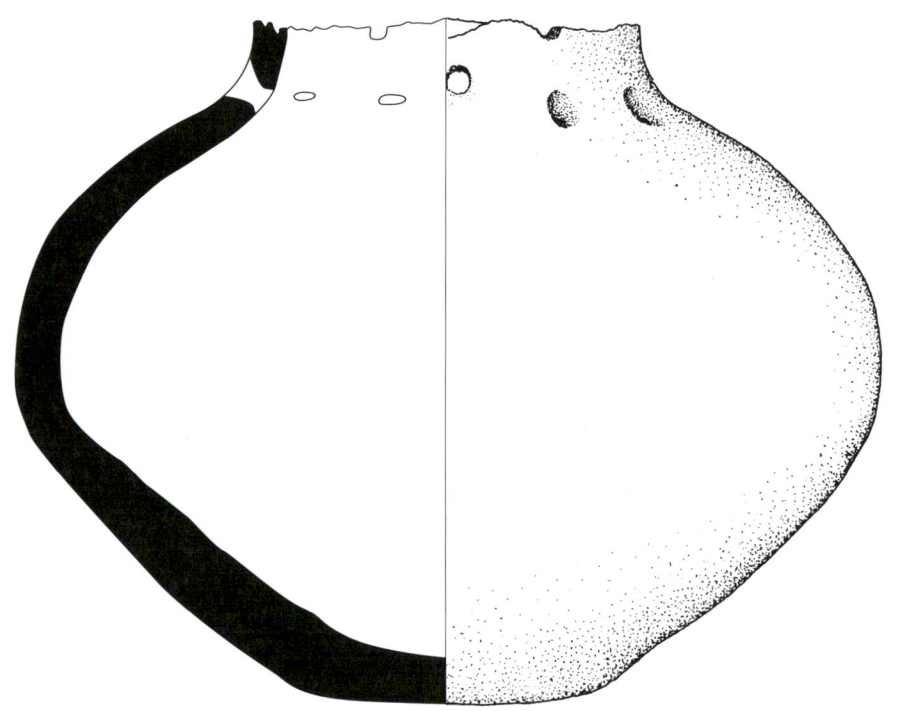

TOMB 1312

Location. The tomb was located c. 70 m southeast of Tomb 1310 on a rock promontory overlooking the pass from a position 25-30 m above the valley floor (fig. 253). The tomb was placed in a position estimated to be 320-325 m above sea level. The rock face falls very steeply downwards to the west, north and east of the burial site. The tomb is surrounded by so-called rock shelter tombs with 16 such features positioned below, above and to the sides of Tomb 1312.

The excavation. Tomb 1312 was excavated in 1971 by N.A. Boas and Bo Madsen while the excavation of Tomb 1311 was in progress. The tomb was found during a previous reconnaissance where it was noted that sherds of painted pottery and soft stone were scattered at the foot of the mound. The chamber and the surrounding area were excavated in horizontal layers from the top. The entrance passage was not excavated.

Structural remains. The tomb was disturbed by a secondary intrusion. Most of the upper construction was removed and lay primarily down the steep slope on the western side of the tomb. The investigation recovered the remains of a ring wall and a central chamber (fig. 273). An entrance passage was not identified during the clearance of the outer periphery and is not mentioned in the fieldnotes, but it appears in photographs of the southern chamber wall. The c. 0.5 m wide opening was blocked with small stones from the outside and more or less aligned with the chamber wall that consists of larger stone blocks.

The chamber had a rectangular plan oriented northwest to southeast with a length of 2 m and a width of 1.6 m (fig. 274). The chamber wall was preserved to a height of 0.8 m with five to eight courses remaining. The eastern side of the ring wall was almost torn down. The ring wall was constructed from rather irregular stones protruding into the chamber. The lowest course contained some large blocks measuring 0.6 to 0.8 m in width. In the south side the wall still had some incline that indicated a corbelled construction.

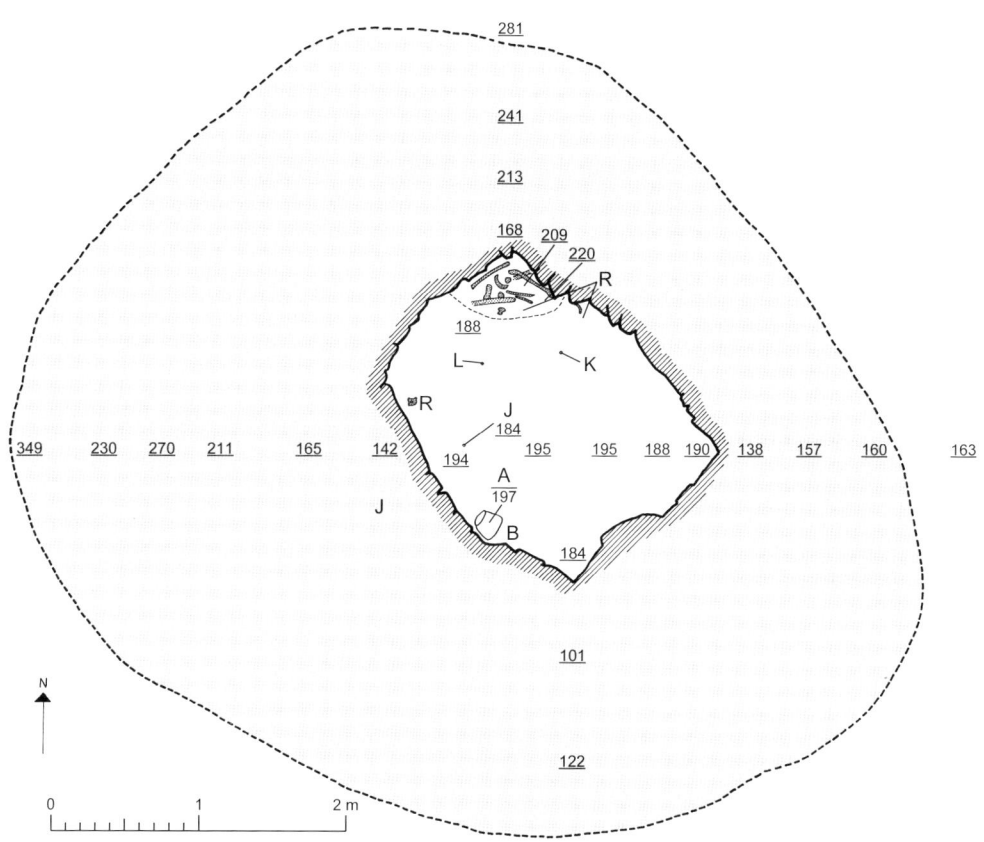

Fig. 273. Plan of Tomb 1312, 1:50. Remains of an Umm an-Nar period interment on the floor and skeletal remains, probably from Hafit period burials, stacked in the north corner.

Only the lower part of the chamber had sediment remains surviving with a thickness of c. 0.5 m. The floor was made up from irregular bedrock; only some larger stone blocks in the north-western part of the chamber seemed positioned in order to form a somewhat level floor.

The original diameter of the ring wall could not be determined, but the wall probably exceeded the 1.2 to 1.8 m that remained of the thickness, suggesting the diameter to be around 6 m.

Finds. The sediments in the eastern and central chamber were much disturbed with the exception of some parts of the lowest level just above the bedrock. At this level a complete softstone beaker of Umm an-Nar date with a shell standing in it was found to the west of the entrance (figs. 275-276). In the northernmost corner was a dense aggregation of redeposited human bones from at least one adult individual, perhaps a Hafit period burial that has been cleared by the later Umm an-Nar burial.

Scattered in the more disturbed sediments among stone blocks fallen from the construction were several carnelian and agate beads that could be both Umm an-Nar and Iron Age. A very fragmented part of a possible lumbar vertebra was observed in the western side.

From the floor level the find list contains:
1312.A: Beehive shaped vessel with concentric lines made of greyish-black softstone of Umm an-Nar date (fig. 277).
1312.B: Jackknife clam, *Ensis*, found inside A (fig. 278).
1312.J: 3 biconical bright red carnelian beads, smoothly polished, L 7.5-8 mm, D 4.6-4.7 mm (fig. 279).
1312.K: Biconical bright red carnelian bead, smoothly polished, L 42.6 mm, D 10.8 mm (fig. 280).
1312.L: Ovate, flat bead of agate, smoothly polished, L 9.9 mm, D 4.3 × 8.8 mm (fig. 281).
1312.R: Human bones, mainly fragmented long bones (the field drawing indicates ribs and a possible humerus) and parts of a cranium from an adult individual (fig. 273).

The remaining objects from the chamber, some probably of Iron Age date, were found in a higher level around 0.5 m above the floor level and concentrated in the south-western side and evidently in disturbed positions (fig. 282).
1312.C: Open finger ring of copper, oval cross section, slightly pointed ends, outer diam. 23 mm (fig. 283).
1312.D: Fragment of copper finger ring with a rhomboid cross-section (fig. 284).
1312.H: Open copper finger ring with oval section, outer diam. 18 mm (fig. 285).
1312.I: Fragment of copper finger ring, c. 21 mm in outer diameter, found on the western chamber wall, conjoins with 1312.C.
1312.M: Side sherd in fine red ware, conjoinable with base found outside chamber (1312.T).
1312.O: 2 potsherds and 1 sherd from softstone vessel.

Additional finds were recovered in the mixed sediments in and above the chamber and inner ring wall, including:
1312.E: Small fragment of copper sheet with hole.
1312.F: Copper fragment.
1312.G: Copper rivet, 1 cm long, 0.35 cm thick, hammered in both ends (fig. 286).
1312.N: 4 potsherds from different vessels.
1312.P: A polished sea shell, bi-valve (*Marcia hiantina*?) with traces of green, cuprious pigment (attacamite?) inside (fig. 287 left), possibly eye-makeup (cf. Potts 1996 and 1997 fig. 13).
1312.Q: Small sea shell (fig. 287 right).

On the surface of the mound and at its foot some scattered sherds were found:
1312.S: 6 sherds from soft-stone vessel, one with 3 dotted concentric single circles, 0.5 cm in diameter.
1312.T: Pottery from at least 6 different vessels, three of which of red sandy ware, with limited conjoining fragments; one conjoining side sherd was found in the disturbed upper part of the chamber-ring wall zone. The latter indicate that the pottery originally came from the chamber rather than being deposited as offerings at the entrance. The pottery had clear Umm an-Nar affinity. The fragments of the largest vessel had a horizontal wavy pattern, like typical black-on-red or buff grave ware (Frifelt 1995 p. 172 and 177, fig. 230, Méry 2000 fig. 80.5).

Fig. 274. The excavated chamber.

Fig. 275. The softstone vessel 1312.A in situ.

Fig. 276. The softstone vessel 1312.A in situ.

171

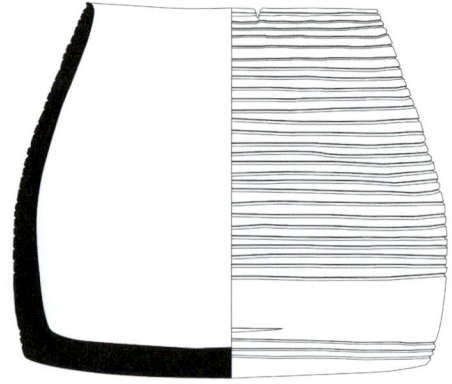

Fig. 277. Softstone vessel 1312.A, 1:2.

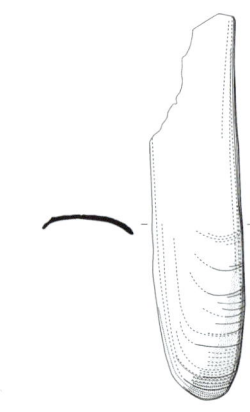

Fig. 278. Jackknife clam 1312.B, 1:2.

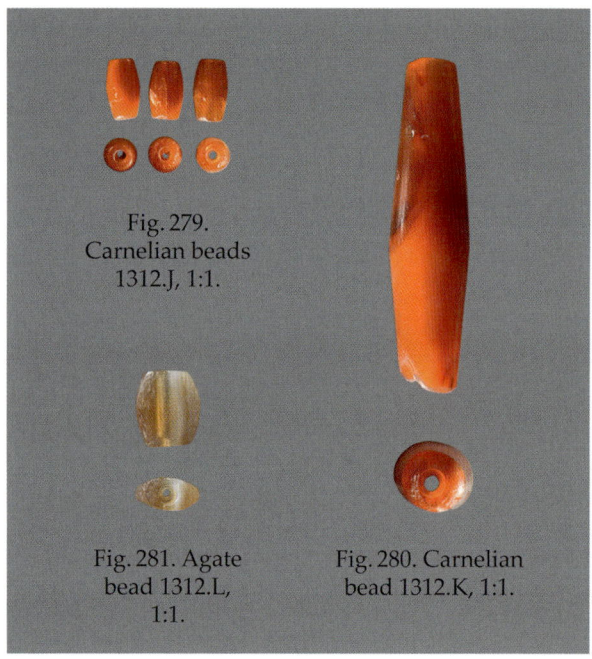

Fig. 279. Carnelian beads 1312.J, 1:1.

Fig. 281. Agate bead 1312.L, 1:1.

Fig. 280. Carnelian bead 1312.K, 1:1.

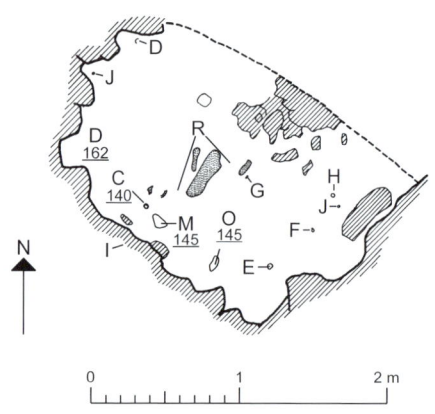

Fig. 282. Plan of the upper chamber level with a mixture of scattered bones and Iron Age small objects, 1:50.

Fig. 283. Open finger ring 1312.C, 1:1.

Fig. 284. Fragment of ring 1312.D, 1:1.

Fig. 285. Open finger ring 1312.H, 1:1.

Fig. 286. Rivet 1312.G, 1:1.

Fig. 287. Shells 1312.P with remains of pigment (left) and Q (right), 1:1.

9. The mounds on the southern plateau

TOMB 1313

Location. Several tombs were surveyed at the most southern end of the valley. It was an almost rectangular area measuring c. 1.5 × 0.8 km. The early mapmakers from the late 1950s named the area, criss-crossed by many narrow paths, *Aqabat Saghir* "small mountain tracks". It is a landscape with eroded hillocks and peaks intermingled with plateaus, slopes and canyons filled with the debris of erosion. For the most part the land exceeds altitudes of 305-310 m above sea level and thus is in contrast to the surrounding plain areas. The northern and eastern part was a veritable mound field with many small groups of prehistoric burial monuments often placed near the bluffs so as to be seen from a distance. The south-eastern flank, along where a major caravan path led to the south was traditionally called *al Kharaijib*, the ruins.

At the northern border of this eroded "plateau landscape" Tomb 1313 was found at an altitude of c. 300 m above sea level (fig. 288). Tombs 1313 and 1314 were part of a local group of grave monuments. Within a distance of less than 100 m four similar mounds were visible.

The excavation. The tomb was excavated in 1971 by N.A. Boas and Bo Madsen. It was investigated from the top where a c. 1 m wide entry hole had been created by grave robbers (fig. 289). The outline of this "shaft" could also be seen in the disturbance to the pavement 1.5 m below. After the chamber wall and the entrance were located the interior was excavated in horizontal levels. With the dumpy level a range of cross levels were taken north-south and east-west in order to construct a section of the remaining structure.

Structural remains. The construction consisted of a central chamber surrounded by a ring wall and a narrow entrance passage leading due south (fig. 290).

The chamber had a rounded to oval plan oriented in line with the axis of the entrance passage. The length was 2 m and the width c. 1.9 m. The chamber wall was preserved to a height of 1.6 m. It was built from elongated stone blocks, from 0.3 to 0.5 m wide, oriented "centripetally" towards the centre of the grave. It was noted that the uppermost stones, where the corbelled construction gradually inclined inwards, were more regular in shape and many were carefully stacked.

The chamber floor consisted of irregular 5 cm thick stone slabs placed on a flat and level subsoil of eroded rubble (fig. 291).

The entrance passage was fully preserved in length. It reached the intact outline of the front of the monument at a distance of 2.2 m from the chamber (fig. 292). It was blocked by densely stacked stones. The eastern wall was slightly curved. The width was 0.45 m at the chamber and 0.5 m for the rest of the passage. The height was c. 0.6 m. The upper construction was corbelled giving the entrance passage a tapering though angular cross section.

The ring wall was 2.2 m thick at the south side where its outline could still be traced. The outer diameter of the tomb was c. 6 m. The outer wall faces and the upper core of the ring wall were demolished by stone plundering.

Finds. As the robber's shaft had been dug through the base of the chamber, burial material was encountered high in the disturbed deposits. Parts of a ceramic vessel, 1313.A, were found about 0.5 m below the top hole and more potsherds occurred further down towards the chamber floor together with splinters of bone. Fragments of 1313.A were also found outside the tomb in front of the entrance passage. No finds were observed in the entrance passage so it is likely that the pottery was associated with the plundering activity.

Fig. 288. Tomb 1313 looking E before excavation.

Fig. 289. Tomb 1313 during excavation looking N.

Fig. 291. The chamber floor during excavation.

Parts of the primary burial layer had survived. At the northern side of the chamber a ceramic vessel was found standing upright among the stone slabs of the pavement (figs. 290 and 292-293). At the eastern side a groups of 75 greenish beads were recovered and approximately 60 of these were conjoined as parts of bead strings (figs. 294-295). Additionally, 29 similar beads and a carnelian bead were found at the eastern side of the chamber. On the eastern side of the entrance was a bead made from an Engina mendicaria shell.

The finds include:
1313.A: Biconical ceramic vessel of Jemdet Nasr type, in yellow-brown ware with small white limestone inclusions broken into nine sherds with remains of plum-red slip with a dark painted ornament on the shoulder (fig. 296).

1313.B: Ceramic vessel, ovoid with conical body and small flat base, of Jemdet Nasr type, in red-brown, micaceous, sand-tempered ware with yellow slip (fig. 297).
1313.C: 5 green-glazed, cylindrical faience beads, L c. 4 mm, D c. 3 mm (fig. 298).
1313.D: Remains of chains of beads: one cylindrical, heated steatite, L 2.9 mm, D 3.4 mm (fig. 299), the rest green-glazed, cylindrical faience beads, estimated to number 99 of which 60 were observed in joined position, L 2-4.6 mm, 2.7-4 mm, and one triple segmented cylindrical, L 8.5 mm (fig. 300).
1313.E: Ring-shaped, milky-surfaced red carnelian bead, L 3.5 mm, D 7 mm (fig. 301).
1313.F: Sea-shell, *Engina mendicaria*, perforated laterally.
1313.G: Skeletal fragments in secondary position.
1313.H: Bone fragment, possibly of lumbar vertebra, found in secondary position in front of the entrance.

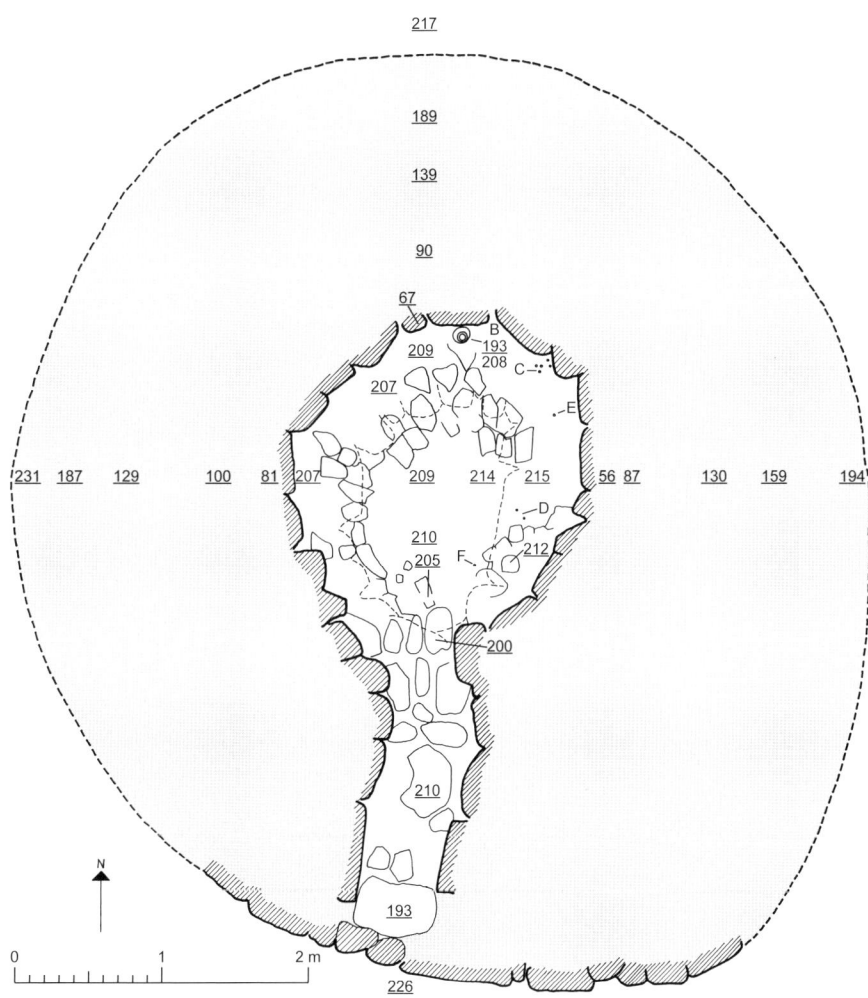

Fig. 290. Plan of Tomb 1313, 1:50. The hatched line in the chamber indicates the upper course of the corbelled roof.

Fig. 292. A view through the entrance passage into the chamber with ceramic vessel 1313.B.

Fig. 293. Ceramic vessel 1313.B in situ.

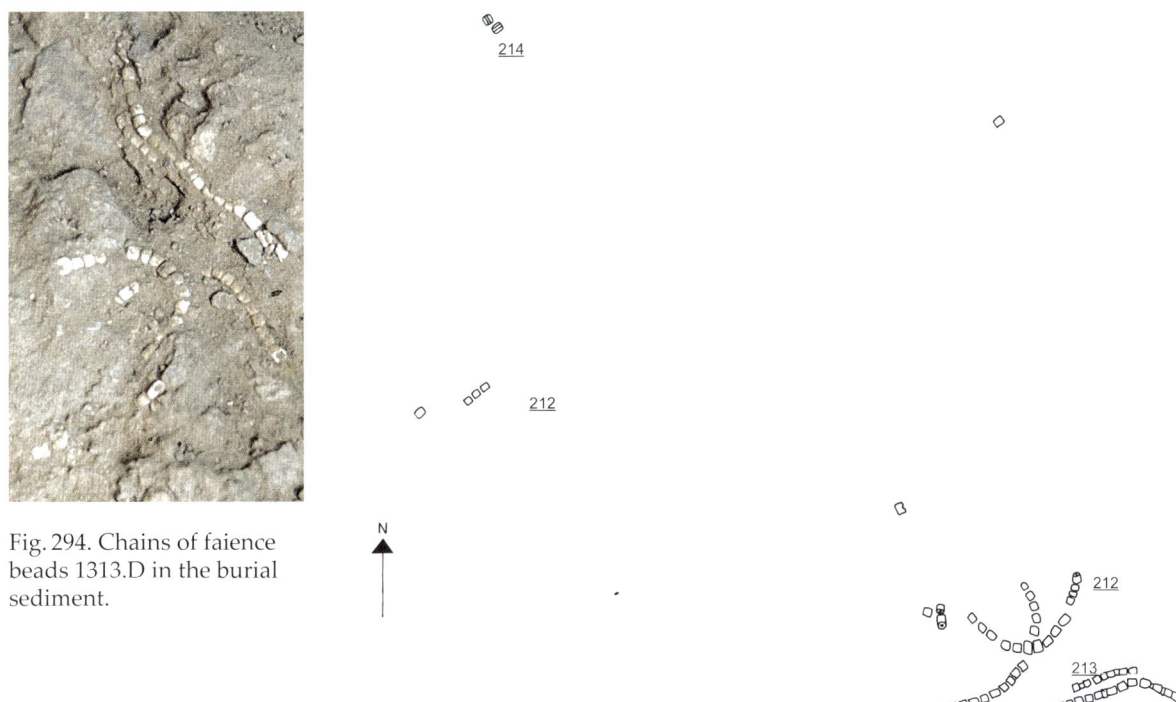

Fig. 294. Chains of faience beads 1313.D in the burial sediment.

> Fig. 295. Plan of faience bead aggregations, 1:2.

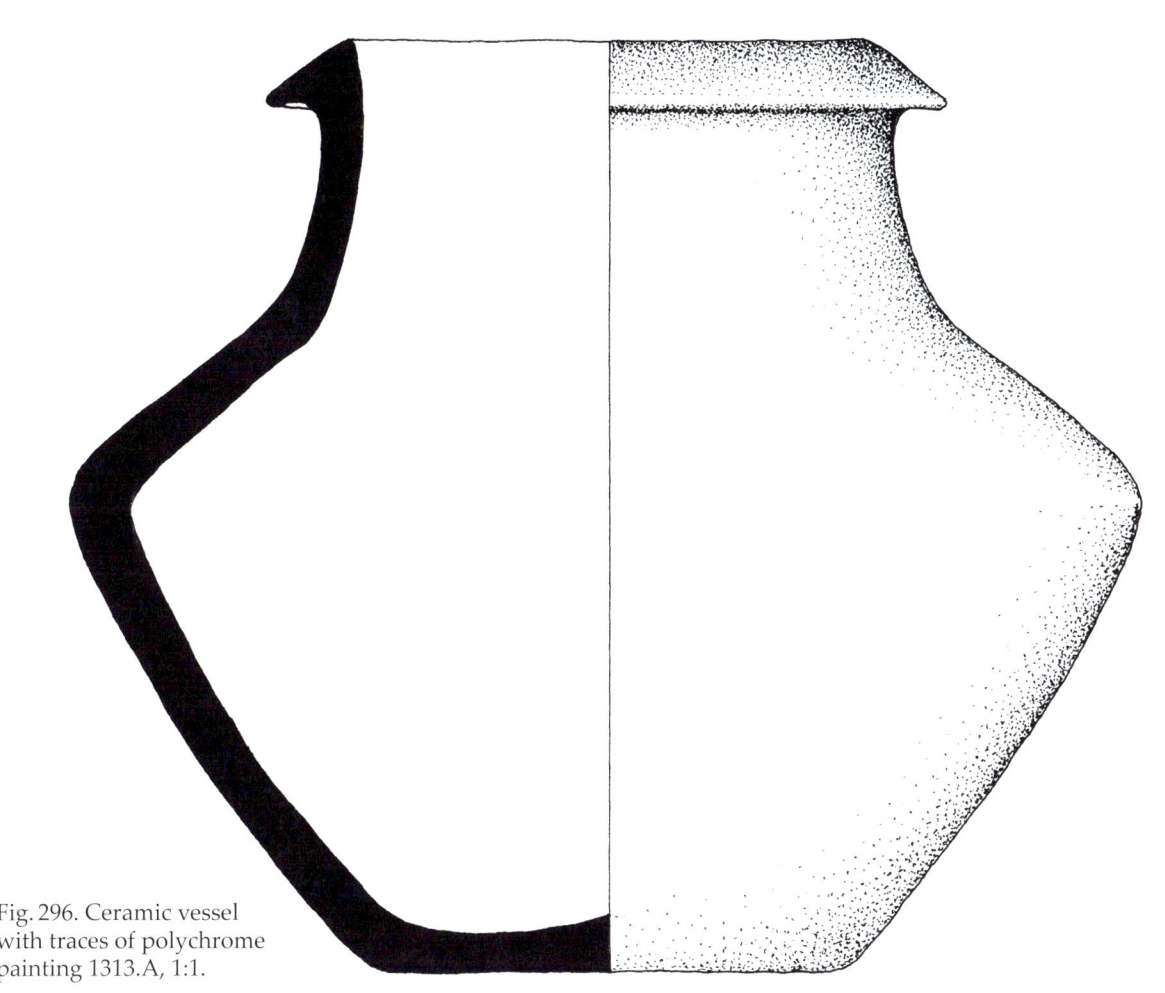

Fig. 296. Ceramic vessel with traces of polychrome painting 1313.A, 1:1.

Fig. 297. Ceramic vessel 1313.B, 1:1.

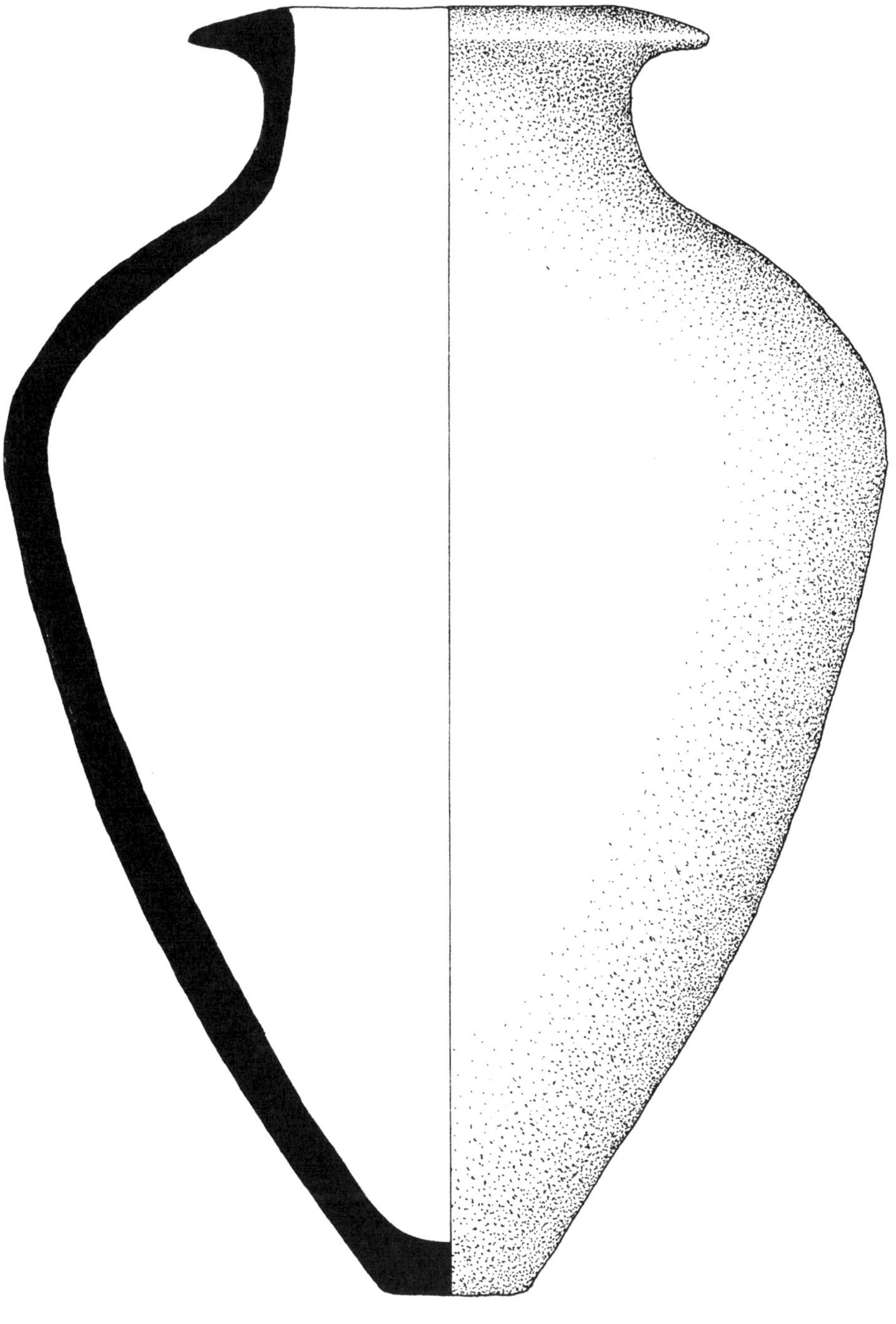

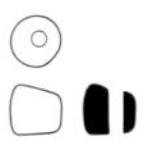

Fig. 298.
Cylindrical bead
in greenish faience
1313.C, 1:1.

Fig. 299.
Heated steatite bead
1313.D, 1:1.

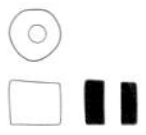

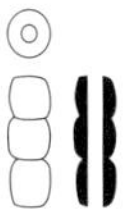

Fig. 300.
Triple-segmented
cylindrical faience
bead 1313.D, 1:1.

Fig. 301.
Carnelian bead
1313.E, 1:1.

TOMB 1314

Location. The tomb was located 70-80 m south of Tomb 1313 at an estimated height of 310 m above sea level. The tomb, like several of the neighbouring tombs, was placed on a hillock, making it appear larger and more visible from a distance (fig. 302).

The excavation. The tomb was excavated in 1971 by Michael Bech, Steen Andersen and Karen Frifelt. It had suffered heavily from recent stone plundering. The top was cleared after which the outline of the chamber wall could be identified. The chamber was emptied by digging carefully with a hoe in the top among fallen stone blocks and later with trowels and a lot of brushing as artefacts started appearing in the finer sediment. The structure was mapped at a scale of 1:20 after the chamber had been excavated. A plan was drawn at a scale of 1:10 showing the skeletal material, diverse artefacts as well as the outline of the chamber wall in a level corresponding to the second stone course (fig. 308).

Structural remains. The tomb had a thick ring wall and a central chamber with an entrance passage to the southeast (fig. 303). The chamber had an almost round plan with a diameter of 2.2 m. The chamber wall was preserved to a height of c. 1.5 m with 10-13 courses (fig. 304). It was largely constructed from large flat blocks with a flat side turned towards the chamber. One block measured 0.9 m in the wall face. The wall stones gradually increased in size in the upper part. The wall construction differed slightly from what had previously been seen during the 1971 campaign by the use of an assortment of larger selected stones.

The curved incline of the wall showed the corbelling starting from 0.5-0.6 m above the floor. In the best preserved eastern side the incline was almost 0.7 m into the chamber and indicated a vault reaching 2 m or more above the chamber floor.

The level floor consisted of regular stone slabs, from four to eight centimetres thick, with sizes varying from 0.1 to 0.4 m. The stone slabs were rather hastily arranged as a round platform 1.5 m across and with a 0.4 m wide unpaved zone along the chamber wall.

The entrance passage had a length of 2 m and a width of 0.6 m at floor level narrowing slightly in the middle. At the chamber it was 0.85 m high decreasing to 0.75 m at the front of the ring wall. The passage was constructed of large stone blocks, up to 0.6 × 0.5 × 0.3 m, in the lower courses and at the joining with the chamber wall (fig. 305). At the outside western corner the entrance passage included a large square block measuring 1.1 × 0.6 × 0.4 m (fig. 306).

Fig. 302. Tomb 1314 looking NW.

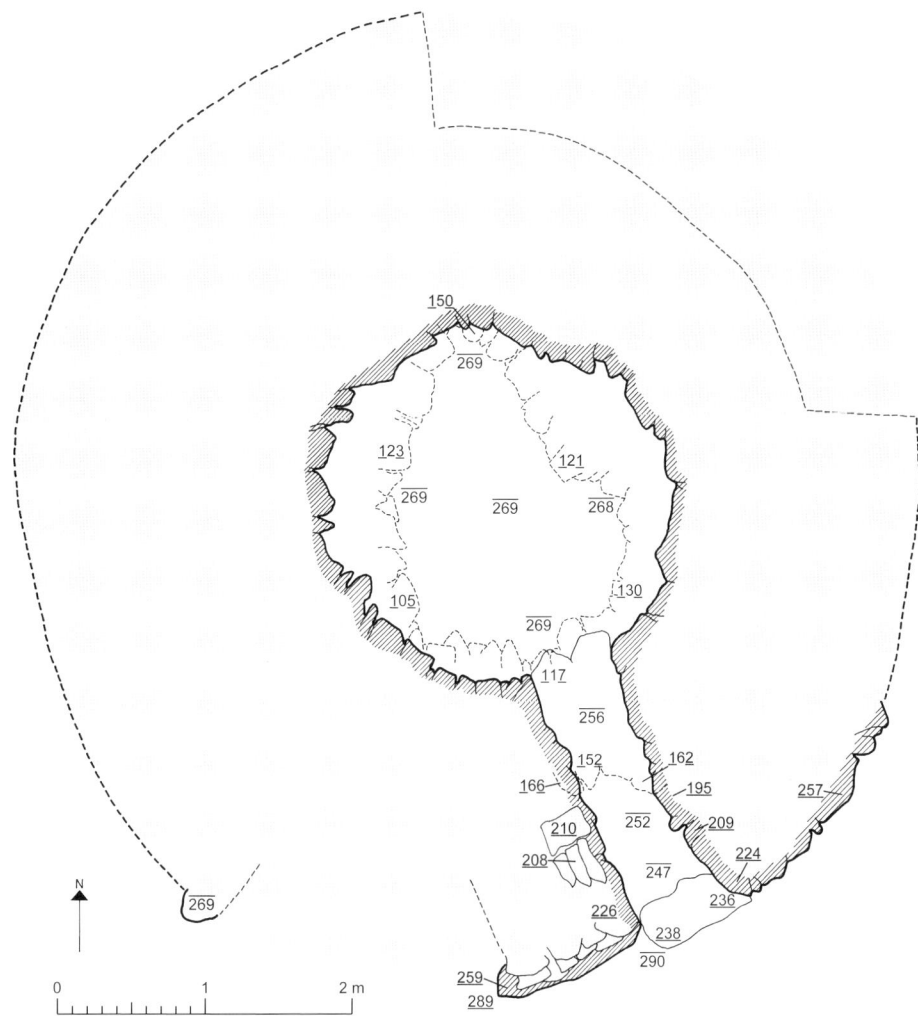

Fig. 303. Plan of Tomb 1314, 1:50. The hatched line in the chamber indicates the upper course of the corbelled roof.

The passage was covered by a low corbelled construction. Towards the chamber, and at the entrance, large stone slabs formed a pavement similar to the chamber floor. The entrance had been carefully closed by a packing of mainly angular blocks at the chamber aligned with the chamber wall and outside with the outer ring wall front.

The ring wall was severely damaged by stone quarrying especially on the north-eastern and south-western sides where stones had been removed in deep cuts that almost reached the chamber. The outline of the ring wall could be identified along three to four meters on both sides of the entrance where the wall has a thickness of c. 2 m indicating an outer diameter of the tomb of 6-6.5 m.

Finds. With a relation to the floor pavement were skeletal remains of at least three individuals (figs. 307-308). Near the entrance passage was a ceramic vessel and in the opposite end of the chamber three copper nails. On the western side a small copper fragment was lying among skeletal parts.

1314.D: 3 copper nails (2.5, 3 and 3 cm long) (fig. 309).
1314.E: Fragment of copper rod, 0.8 cm long, pointed, found by skeleton 1314.B.
1314.G: Rounded biconical ceramic vessel of Jemdet Nasr type, in red-brown to grey-brown sand-tempered ware with grey-yellow slip with a broken-off rim and 11 drilled holes on the upper shoulder and remains of a couple on the neck, was found next to cranium 1314.A near the entrance (fig. 310).

The skeletal remains were not in a good state of preservation, but very fragile. The more or less articulated parts were all found on or closely above the stone pavement. A few scattered smaller fragments were found between the pavement and the chamber wall. The skeletal parts are described according to the level and their stratigraphic relationships (fig. 308).

1314.A: Fragmented cranium recovered in the north-eastern side of the floor pavement, c. 0.2 m above the pavement and above the remains of individual 1314.F. The dislocated skull consists mainly of the calotte without the mandible.

Fig. 304. Tomb 1314 had very regular corbelled construction.

Fig. 305. Ceramic vessel 1314.G in situ.

1314.C: Remains of limb bones. Fragmented long bones from the arms (if from an adult), encountered in a high position in the western side of the chamber c. 0.25 m above the pavement and lying above the pelvis of individual 1314.B.

1314.B: The almost articulated, but only partially preserved skeleton of an adult lying in a contracted position on the right side. The head and torso is directed towards the south, and the body is placed in a slightly bent position. The legs are strongly con-

Fig. 306. The entrance of 1314 with remains of blocking.

Fig. 307. Skeleton 1314.B as excavated.

tracted, and the right foot is almost drawn up to the pelvis. A piece of copper, 1314.E, was found at the waist, located between the lumbar vertebrae. The preserved teeth indicate an elderly adult (Højgaard 1985).

1314.F: The semi-articulated skeletal parts from presumably one adult individual placed in the same level and position as 1314.B, but in the eastern side of the chamber. Feet and leg bones are in their expected anatomical place, but no bones from the torso (truncus) were observed. Some arm bones seem to be almost in their place with an upper arm long bone (humerus) and lower arm bones (ulna /radius) in anatomical order. The cranium is missing. In theory the dislocated cranium 1314.A could derive from the skeleton 1314.F. Under the pelvic area of 1314.F were four dislocated and undetermined long bones from yet another individual. Another skeletal scatter consisted of some cranial fragments 1314.H found next to ceramic vessel 1314.G in the south end of the chamber.

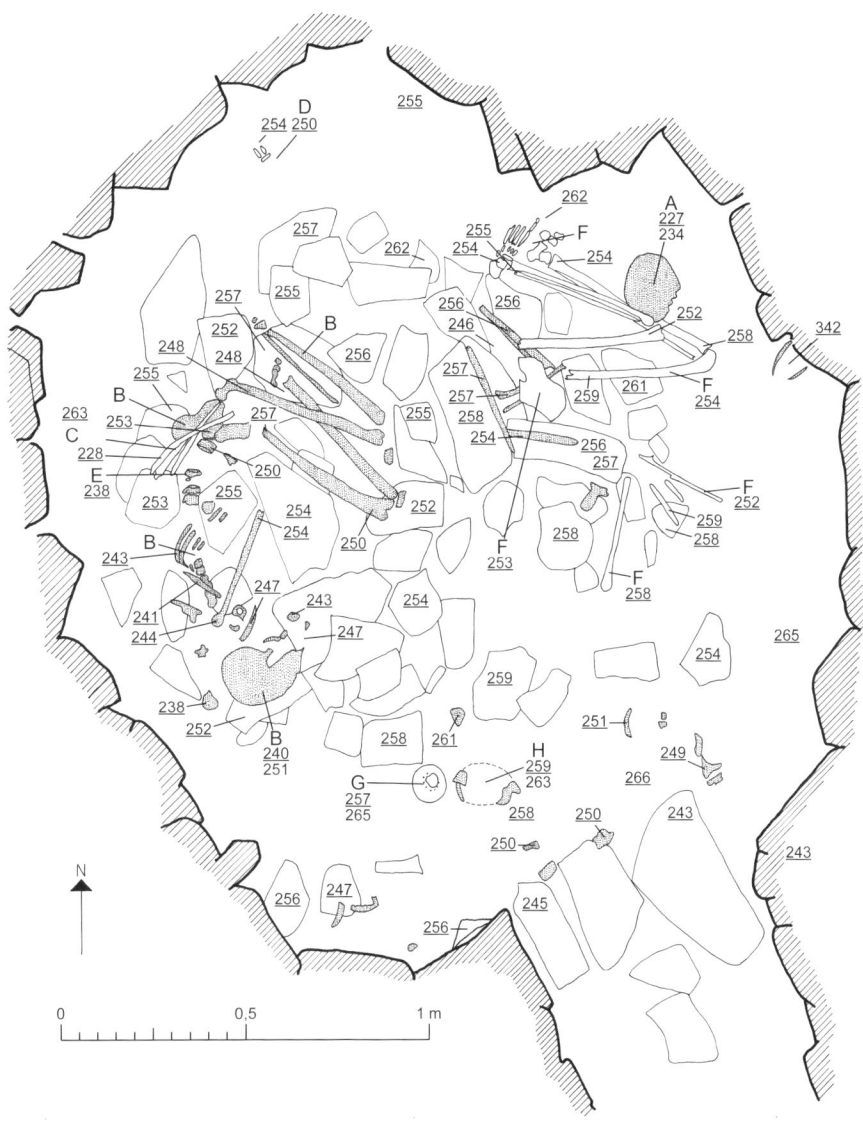

Fig. 308. The chamber floor with skeletal remains and burial goods, 1:20.

Fig. 309. Copper nails 1314.D, 1:1.

Fig. 310. Ceramic vessel 1314.G, 1:1.

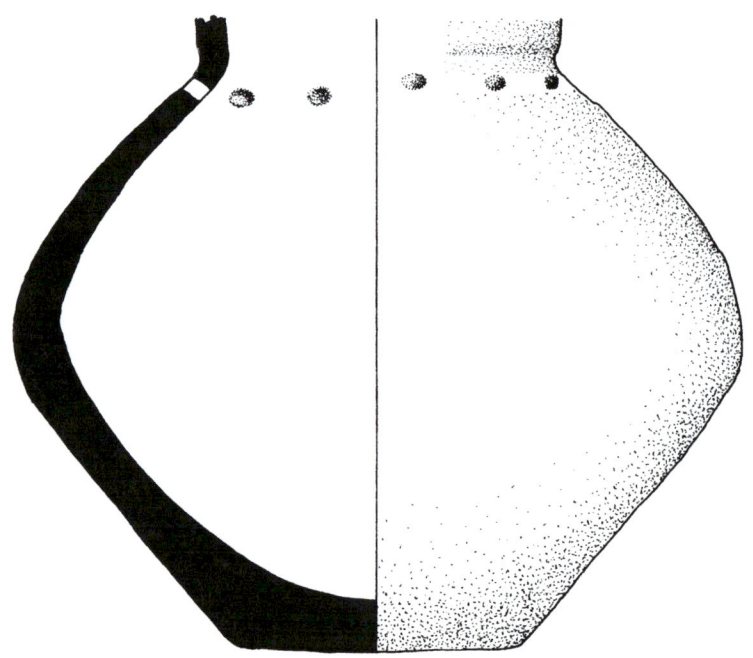

TOMB 1315

Location. The tomb was situated 750 m SSW of Tomb 1314, c. 330 m above sea level. Tomb 1315 lay in a small saddle with barely enough space for a tomb on a westward facing steep crest some 20 m above the surrounding terrain (fig. 311). The crest bordered a large open plain to the north measuring 400 m east-west and some 250 m north-south. In the spring of 1971 this had recently been used as a test site for oil drilling. The area had been flattened on the high spots by bulldozing and some adjacent low lying tombs had been driven on by bulldozers.

The excavation. The tomb was excavated in 1971 by Bo Madsen with mapping assistance from N.A. Boas. The chamber of Tomb 1315 left minimal room for even a single excavator to work. It showed no evident sign of a robber's hole in the top and there was no sign of fresh stone robbing. The entrance passage and the southern part of the chamber were however disturbed at the top and in the entrance area by ancient attempts to access the grave chamber. By clearing the top it was discovered that remains of the corbelled roof were still present in the northern side of the chamber, but had slid into the upper chamber. The upper part of the chamber contained more flat stones that had fallen down from the vaulting.

The chamber was excavated by digging in horizontal layers following the chamber walls and its level stone courses. By clearing the periphery of the southern half the entrance passage was located and could be excavated more or less simultaneously with the lower chamber.

Structural remains. The excavation revealed a relatively small tomb with a ring wall, a central chamber and an entrance passage towards the SSW (fig. 312). The chamber plan was pear-shaped, oriented in line with the axis of the entrance passage, but also very irregular due to collapse of the ring wall. It was 1.6 m long and 1.4 m wide being one of the smallest chambers investigated. The chamber wall was preserved to a height of 1.4-1.5 m. It was built of rather irregular elongated stone blocks with the flattest side, if any at all, facing upwards. Their width varied between 0.2 m and 0.4 m. In the upper part of the chamber flatter stones had been used as the corbelling increased.

Beneath the collapsed roof material, the chamber contained heterogeneous sediments of sand and silt. In the upper part this was compact and hard, probably cemented through the action of percolating water.

Fig. 311. Tomb 1315 looking W.

The chamber floor consisted of a pavement of flagstones of varying size, from c. 0.1 to 0.2 m, scattered mainly in the northern and western part.

The entrance passage had a funnel-shaped plan (fig. 313). It was 1.8 m long and 0.4 m wide at the inside and c. 0.75 m at the outside. The height had been more than 0.8 m. The lack of larger flat blocks among the disturbed stones indicates a low corbelled roof construction made of smaller stones. It is noteworthy that the entrance to this tomb is oriented towards the south in spite of the presence of a deep slope in that direction and not towards the east where the ground is level.

The ring wall had been constructed on uneven ground on both the northern and southern side having been built with part of the base placed on the sloping sides of the saddle. Most of the outer wall had collapsed, but the approximate thickness of the ring wall had been around 1.8 m. The tomb had an outer diameter varying between 5.5 m and 6 m.

Finds. Skeletal remains from at least three adult individuals were found on the irregular floor pavement (figs. 314-315). Grave gifts were represented by 17 beads and a cowry shell as described below.
1315.E: Ring-shaped, milky-surfaced red carnelian bead, L 4.9 mm, D 11 mm, found by cranium A (fig. 316).
1315.F: Cowry shell found southwest of skeleton 1315.A (fig. 317).
1315.G: 16 green-glazed, cylindrical faience beads, L 3-4.4 mm, D 3.2-4.1 mm (fig. 318), one of which was found southwest of skeleton 1315.A, close to the cowry shell.

The skeletal remains consisted of two aggregations in the eastern side of the chamber and some scattered bones in the southern part. The scatter was two cranial upper parts lying to east of the entrance, and parts of scapula and a fragment of a long bone, possibly a humerus, found on the western side. One of the cranial parts 1315.C or D could in theory belong to the skeleton 1315.B, but the bone material is too badly preserved to say more than at least three individuals are represented by the skeletal material.

1315.A: An articulated skeleton, badly preserved, represented by part of the cranium, mainly from the calotte, thoracic vertebrae, a few ribs, remains of the pelvis and long bones from arms and legs. The body was positioned in an extremely contracted position with the head towards the north. The individual had been placed on the left side with the chest and right side turned towards the legs (the collarbone was found under the spine). The arms were lying under the chest. The right arm had been outstretched and the left was bent. The body was in a position as if the deceased had been wrapped as a bundle. At the head was a carnelian bead, 1315.E.

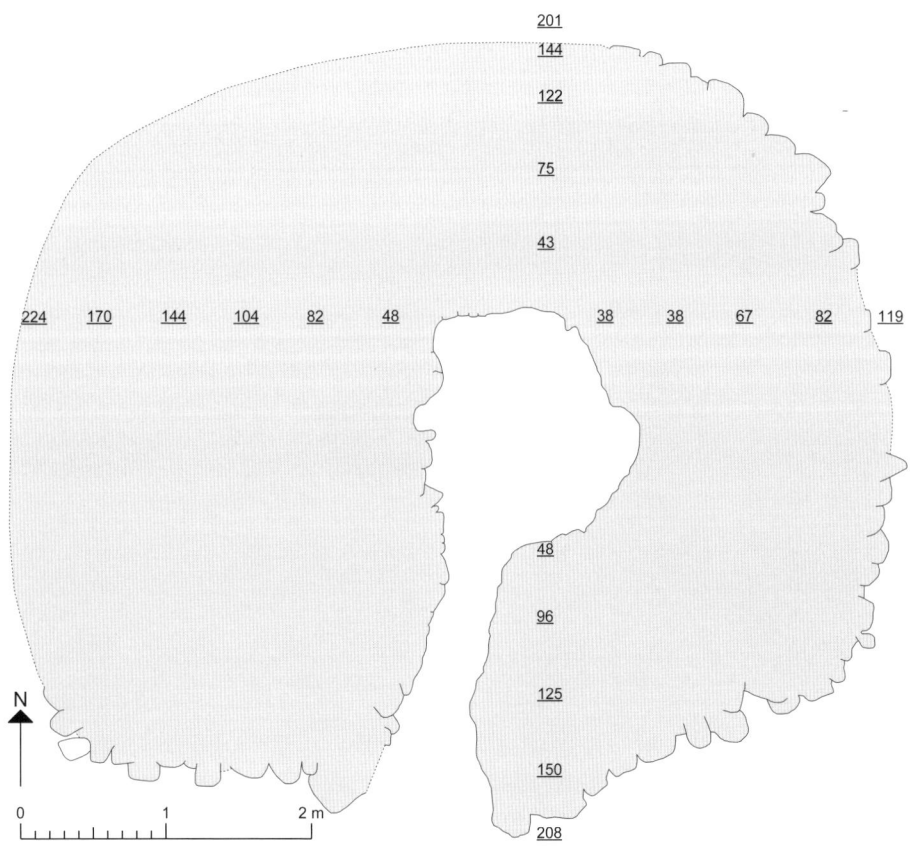

Fig. 312. Plan of Tomb 1315, 1:50. The western part of the ring wall is disturbed.

Fig. 313. The entrance passage with remains of pavement.

1315.B: This aggregation of skeletal fragments contained badly preserved semi-articulated leg bones, diverse vertebrae parts and unidentified bone fragments, which to an extent were superimposed by 1315.A. The position of the leg bones, if in their original position, indicates that the body lay on the left side with the head towards the southwest, the back against the chamber wall and the slightly contracted legs towards the north. Two jaw fragments had teeth which came from an elderly adult and a young adult respectively (Højgaard 1985).

1315.C: A very fragmented calotte was evidently in secondary position lying on the upper part of the left femur from 1315.B. As with the skull parts from 1309.I, the previously excavated tomb at the western mountain ridge, this calotte had marks of trepanation. The cranium was represented by large fragments of the cranial roof, no facial bones were preserved and also a large part of the right side was missing. The relatively thick skull belonged to a young to middle aged adult, possibly a male. Four trepanations marked as oval lesions from c. 1.5 to 3.4 cm long were identified, apparently the surgery was carried out during several sessions (Littleton and Frifelt 2006).

1315.D: Parts of a cranium, the calotte with the remains of the eye brows, was lying upside-down half a meter from cranium 1315.C.

Fig. 314. Skeletal remains in the eastern part of the chamber.

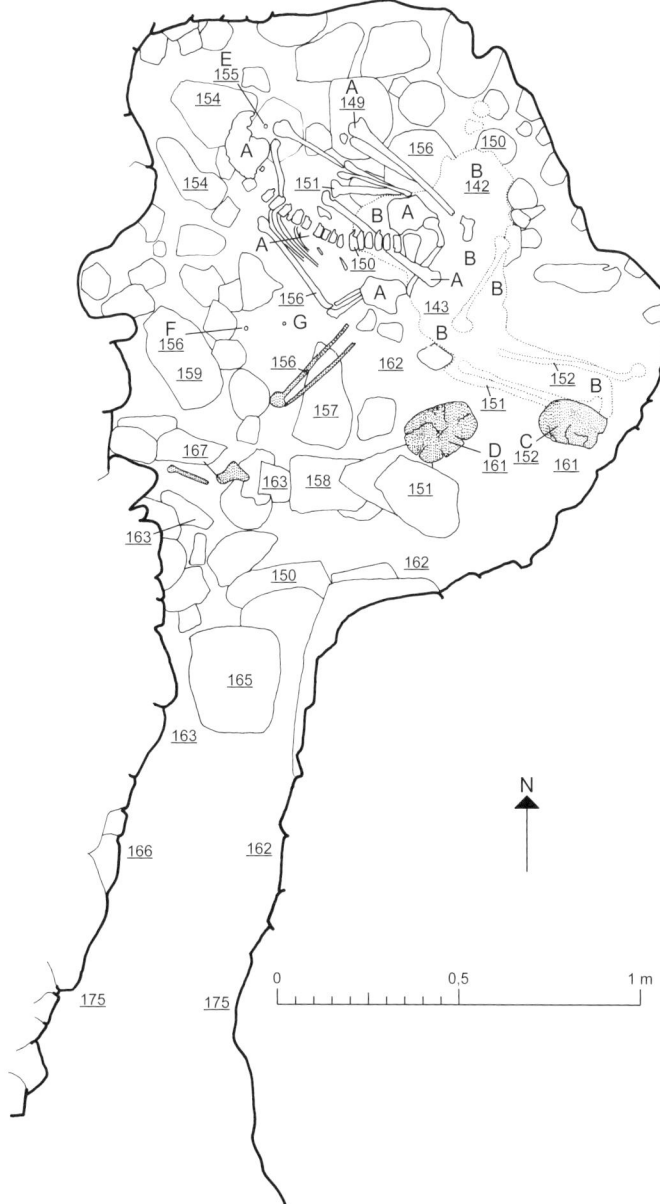

Fig. 315. Positions of skeletal material, 1:20; the trepanned calotte 1315.D is indicated. Note the extreme contracted position of individual 1315.A.

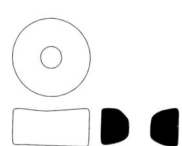

Fig. 316.
Ring-shaped carnelian bead 1315.E, 1:1.

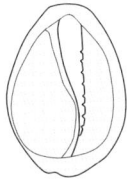

Fig. 317.
Cowry bead 1315.F, 1:1.

Fig. 318.
Green faience bead 1315.G, 1:1.

TOMB 1316

Location. The mound was situated c. 100 m west of Tomb 1315, at the foot of the rock at the southern side of a plain where, as mentioned, test drillings had taken place (fig. 319). Some 30 m further to the west yet another severely damaged mound was located in a similar position at an altitude of c. 310 m above sea level.

The excavation. The tomb was excavated by N.A. Boas in 1971. The tomb was damaged by stone plundering down to the level just above the entrance passage. The mound was uncovered from the top and the outline of the chamber and entrance identified after which they were excavated in horizontal layers. A section was established across the lowest level of the chamber in order to identify the surface of the chamber floor.

Structural remains. The excavation resulted in the identification of a tomb consisting of a ring wall around a central chamber with an entrance passage aligned almost due south (fig. 320). The chamber had a rounded square plan, 1.9 m long along the line of the axis of the entrance passage and 1.8 m wide. The eastern side seemed out of position and appeared to be caved in with many loose stone blocks. The chamber wall was preserved to a height of c. 1.1 m. It was constructed from a mixture of stone placed in more or less horizontal courses. Flat and elongated blocks were exposed at the upper levels, where the wall had a considerable inward incline of 0.4-0.6 m, which pointed to a rather low, corbelled construction.

The lower chamber sediment consisted of a compact sandy soil with a high content of small stones and gravel. The floor was difficult to identify with certainty. The section through the level of the assumed floor showed that the tomb was constructed on a layer of c. 0.3 m thick mixed sediment which derived from the erosion of the limestone slopes (fig. 321).

The entrance passage was 2-2.2 m long and the width expanded from 0.4 m at the chamber to 0.7 m at the outer periphery of the ring wall. The flanking walls were constructed from larger stone blocks up to 0.6 m in size used along the line of the entrance. The floor was paved with flat stone slabs up to 0.3 × 0.4 m in size. The innermost cap-stone was still in place, a block measuring 0.9 × 0.25 × 0.2 m, giving a height of the passage of 0.8 m.

Fig. 319. Tomb 1316 looking N.

The ring wall was very damaged by recent stone quarrying. The area in front of the entrance was examined but the rest of the circumference was not cleared. The diameter of the disturbed mound was around 7 m. The ring wall was constructed with a very high content of gravelly soil and small stones. Apparently, the local subsoil had been used to fill the gaps between the stone blocks.

Finds. C. 1 m west of the ring wall some small ceramic sherds were found, 1316.F. In front of the entrance were some bone splinters and a flat hammered copper pin. In the grave chamber were only 3 scattered faience beads and a bone splinter in the probably disturbed fill.

1316.A: 2 green-glazed, cylindrical faience beads (one crumbled), L 3.5 mm, D 3.6 mm.
1316.B: 1 green-glazed, cylindrical faience bead, L 6 mm, D 3.8 mm.
1316.D: Copper pin, c. 15 cm long, 1 cm thick, flat-hammered near the pointed end (fig. 322).
1316.F: 3 side sherds and 1 base sherd in a fine red, hard fired ware with a red slip of Umm an-Nar date.
1316.C: Skeletal fragment found in the western side of the chamber.
1316.E: Skeletal fragments, bone splinters, found in front of the entrance near the copper pin 1316.D.

Fig. 320. Plan of Tomb 1316, 1:50. The hatched line in the chamber indicates the upper course of the corbelled roof. The innermost lintel block was anchored in the line of the corbelled chamber wall.

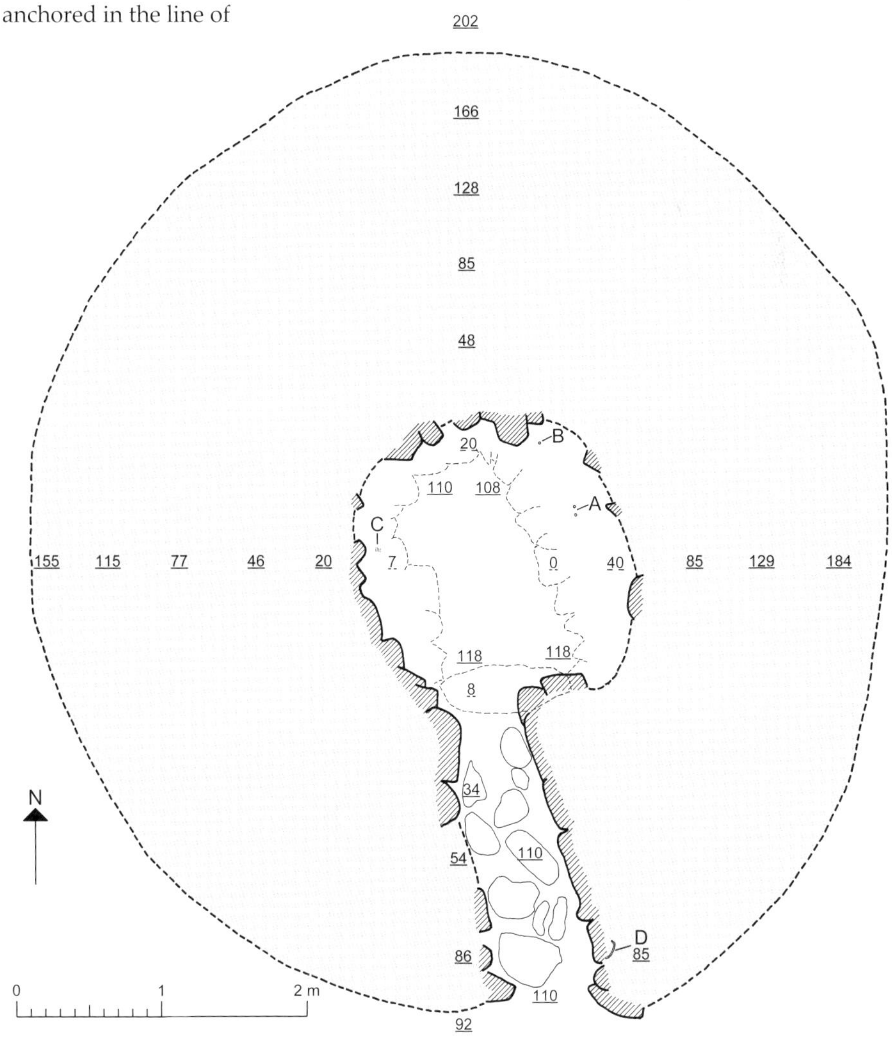

Fig. 321. Excavating a section through the floor level of Tomb 1316.

Fig. 322. Copper pin 1316.D, 1:1.

10. The mounds on the eastern side of the mountain

TOMB 1317

Location. This tomb and four others were excavated on the east side of Jebel Hafit c. 5 to 6 km to the northwest of the village of Mazyad and almost due west of what is today, Al Zahir. The present tarmacked road to Ibri was, at the time of the fieldwork, a dirt track leading off to the south and cutting many of the washes flowing east from the mountain. Driving the Land Rover up these wadis from the plain was the only way to get to the base of the mountain. For the last part of the way, the equipment had to be carried by foot. This, to a certain extent, influenced the choice of tombs excavated.

Tomb 1317 was located on a rounded terrace at the end of a dry wadi which had a dirt track running parallel. The tomb was located at an altitude of c. 352 m above sea level (fig. 323).

The excavation. The tomb was excavated in 1971 by Steen Andersen, Karen Frifelt and Michael Beck. On the southern half of the mound stones that had slid down from the construction were removed until the outer ring wall with a blocked entrance was found. Part of the area to the southern side was cleaned in order to search for material from inside the chamber. The top of the mound was cleared of stones in secondary position and remains of the uppermost part of the corbelled construction came to light (fig. 324). Part of this was removed until a safe entry was established. The sediments in the chamber were excavated in horizontal layers and when the level of the intact entrance passage was reached, it was carefully emptied from stone packing and sand digging with trowels from both inside and outside. The excavation work involved some tricky climbing into the chamber, but the uppermost courses of the roof were still, after 5000 years, wedged in position by the massive pressure from the outer wall. The main obstacles were taking accurate levels inside the chamber and the limited light for photography.

Structural remains. The investigation revealed a relatively large tomb with considerable remains of a regularly constructed ring wall with a base of large stone blocks (fig. 325). The central chamber had an almost circular plan and a nearly intact corbelled roof (fig. 326). A long entrance passage was directed towards the southwest.

The chamber had a diameter of c. 2.5 m and stood to a height of c. 2.1 m. Between 13 and 16 courses could be counted from the base to the top. In the lower c. 1.3 m, the chamber wall was constructed from very large stone blocks with dimensions up to 0.6-0.7 m and a thickness of around 0.2-0.3 m. These blocks were stacked with a flat side towards the chamber. Above these solid blocks came courses of smaller oblong stone blocks gradually more inwardly placed and stacked with their pointed ends directed towards the centre of the chamber. This part of the chamber wall was more irregular and some larger earth filled voids could be seen as if sections of the inner wall (on the eastern side) had settled to a secondary stable position. If this in fact was the case it could have affected the incline of the upper chamber wall.

At the top of the corbelled construction the wall had a higher amount of large stone slabs, sizes c. 0.4-0.5 m. Some long and narrow slabs, 0.1-0.2 m wide, with a long side turned inward, were used in the final closing of the corbelled roof. On top of the vault still rested some large stone blocks.

The burial chamber was filled with windblown sand in the upper part, below which were compacted sand sediments. Burial levels were encountered from a depth of c. 1.5 m where several floor pavements were documented. The base of the chamber consisted of bedrock.

The entrance passage was well constructed. It was 2.5 m long, at the chamber it was 0.5 m wide and expanded to 0.6 m at the outside of the ring wall. The height was 1.2 m and 1 m respectively.

The flanking walls were almost vertical and built from large stone blocks, up to 0.8 m long/wide, with smaller stones between. The passage was covered with three very large and flat stones giving it a rectangular cross-section. The outer end of the passage was completely blocked by larger stones whereas the inner part was only partially filled to a height of c. 0.4 m. In front of the entrance lay a very large stone slab which sloped to south (fig. 327) and may originally have sealed the doorway (fig. 328). It measured 1.45 × 0.7 × 0.35-0.40 m.

The tomb seemed to have been exposed to a limited degree of stone plundering. The top of the ring wall and above the chamber had been disturbed with some of the largest stone blocks having been dragged out of position. The almost vertical outer face of the ring wall was preserved to a height from 0.8 to 1.25 m. Meter-sized stone blocks had been positioned in the first course and some large blocks had also been placed in both the second and third courses. This was observed in the southern excavated half of the wall but could also be noted behind the displaced stones lying around the ring wall on the opposite side. The most regular angular blocks had been used at both sides of the entrance where the wall was constructed as a regular facade. The ring wall had a thickness of 2.4 m and the total diameter of the tomb was 7-8 m.

Frifelt wrote that the chamber of this tomb was surrounded by two circular walls (Frifelt 1975b p. 61, fig. 14), but this is not in concurrence with the observations made during excavation. The notch/crevice on Frifelt's published black ink plan represents a misunderstanding of the field drawing. The original field plan clearly shows that this line indicates the limit of investigation (fig. 325).

Outside the ring wall in the southern half, a pavement of fist-sized stones was encountered. It was c. 0.7 m wide and must have been placed either as an *ad hoc* levelling of the terrain around the southern side of the monument or as part of the funerary architecture. A possible parallel may be seen in Tomb 1137 excavated some years later at Bat, which had a more regular plinth-like pavement around the ring wall. This was even more pronounced in Tomb 1138 from the same Omani grave field. Both are basically similar to the Hafit tombs but both chambers are more angular and have a rudimentary supporting wall (Frifelt 1975a).

In front of the entrance of Tomb 1317 six, 0.3-0.6 m large stone slabs were found lying horizontally.

The different building material used in this tomb can be explained by the characteristics of the local stone material. The nearby wadi was rich in larger and smaller regular blocks and some slabs had fallen from an exposure of stratified limestone south of the wadi.

Finds. Three burial levels were encountered from c. 40 cm above bedrock and below. They were indicated by the remains of three pavements made from stone slabs of varied size.

Fig. 323. Tomb 1317 looking N before excavation.

The upmost level (I) contained skeletal remains of one individual in a contracted position on the left side with the head towards the east (fig. 329). In the same level were three copper rivets of which one was lying at the waist of the skeleton (1317.A).

The middle burial level (II), separated by five cm of sand from level I contained a few completely scattered and disarticulated skeletal remains and 5 green faience beads (fig. 330).

The lower level (III) was partly mixed with level II and contained badly preserved remains of a minimum of one individual (fig. 331). The skeletal remains were in a bad state of preservation and were very scattered mainly to the eastern side of the pavement.

Outside the tomb on the left side of the entrance were scattered sherds of a ceramic vessel (1317.N) and above the door stone was a copper rivet (1317.O), most likely objects that ended outside the tomb due to a clearance of the grave chamber.

The finds are described according to their relative level in the chamber.

1317.A: Copper rivet, c. 5.5 cm long and c. 0.8 cm in diameter of the flat-hammered ends, from level I (fig. 332).

1317.C: Copper rivet from level I, c. 4.8 cm long, 0.6 cm thick and c. 0.7 cm in diameter of the flat-hammered ends (fig. 333).

1317.E: Copper rivet from level I, c. 5 cm long and c. 1 cm in diameter of the flat-hammered ends (fig. 334).

1317.F: 1 double segmented, cylindrical greenish faience beads, L 8.2 mm, D 4.6 mm. Level II (fig. 335).

1317.H: 1 green-glazed, cylindrical faience bead, L 4.7 mm, D 4.9 mm. Level II.

1317.J: 1 double segmented, cylindrical greenish faience bead, L 9.2 mm, D 4.4 mm. Level II, scatter find.

1317.G: 1 double segmented, cylindrical greenish faience bead, L 10.1 mm, D 4.6 mm. Scattered find from level II.

1317.K: 1 green-glazed, cylindrical faience bead, L 3.6 mm, D 4.3 mm. Scattered find, from level II?

1317.I.: Skeletal fragments found in level II.

1317.M: Skeletal remains in level III, two unspecified long bones and some finger or toe bones.

1317.B: Skeletal fragments found in level I. The individual is represented by an articulated spine, pelvis and long bones in a contracted position (2 femora and 1 tibia), shoulder and upper arm bones lie slightly out of their anatomical position. Teeth fragments indicate an elderly adult (Højgaard 1985).

1317.D: A fragmented cranium found in level I, adjacent to 1317.B, north of the spine. It included the upper cranium, mandible and some almost worn down teeth.

1317.N: 28 sherds of a biconical ceramic vessel with faint marked shoulder of Jemdet Nasr type, in red sand-tempered, micaceous ware with greyish slip, found outside the entrance (fig. 336).

1317.O: Small copper rivet found on the door stone in front of the entrance (fig. 337).

Fig. 324. The corbelled vault viewed from above. It was capped with flat blocks. A large amount of stone has been removed from above the vault.

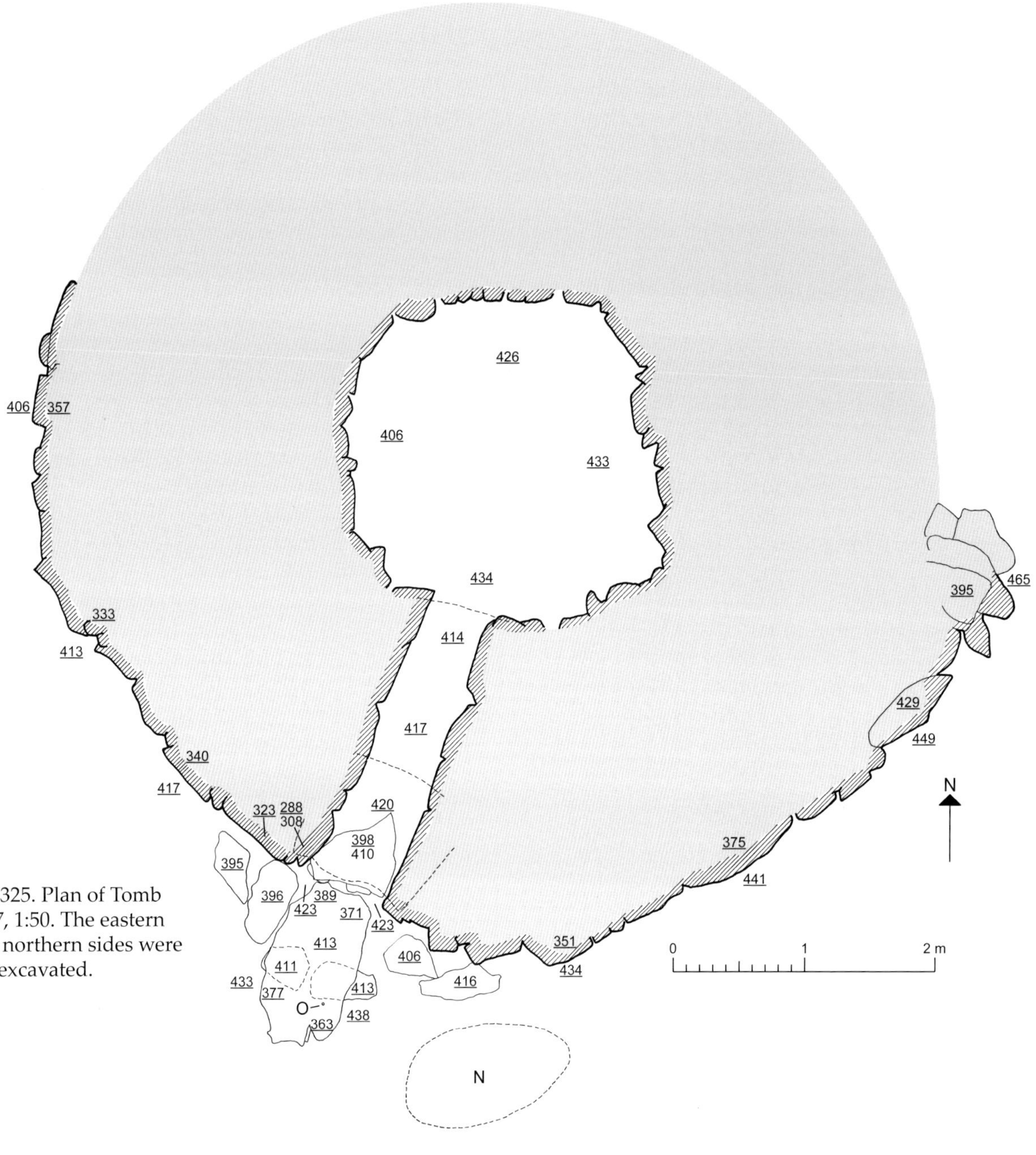

Fig. 325. Plan of Tomb 1317, 1:50. The eastern and northern sides were not excavated.

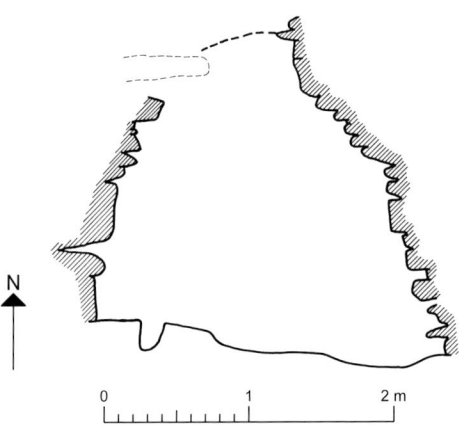

Fig. 326. Cross section of chamber, 1:50. The stone in thin hatched line lies from 10 to 50 cm south of section. The bold hatched line indicated removed roofstones.

Fig. 327. The large slab in front of the entrance standing as found during the excavation.

Fig. 328. The slab positioned as door stone.

197

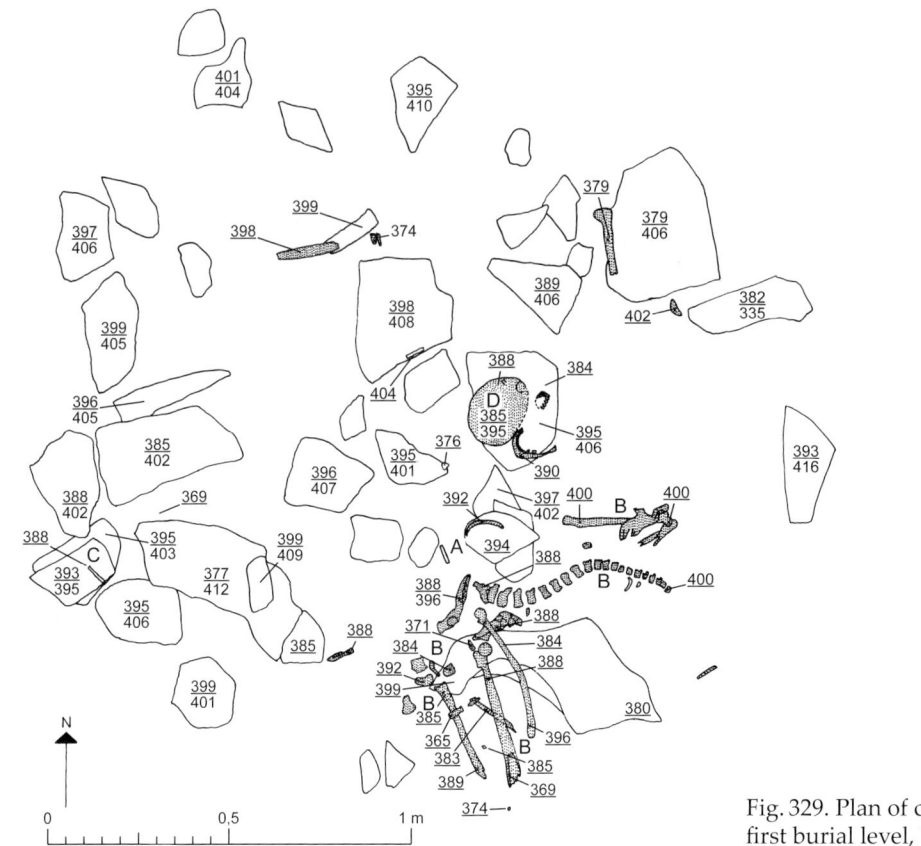

Fig. 329. Plan of chamber, first burial level, 1:20.

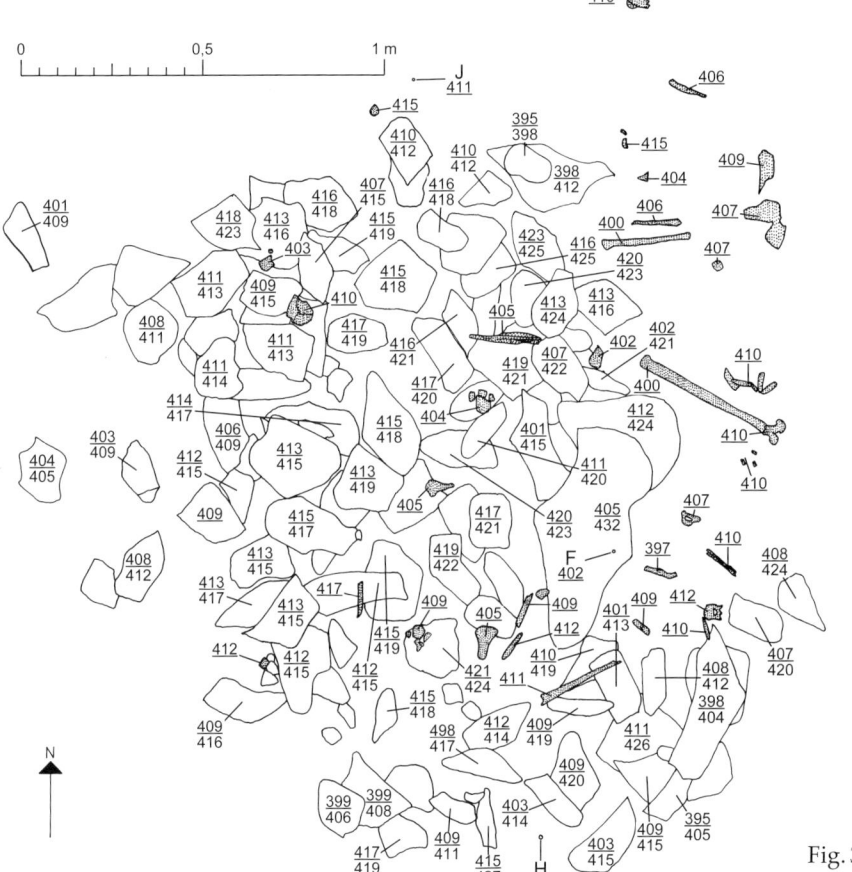

Fig. 330. Plan of chamber, second burial level, 1:20.

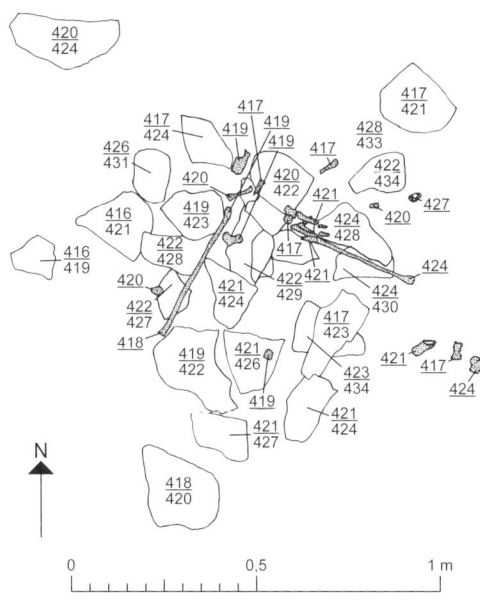

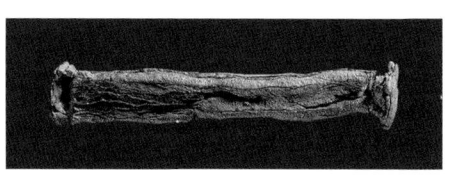

Fig. 333. Rivet 1317.C, 1:1.

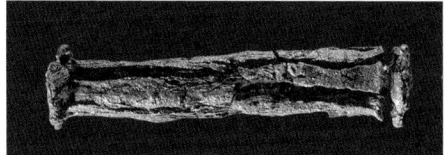

Fig. 334. Rivet 1317.E, 1:1.

Fig. 331. Plan of chamber, third burial level, 1:20.

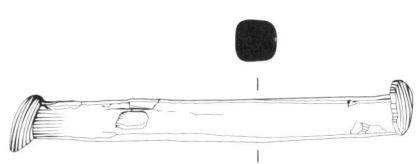

Fig. 332. Copper rivet 1317.A, 1:1.

Fig. 335. Double segmented, green faience bead 1317.F, 1:1.

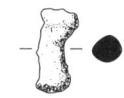

Fig. 337. Copper rivet 1317.O, 1:1.

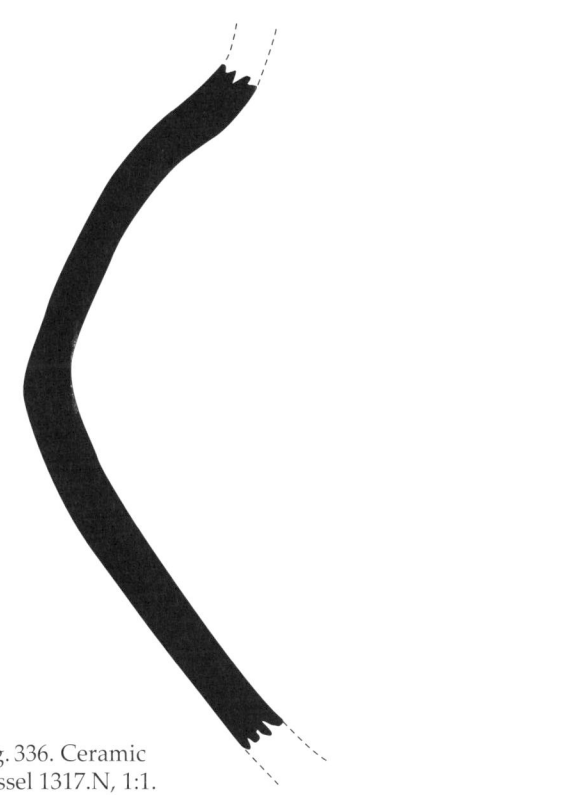

Fig. 336. Ceramic vessel 1317.N, 1:1.

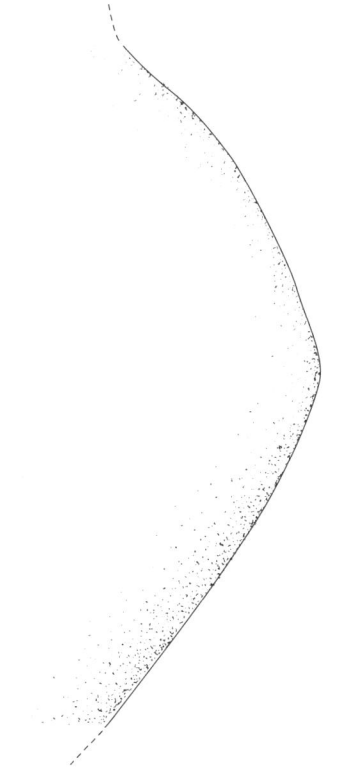

199

TOMB 1318

Location. The tomb, named "The Scorpion Tomb" because of its wildlife content, was positioned 50 m WNW of Tomb 1317 at an altitude of c. 355 m above sea level. It was situated on sloping terrain on a raised area in the middle of a 30 m wide wadi near the edge of the steep talus (fig. 338). The tomb was surrounded by nine other tombs of similar size and construction. Two tombs could be seen to the northwest and seven towards the east and the south.

The excavation. The tomb was excavated by N.A. Boas and Bo Madsen in 1971. The chamber was excavated from a robber's hole in the south-eastern side of the chamber. Most of the chamber was filled with stones due to a collapse of the south-eastern chamber wall. Both ends of the entrance passage were excavated but the central part had collapsed.

Structural remains. The investigation revealed the remains of a relatively intact tomb with a ring wall, a central chamber and an entrance passage aligned almost due south (fig. 339). The chamber had an oval plan oriented perpendicular to the axis of the entrance passage. It measured 2.2 × 1.9 m. The chamber wall and most of the corbelled roof were preserved in the western side and stood to a height of 2.7 m (figs. 340-341). It had 16 to 18 courses of elongated horizontally placed stones pointing towards the centre of the chamber. A cross-section measured just to the west of the centre of the chamber at the hypothetically highest point documents the corbelled construction. The opposing sides of the chamber are inclined in two almost straight lines until 2.4 m above the chamber floor from where the vaulting commences. This upper corbelled construction was made by the use of rather flat and long stone blocks with a gradual displacement upwards. The vault by this rather high ogival profile in reality only spans a relatively short distance of c. 1 m. In the centre of the chamber the inner height of the chamber may have reached 2.8 m.

One third of the south-eastern chamber wall had collapsed in ancient times and filled most of the chamber with stones. The lowest part of the chamber above the natural stone bedrock consisted of c. 0.2 m thick and hard cemented sand.

The entrance passage was 1.8 m long and 0.6 m wide at the chamber and 0.5 m at the outside of the ring wall. The inside had collapsed and a height could not be measured with any certainty.

The ring wall had a thickness of 1.8-2 m. The diameter of the tomb was 6-7 m. During cleaning of the north side it was observed that a secondary wall, 0.6 m wide and almost 1 m high, had been constructed against the face of the ring wall and continuing around the east side of the mound, maybe to support the eastern unstable part of the chamber wall (figs. 339 and 341).

No finds were observed, neither inside nor outside the chamber.

Fig. 338. Tomb 1318 looking SSW. Excavation has commenced along the northern and eastern part of the ring wall.

Fig. 340. The chamber seen from above.

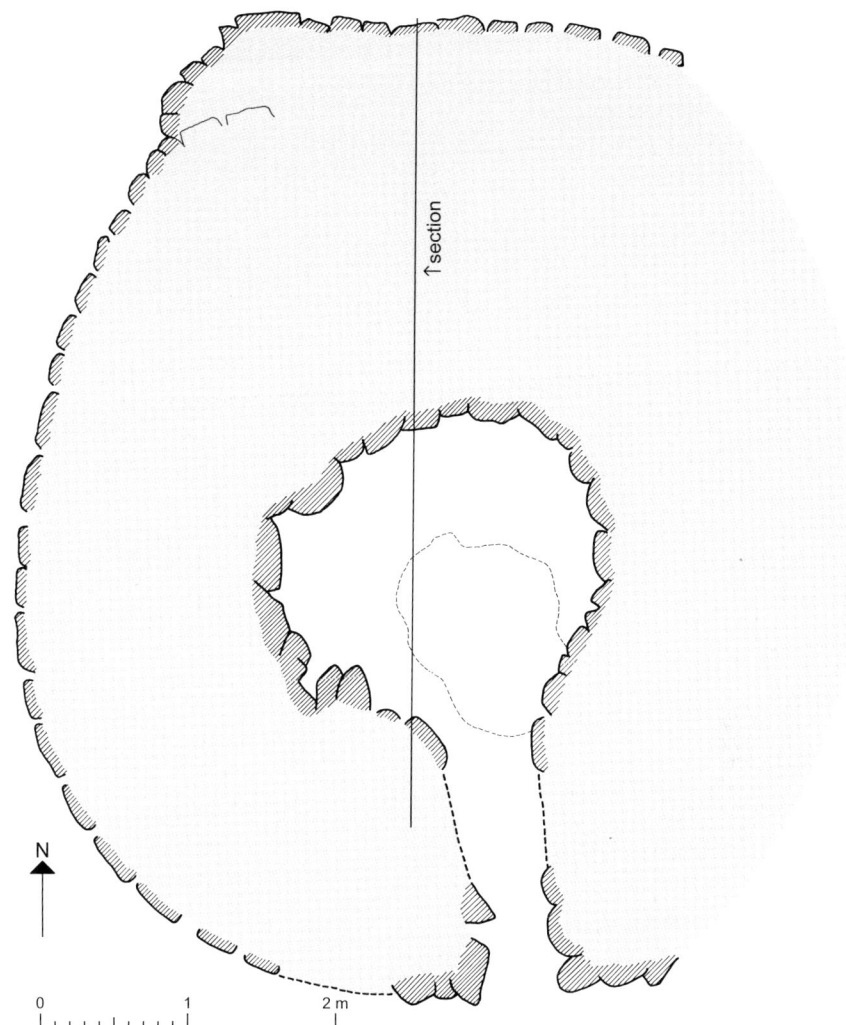

Fig. 339. Plan of Tomb 1318, 1:50. The hatched line in the chamber indicates the robber's hole through the corbelled roof.

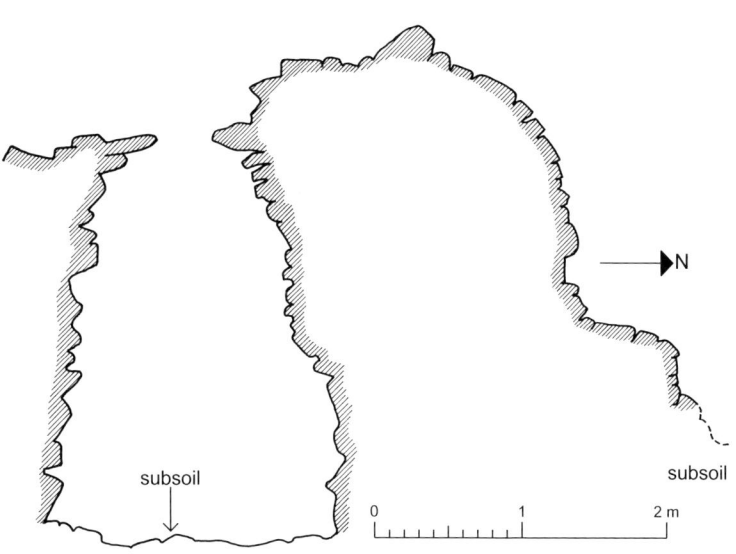

Fig. 341. Elevation of chamber in Tomb 1318, 1:50.

TOMB 1319

Location. The tomb was located 500 m northwest of Tomb 1318 lying in a group of tombs where Tomb 1320 was also situated. It is positioned just above the north side of a steep sloping canyon filled with large boulders and a variety of smaller stone blocks (figs. 342-343). The altitude was c. 368 m above sea level.

The excavation. The tomb was excavated by N.A. Boas and Bo Madsen in 1971. The top of the tomb appeared flattened as if some clearing of stones above the chamber had taken place. The excavation was commenced from a rather small hole in the centre of this level left by grave robbers. The hole, almost 3 m above the chamber floor, was enlarged from 0.6 m to 0.8 m to allow some light and air to enter into the deep chamber. The chamber sediments were excavated in horizontal layers until the subsoil was reached. The entrance was emptied and investigated for secondary finds. Part of the southern and northern exterior ring wall was cleared. Besides the standard mapping procedure the outer tomb structure was mapped at an arbitrary level from 2.2 to 3 m above the base. The plan documents the plundering hole in the flattened top and the position where a secondary wall reaches and partly overlaps the outer ring wall. The cross-section cuts through the ring wall with chamber and the entrance and not least through the secondary wall.

Structural remains. The investigation led to the identification of a rather intact tomb with a central chamber surrounded by a ring wall and an entrance passage facing to the south (fig. 344). Additionally, a secondary wall, circumscribing the primary ring wall and the entrance was documented.

The grave chamber had a pear-shaped plan and measured 2.1 m along the axis of the entrance passage. The width was 2 m. The chamber wall was standing to a height of c. 2.5 m and was built of c. 17 courses of medium sized stone blocks with the largest being used in the lower wall. Above this, more elongated irregular stones were used with one of the narrow ends pointing towards the chamber. Characteristically they were closely stacked in horizontal lines with a tendency to have been placed with the most flat side upwards. The wall inclined only slightly until a height of c. 1.6 m. From here the wall stones became larger and flatter with a gradually increasing central placement. Below the corbelled roof, the chamber is likely to have reached a height of 2.6-2.7 m (figs. 345-346).

A burial level was found at the base of the chamber which consisted of alluvial subsoil composed of small stones and gravel.

The entrance passage was 1.6 m long, funnel shaped, 0.7 m wide at the chamber end tapering to 0.5 m at the outside of the primary ring wall. It was 1.3 m high with an almost triangular cross-section covered by flat cap-stones exposed in the flat ceiling that was 0.1 to 0.2 m wide. The passage was filled with densely stacked stones filling the lower two-thirds (figs. 347-348).

Fig. 342. Tomb 1319 looking S before excavation.

Fig. 343. Tomb 1319 before excavation. Entrance opening with lintel stone can be seen behind the down fallen blocks from the ring wall.

A minor section of the ring wall had collapsed on the northeast side but most of the outline could be traced. It was preserved to a height of about 3.2 m and had been 1.6-1.7 m thick at the base. The diameter of the structure would then have been in the range of 6 m and the original height above the chamber close to 4 m. The upper part of the structure had a slightly asymmetrical square or rhomboid form with one corner extended over the entrance area.

Against the ring wall was a partially preserved secondary wall (fig. 349). It was c. 0.5 to 0.6 m thick, enlarging the diameter of the tomb to c. 7 m and built to a height of about 1.5 m. It was stacked as an outer shell covering the primary wall and followed its shape evenly. It was made from similar sized and shaped stones. This shell wall had also covered the entrance but had been removed in a wedge-shaped cut that revealed the top of the entrance. The secondary wall adds a considerable volume and visibility to the monument and may have been associated with a secondary burial phase.

When excavating outside the ring walls, sand and gravel sediment was encountered still covering the foot of the wall; this was left untouched.

Finds. The sediment inside the chamber consisted of loose sand, apparently alluvial deposits, and some loose blocks fallen from the structure. On and slightly above the base level lay a copper pin and a copper rivet. The chamber was looted in the past. The intruders tried to get through the entrance passage by making a cut through the secondary wall shell, but gave up before removing the interior blocking. Instead, they cleared the top of the mound to reach the top of the vault and entered the chamber from above. The alluvial sand indicates that the chamber was left open for quite some time. This might also explain why there was not even the faintest trace of skeletal material preserved. If skeletal remains were exposed to open air they would disintegrate.

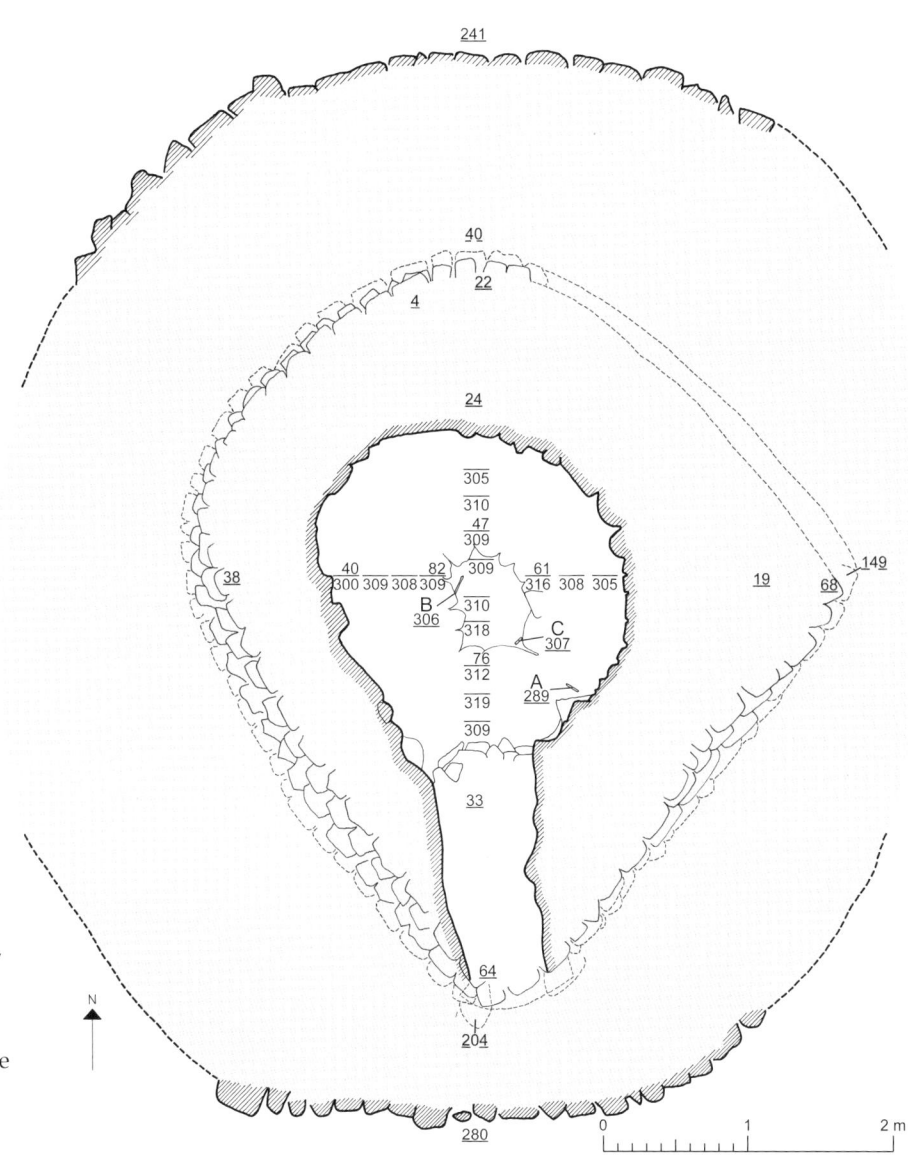

Fig. 344. Plan of Tomb 1319, 1:50. The outline has been drawn in two levels: at the base and just above the top of the secondary wall. In the centre of the chamber the robber's hole through the corbelled roof is indicated.

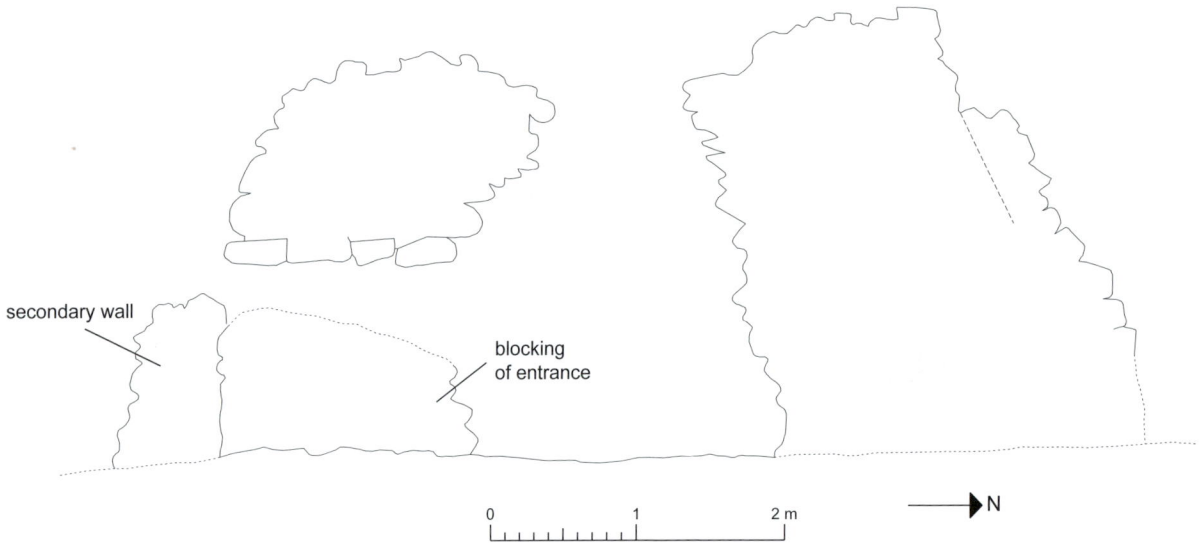

Fig. 345. Cross section of Tomb 1319 in the axis of the entrance passage, 1:50.

1319.A and B: Copper pin in two halves, with round section and partly flat-hammered at one end, c. 12.5 cm long (fig. 350).

1319.C: Copper rivet, c. 4.5 cm long and 0.4 cm thick, flat-hammered in both ends (fig. 351).

Fig. 346. The corbelled construction is made from carefully stacked oblong stone blocks.

Fig. 347. The entrance with blocking viewed from the chamber.

Fig. 348. The cleared entrance with stone pavement viewed from the chamber.

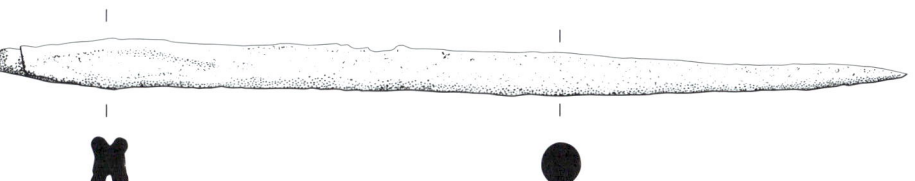

Fig. 349. The secondary ring wall.

Fig. 350. Copper pin 1319.A, 1:1.

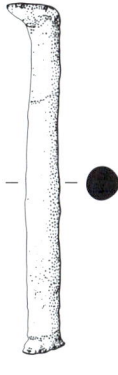

Fig. 351. Large copper rivet 1319.C, 1:1.

TOMB 1320

Location. The tomb was situated c. 40 m southeast of Tomb 1319, in the same wadi but ten metres lower and at the edge of more sand covered slopes (fig. 352). The altitude is estimated to be c. 358 m above sea level.

The excavation. The tomb was excavated in 1971 by Steen Andersen, Michael Beck and Karen Frifelt. It had recently been damaged by stone plundering with many fresh holes from removed stones. The top of the mound was cleaned of secondary material in order to locate the chamber wall and entrance passage (fig. 353), afterwards the chamber was excavated in horizontal layers and the entrance passage emptied from its stone packing. The damaged periphery of the ring wall was cleared towards the south and the west revealing most of the lower course of the ring wall.

Structural remains. The investigation uncovered a tomb with a ring wall, a central chamber and an entrance passage pointed due south (fig. 354). The plan of the chamber was almost round and measured c. 2 m in diameter. The chamber wall was preserved to a height of 1.2-1.4 m and had been built from larger elongated blocks 0.4 to 0.5 m long, stacked in horizontal courses with pointed ends towards the chamber (fig. 355). The uppermost stones were flatter. Some large slabs were placed in the uppermost two surviving courses indicating the upper corbelled construction starting from c. 1.3-1.4 m above the chamber floor.

The chamber floor consisted of level bedrock on which the burial layer rested.

The entrance passage was relatively long, measuring c. 2.5 m. The width varied from 0.4 at the chamber to 0.7 m at the outer periphery. It was constructed from medium blocks up to 0.4 m. Some protruding stones in the lower course narrowed the chamber floor somewhat in the middle. The entrance was covered by a low corbelled construction. The height was not noted in the field notes, nor were any levels taken, but judging from the excavation photos the entrance passage had a height of 0.7 to 0.8 m. At the chamber end, three stone slabs from an entrance floor were uncovered.

The ring wall had a thickness of 2 m, and it was preserved to a height of 1.6 to 1.8 m. It was constructed of stone blocks and a considerable amount of sand and rubble, which could be found in plentiful supply around the tomb. The outer diameter of the monument was c. 6 m.

Finds. In the lowest 0.25 m of the chamber a disturbed burial was found lying in mixed sand in a semi-circular zone around a large empty area in front of the entrance. In the burial sediments two ceramic vessels were recovered, as were the disarticulated skeletal remains of at least three individuals and a spread of beads of faience, carnelian, rock crystal, and other stone (fig. 356). The two ceramic vessels stood in the north-western part of the chamber near crania 1320.J and 1320.K (figs. 357-358). The position of the beads does not reveal any distinct pattern except that a majority lay north of cranium 1320.T and an aggregation of long bone fragments and a piece possibly from the pelvis.

The finds are described in the following:

1320.P: Rounded biconical ceramic vessel of Jemdet Nasr type in red-brown micaceous, sand-tempered ware, with traces of a slip (fig. 359).

1320.S: Rounded biconical ceramic vessel of Jemdet Nasr type in brown micaceous ware (fig. 360).

1320.Z: Sherd in brown micaceous ware, undoubtedly from vessel S.

1320.AC: Sherd in brown micaceous ware, undoubtedly from vessel S.

1320.A: 1 side-sherd of 1320.S.

1320.B: Ring-shaped, milky-surfaced red carnelian bead, irregular polished surface, L 3.4 mm, D 7.8 mm (fig. 361).

1320.F: Biconical ring-shaped milky-surfaced red carnelian bead, irregular polished surface, L 4.2 mm, D 8.7 mm.

1320.O: Biconical ring-shaped, milky-surfaced red carnelian bead, irregular polished surface, L 2.4 mm, D 7 mm (fig. 362), and 7 greenish cylindrical faience beads, L c. 3 mm, D c. 3 mm.

1320.AA: Biconical ring-shaped, milky-surfaced red carnelian bead, irregular polished surface, L 5.2 mm, D 10 mm (fig. 363).

1320.C: Green-glazed cylindrical faience bead, L c. 3 mm, D c. 3 mm.

1320.D: Small green-glazed faience bead, like 1320.C.

1320.L: Green-glazed cylindrical faience bead, c. 0.3 × 0.3 cm.

1320.Q: 36 green-glazed cylindrical faience beads (18 complete), L 2.9-3.5 mm, D 2.8-3.7 mm.

1320.M: Barrel-shaped bead of pinkish, very fine-grained material with a cellular structure, finely polished surface, L 4.6 mm, D 6.1 mm, perforated from two sides (fig. 364).

1320.N: Barrel-shaped bead of pinkish, very fine-grained material with a cellular structure, finely polished, L 4.6 mm, D 5.8 mm, perforated from two sides (fig. 365).

1320.U: Cylindrical ring-shaped pink bead of unidentified silicious material, ring-shaped, irregular polished surface, L 4 mm, 9.2 mm (fig. 366).

1320.V: Cylindrical ring-shaped, pink bead of unidentified silicious material, irregular polished surface, L 3.5 mm, D 7.8 mm (fig. 367).

Fig. 352. Tomb 1320 during excavation looking N. The flag of Abu Dhabi is hoisted on top.

Fig. 353. The top of the intact vault.

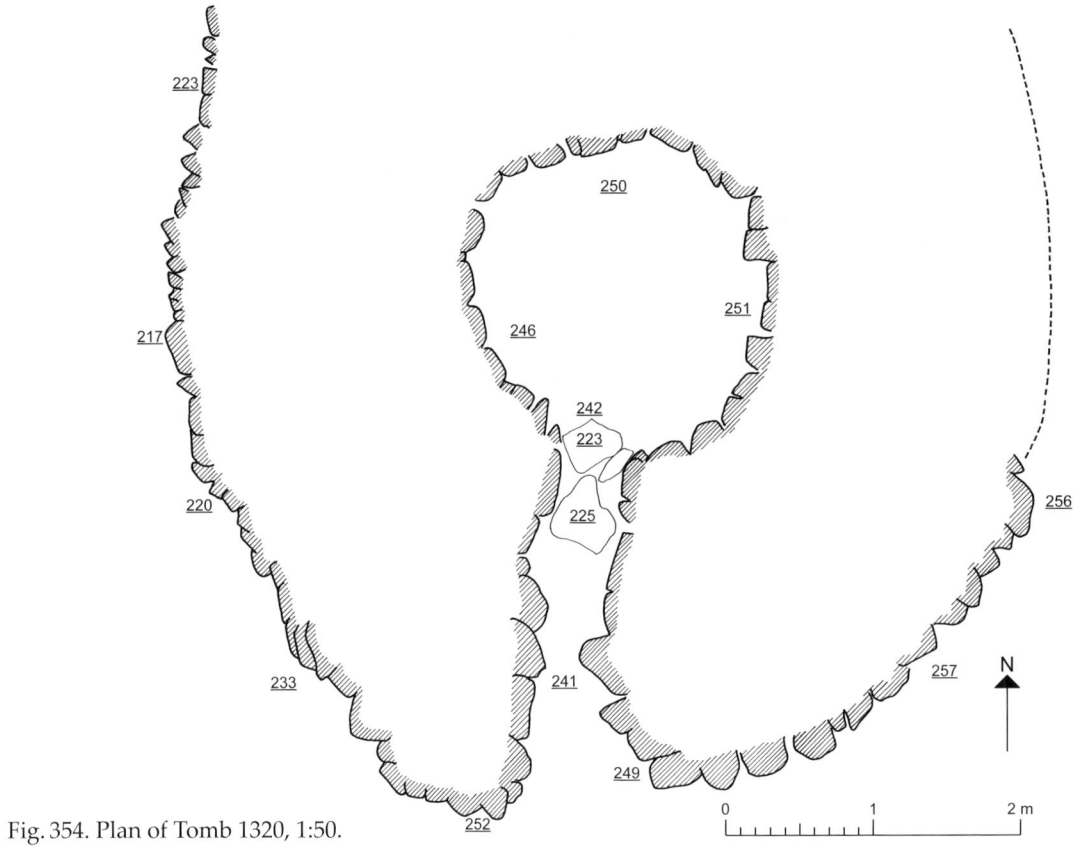

Fig. 354. Plan of Tomb 1320, 1:50.

Fig. 355. The chamber during excavation.

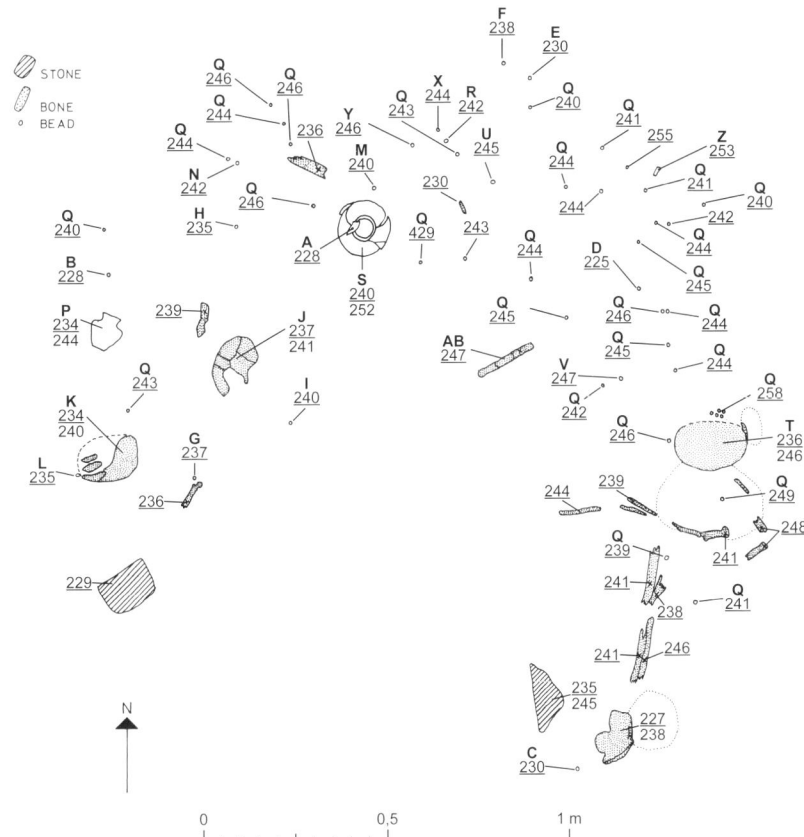

Fig. 356. Plan of the chamber area with finds, amongst two ceramic vessels, beads and remains of three crania, 1:20.

Fig. 357. Ceramic vessel 1320.S during excavation.

Fig. 358. Ceramic vessel 1320.P and skeletal remains in the bottom level of the chamber.

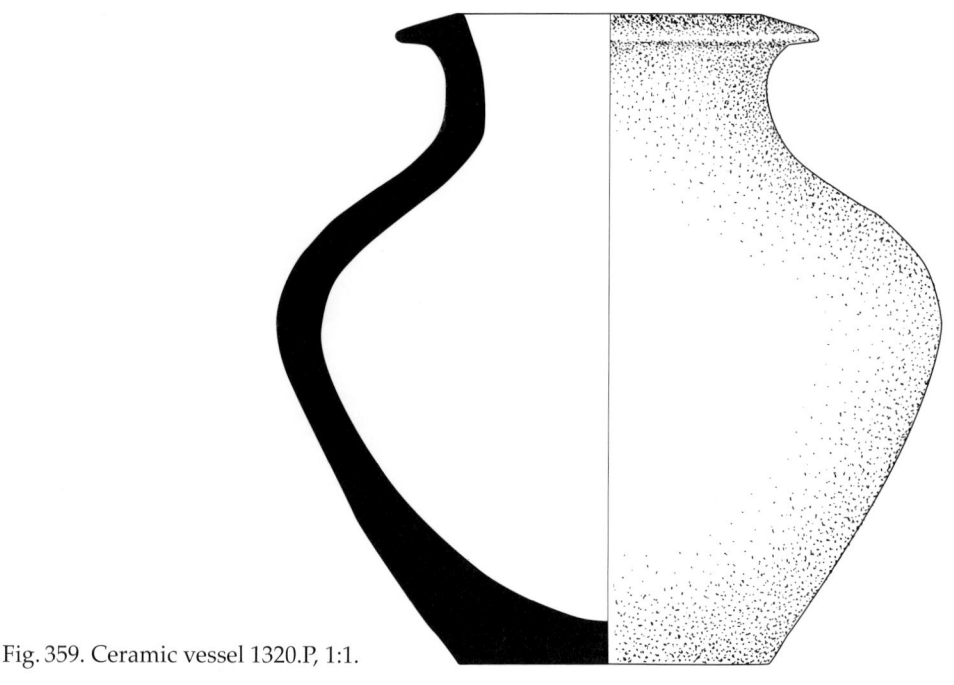

Fig. 359. Ceramic vessel 1320.P, 1:1.

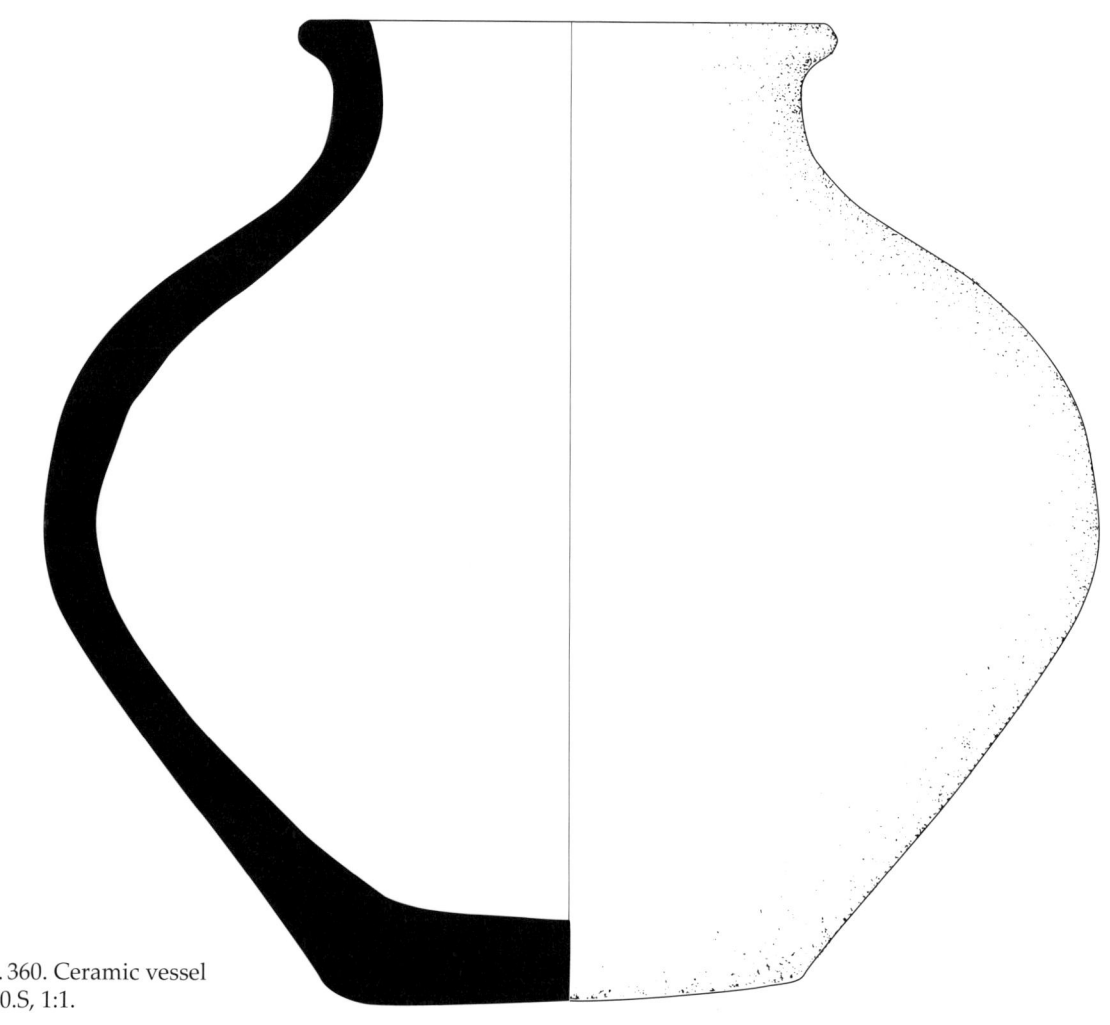

Fig. 360. Ceramic vessel 1320.S, 1:1.

1320.E: Disc-shaped rock crystal bead, irregular polished surface, L 3.1 mm, D 9.8 mm (fig. 368).
1320.H: Disc-shaped rock crystal bead, irregular polished surface, L 3.2 mm, D 8.2 mm (fig. 369).
1320.I: Disc-shaped rock crystal bead, irregular polished surface, L 2.6 mm, D 6.6 mm (fig. 370).
1320.R: Disc-shaped rock crystal bead, irregular polished surface, L 3 mm, D 8.3 mm (fig. 371).
1320.G: Bead from *Engina mendicaria*, perforated laterally (fig. 372).
1320.J: Cranial parts, mainly calotte.
1320.K: Cranial parts.
1320.T: Cranial parts and other skeletal parts in the eastern side of the chamber.

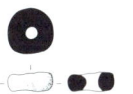

Fig. 361.
Carnelian bead
1320.B. 1:1.

Fig. 362.
Carnelian bead
1320.O, 1:1.

Fig. 363.
Carnelian bead 1320.AA, 1:1.

Fig. 364. ›
Pinkish bead in fine grained material
1320.M, 1:1 and 10:1.

1320.AB: Remains of long bone.
1320.X: Barrel-shaped bead of pinkish, very fine-grained material with a cellular structure, finely polished, L 4.5 mm, D 5.8 mm, perforated from two sides (fig. 373).
1320.Y: Disc-shaped bead of rock crystal, irregular polished surface, L 2.7 mm, D 9.5 mm (fig. 374).

Fig. 365.
Pinkish bead in fine grained material
1320.N, 1:1.

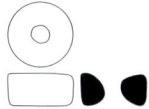

Fig. 366.
Bead of pink silicious material 1320.U, 1:1.

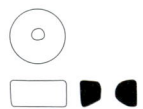

Fig. 367.
Bead of pink silicious material 1320.V, 1:1.

Fig. 368.
Rock crystal bead
1320.E, 1:1.

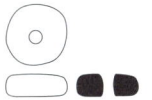

Fig. 369.
Rock crystal bead
1320.H, 1:1.

Fig. 370.
Rock crystal bead
1320.I, 1:1.

Fig. 371.
Rock crystal bead
1320.R, 1:1.

Fig. 372.
Bead of Engina Mendicaria shell,
1320.G, 1:1.

Fig. 373.
Bead in pink, fine grained material
1320.X, 1:1.

Fig. 374.
Rock crystal bead
1320.Y, 1:1.

TOMB 1321

Location. The tomb was located 350 m northeast to north of Tomb 1320 at an altitude of 353-355 m above sea level. It lay at the foot of the rocky escarpments of the mountain overlooking a flat plain, 5-6 m lower (fig. 375).

The excavation. The tomb was excavated in 1971 by N.A. Boas and Bo Madsen. Extensive damage had been the result of recent stone plundering on the exterior (fig. 376). The excavation was started by cleaning the top of the mound and identifying the outline of the chamber and the entrance passage. The chamber sediments were excavated downwards in thin horizontal layers.

Structural remains. The excavation recovered a ring wall with a central chamber and an entrance passage from the southeast (fig. 377). The chamber had a slightly irregular rounded, rhomboid plan. The length along the axis in line with the entrance passage was 2 m and the width was 1.8 m narrowing towards the back of the chamber. The chamber was filled by stone collapse and disturbed by stone quarrying down to the level of the chamber floor. The disturbed sediments were mixed with slabs from the pavement (fig. 378).

The chamber wall was preserved to the level of the top of the entrance passage, barely a meter in height. It was disturbed on the eastern side. The wall was constructed from elongated stone blocks with slab-like blocks mixed in. The character and incline of the wall clearly pointed to a corbelled construction.

Scattered stone slabs indicated that the chamber had a paved floor.

The entrance passage was c. 2.2 m long and 0.5 m wide and c. 0.9 m high. It had been covered with large and thin stone slabs. One had been left by the looters almost in place at the entry to the chamber. Two flat stones at the entry indicated that the passage had at least a partial floor pavement.

The ring wall was too damaged to determine its thickness, but considering the length of the preserved entrance passage it must have been around 2 m and suggests a diameter of the burial monument of at least 6 m.

Fig. 375. Tomb 1321 looking N at the east side of Jebel Hafit.

Fig. 376. The tomb before excavation showing fresh stone robbing.

Fig. 378. The chamber with disturbed pavement.

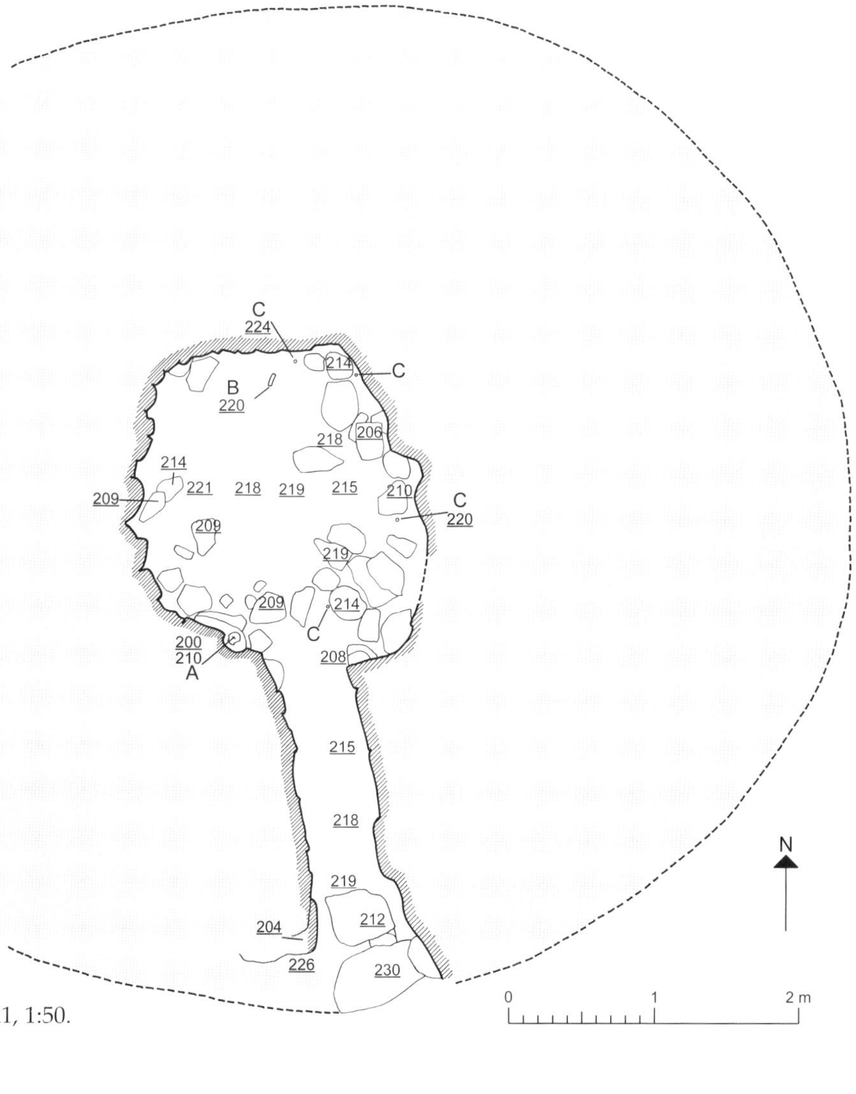

Fig. 377. Plan of Tomb 1321, 1:50.

213

Finds. In the bottom of the chamber, standing in a cavity in the chamber wall very near to the western side of the entrance was a ceramic vessel of Jemdet Nasr type (1321.A) (fig. 379). Sherds from another Jemdet Nasr vessel were found in the debris pushed against the northern chamber wall. Four greenish faience beads lay among the pavement stones in the eastern side of the chamber together with a bone splinter and two small flint flakes.

1321.A: Biconical ceramic vessel with ridged shoulder of Jemdet Nasr type, very thin-walled, fine greenish ware (fig. 380).

1321.B: 3 large ceramic sherds, incl. a rim, similar to that of fig. 359 and other Jemdet Nasr vessels, standard red-buff micaceous ware (fig. 381).

1321.C: 4 green-glazed, cylindrical faience beads, L c. 3 mm, D 3 mm; 1 thin tube from *Dentalium* shell (fig. 382); 2 flakes of a fine grained flint, c. 0.8 × 0.5 and 0.5 × 0.5 cm. The morphology indicates that they are flakes from edge trimming of a larger artefact like a biface preform or a core. The presence of the flakes has no evident explanation as they are too small for use as "strike a light" or cutting tools. Maybe they are by-products secondarily redeposited from a settlement context.

1321.D. Bone fragment, 3.5 cm.

Fig. 379. The ceramic vessel 1321.A as it was uncovered.

Fig. 380. Ceramic vessel 1321.A, 1:1.

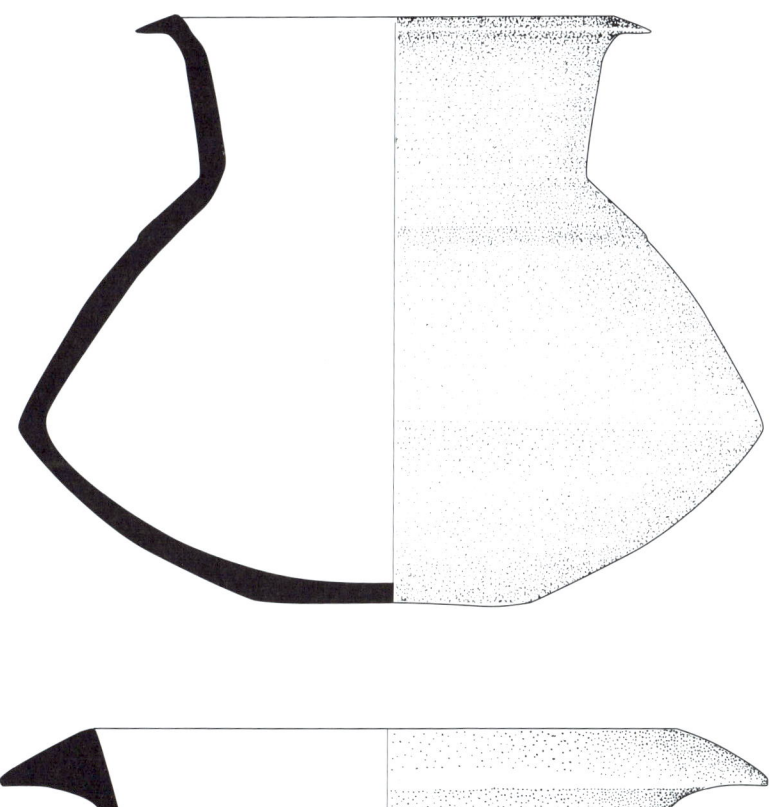

Fig. 381. The rim of 1321.B, 1:1.

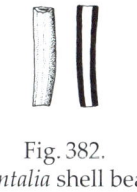

Fig. 382. *Dentalia* shell bead 1321.C, 1:1.

11. The finds and their context

Of the 50 tombs presented here 46 belong to the Hafit type, including one with a rather narrow chamber (Tomb 1050) and the bottoms of three demolished tombs (1055.B, 1055.E and 1055.L). One of these Hafit type tombs had a secondary oval chamber with an uncertain date (Tomb 1053).

Besides, one tomb covered an especially narrow chamber, apparently without a passage (Tomb 1304), and three tombs were of a completely different type constructed up against a vertical rock face (Tombs 1301, 1307 and 1308); these rock shelter tombs all belong to the Iron Age.

Of the 50 tombs 37 contained remains of burial furniture, whereas 8 exclusively had skeletal remains, and 5 tombs were devoid of any finds.

The gravegoods belong to the following periods: The Hafit, the Umm an-Nar, the Wadi Suq periods or the Iron Age. Most finds can be ascribed to the Hafit period, and they have generally been recovered in the lowest levels of the burial chambers. In this level, some finds from the Umm an-Nar period were also retrieved as well as objects which elsewhere occur in both Hafit and Umm an-Nar contexts. There can be no doubt that the Hafit tombs were constructed in the Hafit period and that the post-Hafit period objects belong to secondary burials in original Hafit tombs. The secondary burial features as well as tombs of later type will be described in chapter 14.

In the Hafit type tombs with datable remains from the primary burial phase there was a tendency that major objects like pottery were found along the chamber walls or wedged between protruding stones of the chamber wall. This may either be explained as an expression of burial custom or as a result of repeated burial in the same chamber, where old burials were pushed aside to make room for new ones.

Evidence of secondary burials is primarily documented by either datable artefacts or by relative stratigraphy. Intrusions from prehistoric looting is more difficult to assess. In some instances, the human skeletal material also in the lower burial sediments and floor level indicates considerable disturbances by its fragmented nature and dislocation. This was mainly observed in the centre of the chamber and the area towards the entrance passage, as in the case of Tomb 1320, where the passage also had no blocking; it could have been removed by looters in search for metal. This activity has been practiced on a systematic scale throughout the late Bronze Age and early Iron Age all over the region, exemplified by hoards of metal artefacts, probably looted from prehistoric graves (Yule and Weisgerber 2001 p. 38). This is to say that in even some of the earliest burial levels with few and small copper objects, prehistoric looting may have affected the number and size of metal objects preserved. The largest number of copper artefacts and the most intact skeletal material from the Hafit tombs were found during the 1971 campaign. The Hafit tombs excavated previously were situated closer to the oasis areas and later settlements and they had suffered more from the effects of stone quarrying including being disturbed down to the floor level.

Hafit period finds

The assumed primary burial furniture from the Hafit type tombs counts around 773 objects, comprising 29 ceramic vessels, 23 copper objects, 1 retouched blade of flint and c. 720 beads and pendants which are described in detail below. The objects within these groups are quite homogenous.

To this comes a range of objects which are clearly of later date, belonging to the Umm an-Nar/Wadi Suq/Late Bronze Age periods or the Iron Age. They are described in detail in separate sections at the end of this chapter.

Pottery. 29 ceramic vessels with affinities to Mesopotamian Pottery from the Jemdet Nasr period were found inside 21 different tombs. The main typological form is a rather low and wide vessel, the *vases "larges"* of Méry (2000 p. 169 ff.), with heights around 12 cm and slightly larger widths; one vessel is 22.4 cm high and 25.7 cm wide (fig. 150). The majority of these vessels are biconical with a carinated or marked shoulder (e.g. fig. 36), a few are biconical without any accentuation of the shoulder (e.g. fig. 296) and some are rounded biconical (e.g. fig. 98) or globular (fig. 167). The biconical vessels with a carinated shoulder are almost always decorated in several colours in a broad band between the shoulder carination and the maximum width of the body or covered in plum-red paint, whereas the other shapes are mostly undecorated.

Another form of vessel are small ovoid jars with pointed bases, the *vases "hauts"* of Méry (2000 p. 173). The height of these varies between 13 and 18 cm (figs. 47, 248, 297).

The fabric typically has a high content of sand used as a temper. The colour is light yellow to light brown. In two instances the ware differs: Vessel 1321.A (fig. 380) is small and thin-walled with an almost round base made from a fine grained, pale green ware. A similarly well-thrown thin-walled vessel of fine creamy ware without slip or paint is represented by 1052.B (fig. 168).

Some technical traits suggest that the pottery was wheel thrown, e.g. sections showing wavy profiles from the pulling of the wet clay, carination lines and striae (cf. Méry 2000 p. 179).

Frifelt and During Caspers agreed in dating the pots described above to the Jemdet Nasr period (Frifelt 1971. During Caspers 1971), whereas Potts has argued for a wider dating, pointing to indications for a dating also to the ED I-III periods (Potts 1986).

26 pottery vessels from the Danish excavations at Jebel Hafit have previously been analysed morphologically and petrographicall(y by Méry (2000 p. 169-189) and compared to vessels from Mesopotamia. The conclusions were that the vessels found in Hafit graves represent a small part of the total ceramic corpus of the Jemdet Nasr and ED I-II periods in Mesopotamia, and it is extremely likely that they were imported from Mesopotamia to southeast Arabia.

The polycrome painted biconical vessels with carinated or marked shoulder make out a large proportion of the vessels found in the tombs at Hafit, and they are so strikingly similar to each other with respect to several features of morphology and decoration that they must have been produced over a rather limited period of time. A broad dating of such distinct and uniform vessels extending from the Jemdet Nasr period into the ED I-II or even III period, i.e. several hundred years (c. 3100-2700 BC), does not seem likely and is probably an expression of the lack of precise stratigraphical information from rather old excavations at sites in Mesopotamia. Whether the dating of these pots should cover the whole Jemdet Nasr period, or just the end of the Jemdet Nasr period (as suggested by Frifelt 1971 p. 378), or even extend into the ED periods is impossible to decide with the current level of knowledge. New information from well excavated and well studied Mesopotamian sites is probably needed to clarify the matter. The point accentuated here is that the uniformity of this assemblage suggests that it covers a rather short period of time.

Whether the remaining vessels, the biconical without any accentuation of the shoulder and the rounded biconical or globular, belong to the same or perhaps to a slightly later period is uncertain. Likewise, further investigations are needed in order to decide whether all these pots were imported or whether some of them were produced locally.

The finds from the Eastern Province of Saudi Arabia represent a warning not to extend the dating of the Hafit pots well into the ED I-III periods, as recently pointed out (Laursen & Steinkeller in press). If the pottery found in the Hafit tombs belonged not only to the Jemdet Nasr period but also to the ED I-III periods, it is remarkable that not a single unequivocal example of this type of pottery has been found in the Eastern Province of Saudi Arabia, where such a rich inventory of imported Mesopotamian pottery from the ED I-III periods has been discovered, from both graves and settlements (Piesinger 1983).

Two considerations are worth repeating: Méry notes that most of the Mesopotamian parallels to the Hafit pots comes from the Jemdet Nasr or the ED I period (2000 p. 177), and Wilson notes that most of the polychrome pottery from the Inanna Temple at Nippur comes from the Jemdet Nasr levels and only small amounts from later levels (Méry 2000 p. 177, note 22).

The tentative conclusion drawn from the present study is that the Hafit pots belong to a rather short period that can be centered on the Jemdet Nasr period, and that there is no evidence that this pottery type should be given a very long life time, extending far into the ED periods.

The Jemdet Nasr vases found deposited in the Hafit tombs are quite worn when compared to the later Umm an-Nar burial pots, even if one considers the influence of saline soils, the time difference and its impact on the seemingly less hard fired Hafit pots. In addition, two Hafit vases with broken off necks (figs. 272 and 310) have a series of drilled holes along the break showing that the vessels were carefully mended in Antiquity as pointed out for another similar vase from the Hafit area (During Caspers 1971 p. 28. Mitchell 1972 Pl. LVI:d left). This seems to suggest that these vessels were considered to be valuable in their own right, but perhaps also as containers of some kind of substance essential in burial rituals. One can speculate whether the direct trade relations to Mesopotamia was at some point terminated, cancelling continued import of prestigious pottery.

Copper objects. Pins with round or square sections have been found in nine cases. Three of them have a flattened part near one end (fig. 322)(cf. Vats 1940 pl. CXXV:1. Begemann et al. 2008 pl. 19, Louvre 47-48). A very long specimen (fig. 39), has a fine hole in one end. It could have been applied with a string and used to hold a mantle. Frifelt points to their use as hair-pins or for the application of cosmetics like some Mesopotamian counterparts (Frifelt 1975c).

Common are also rivets (7) and nails (4). The rivets have square or rounded sections and are in some cases quite long, up to 5.5 cm, with traces of heavy hammering at the ends, often obliquely inclined (fig. 217). Their function is un-explained. They seem too long for use in knife or dagger handles, even if these had very thick pommels. A different type is the very short rivet (fig. 337), which resembles the rivets attached to daggers and knives.

Two curved objects made from rather thin copper sheet may belong to the same object, perhaps a bowl or a spout (figs. 82 and 85).

A 21.7 cm long blade has a tongue-shaped outline and a thin and flat section with a fine central midrib (fig. 171). Two rivet holes with rivets *in situ* are placed at the base for a handle. The blade is probably cast. Today the thin-hammered edges expose the most pronounced corrosion. A close parallel has been found in a Hafit/Beehive tomb at Dhank (Williams & Gregoricka 2013 fig. 14a).

Beads. Beads are the most common finds in the Hafit period burial assemblages, and they occur in a number of around 720 in a variety of materials: faience, heated steatite, carnelian, rock crystal, and a few other materials. Two tombs produced by far the largest numbers: Tomb 1051 with 379-394 and Tomb 1313 with 105 beads.

Most beads (492-507) were made of *faience*, a soft material, easily damaged or broken, of white, sintered quartz, usually with a greenish, sometimes white, glazed surface (e.g. figs. 152 and 258). The shapes are rather indistinct, but normally cylindrical, barrel-shaped or more rounded, L 2-6.5 mm, D 2.5-5.1 mm. A few are double or triple segmented (e.g. figs. 335 and 300).

Many beads (178) were made of *heated steatite* (cf. Frifelt 1991 p. 114), a hard, fine-grained, cream-coloured material, which occurs in three shapes; most are cylindrical (136) (figs. 157-158), a few are biconic (7) (figs. 159-160) and some (35) square ("spacers") (figs. 262-264), all well-preserved with sharp, well-defined edges. The size of the cylinders varies, L 2-4.3 mm, D 2.5-3.7 mm; the biconic L 1.5-3 mm, D 2.2-3.8 mm; and the square 5.8-7.5 × 5.8-7.3 × 2.3-3.6 mm.

All surfaces on the square beads, both narrow and broad, show clear sawing marks. The marks on two opposing broad faces are always parallel, i.e. they are sawed from the same direction. The marks on the narrow sides are always transverse to the short side, showing that first a long, square stick was sawn into shape, followed by the sawing of the small square slabs (figs. 262 and 383). The holes through the corners were drilled from two sides (cf. figs. 182, 263-264) meeting at an angle in the interior (rotation marks from the drilling clearly visible under microscope), and not in a straight line as indicated in published drawings (Cleuziou & Tosi 1989 fig. 1).

The sawing marks combined with the remarkably sharp edges make it unlikely that these square beads were fabricated out of a soft paste. They must have been cut out of a hard material, such as steatite, and then achieved an extra hardness and white colour through firing to a high temperature, thus the preferred name *heated steatite* (cf. Panei et al. 2005).

The sawing marks are identical to marks left on unfired steatite debitage found at Qala'at al-Bahrain (Højlund & Andersen 1994 figs. 1981-1984).

The square beads have been found in Tombs 1055 and 1310, in the latter case with Jemdet Nasr type pottery (figs. 182, 262-264). They are known from Mesopotamia (Delougaz and Lloyd 1942 p. 229 and fig. 198) as well as from Iran and Bahrain (Laursen 2013 p. 129, figs. 6-7) and date from Jemdet Nasr to ED II times (Cleuziou and Tosi 1989 fig. 1 p. 30).

The cylindrical beads of heated steatite also show marks from their fabrication, sawing marks on their perforated ends and striations along the length of the bead (from grinding?). The perforation is made from opposing sides, and the rotation marks are clearly visible under magnification. Since the perforation marks has the same white surface as the external side of the bead, the piercing must have taken place before the bead was heated.

Carnelian beads are rather few. They are mostly ring-shaped (fig. 316), sometimes slightly biconical (fig. 363), and rather irregularly knapped and polished, of a pale red hue, often with a milky white surface, possibly an effect of heat-treatment to bring out the red colour. One very small carnelian bead is disc-shaped (fig. 143), similar to the rock crystal beads described below.

Only two spherical carnelian beads were found in Hafit tombs (figs. 126 and 220), but none in good Hafit period contexts. They belong rather to later, secondary burials (see below).

Disc-shaped beads in rock crystal were found in two graves, two light green in Tomb 1300 (fig. 189), and five colourless in Tomb 1320 (figs. 368-371 and 374).

Almost all the beads in hard stone, i.e. carnelian and rock crystal, that can be referred to the Hafit period (fig. 384, above the hatched line), are characterized by having a length less than half of the diameter, thereby reducing the distance that had to be pierced. This is understandable when the simple piercing technique is observed. More studies may decide the exact technique, pecking, flaking and/or rotary drilling (cf. Chevalier et al. 1982 p. 55). The simple piercing technique is matched by the irregular, roughly polished surface.

Only one bead (fig. 53) and one pendant (fig. 81) were made of white shell.

Shell. Apart from the shell bead and pendant just mentioned, a relatively large plaque of mother-of-pearl with two holes were found in Tomb 1310 (fig. 257). Similar plaques are known from Hafit tombs near the southern plateau excavated by the French team (Cleuziou 1977 p. 17, fig. 17:2c, Cleuziou and Tosi 2007 fig. 100:7).

Cowry shells have been found in two tombs (figs. 37 and 317) as well as a bead made from *Dentalia* shells (fig. 382). The remarkable beads of *Engina mendicaria*, which are probably imported from their habitat in the Oman Sea or the Arabian Sea, were found in three tombs (figs. 258 and 372). The Engina mendicaria is known from several Jemdet Nasr and Early Dynastic contexts in Mesopotamia (Gensheimer 1984 p. 67. Cleuziou et al. 2011 p. 36).

Flint. In Tomb 1036 was a large retouched blade of light grey, good quality flint (fig. 74). The blade has been detached from a large regular blade core as part of a series of several blades. The platform remnant is facetted (dihedral) and flat. The bulbar area, which is partly retouched, indicates that the detachment was done by percussion, probably by the punch method. The flint is a local variant of high quality Eocene flint. Both lateral sides of the blade are fully retouched; one side has a curving back and the other, with a finer flat retouch, probably a resharpening of the edge. The artefact has most probably served as a knife.

Umm an-Nar, Wadi Suq and Late Bronze Age finds

Scattered remains of one or several Umm an-Nar burials were found in Tomb 1312. A beehive-shaped soft stone vessel of late Umm an-Nar date lay on the chamber floor (fig. 277) (cf. from the Hili Grand Tomb, Frifelt 1975a, fig. 17e and from Tomb A, Hili North, Cleuziou et al. 2011 fig. 227). Further fragments of soft stone vessels, as well as sherds of red-buff ceramic ware with horizontal black-brown wavy lines were found scattered outside the tomb. They probably represent Umm an-Nar type bowls or jars in the local sandy ware. From the disturbed sediments above and outside of the tomb come two unworked shells, as well as a large slender biconical bead (cf. Cleuziou et al. 2011 fig. 252: DLA/m96, from Hili North Tomb A; Benton 1996 fig. 144.1 from Al Sufouh) from intense red carnelian, three biconical carnelian beads of similar colour, an agate bead and some finger rings, all probably dating to the Umm an-Nar period or later.

In Tomb 1034 the only find was a large fragment of an Umm an-Nar period vessel of red-brown sandy ware with a now faint, wavy band painted on the shoulder (fig. 66). This decorative band might have been infilled as on a necked jar from the large Tomb A at Hili North possibly representing a local imitation of either Dasht or Indus ware (Cleuziou et al. 2011 fig. 156: DLA/v353). In Tomb 1033 a Wadi Suq type soft stone bowl was the only find in the chamber (fig. 60) (cf. Velde 2003 fig. 5:11 and 13 p. 108).

The copper arrowhead in Tomb 1051 (fig. 151) is probably not earlier than the Late Bronze Age, but may belong in the Iron Age (Velde 2003 fig. 8, p. 112. Jasim 2012 p. 295).

The two spherical carnelian beads mentioned above probably post-dates the Hafit period.

The finely polished biconical carnelian bead 1310.C (fig. 261) resembles in surface treatment and colour the three biconical beads from Tomb 1312 (fig. 279) that are thought to post-date the Hafit period.

Iron Age finds

The secondary burial in Tomb 1049 probably dates to the Iron Age. The short-sword of copper-bronze (fig. 136) was compared by Bibby to similar weapons from Talish in the Caspian area and from Luristan, suggesting a date to the 14th-13th centuries BC. Related rim-flanged daggers (and the Talish weapons) have since then been given a late second millennium date by Dyson, compatible with Potts' date to between the thirteenth and eleventh centuries (Frifelt 1971 p. 377. Bibby 1965 p. 109. Dyson 1964 p. 32-45, figs. 1-2. Potts 1990 I p. 386-387. Cf. also Yule and Weisgerber 2001 p. 21). The type, however, continues into the Iron Age (Velde 2003 p. 111-112. Jasim 2012 figs. 350, p. 294).

The scabbard was not preserved, but a belt is indicated by a possible belt-hook. The sword hilt or the belt was equipped with a large polished shell button with three V-shaped holes on the interior, concave side (figs. 137-138), made from the *Xanxus gravis dillwyn* imported from the Indian Ocean (Frifelt 1971 p. 364). As Frifelt points out, this large button has exact parallels from Nimrud dating to the ninth-eighth centuries BC (Mallowan 1966 p. 125 and fig. 66).

A similar, though smaller, shell button, also with three V-shaped drilled holes on the interior side (fig. 193) was found in rock shelter tomb 1301.

Tomb 1307, another rock shelter tomb, contained a double-edged long sword of iron with a bronze chape, along with a bundle of iron objects, possibly arrows. Parallels to the sword and arrows are known e.g. from Ed-Dur (Mouton 1992 figs. 23, 42, 115-116) and indicate a dating from the 3rd century BC and onwards. A similar square chape is apparently found with a double-edged long sword of iron in Tomb 88 at Jebel Buheis (Jasim 2012 figs. 317-319).

An intrusive burial in Tomb 1303 contained an iron cylinder, possibly a spear socket. The burial resembles a late pre-Islamic interment found at Jebel al-Emalah in Sharjah, where a male skeleton was found in the same flexed posture "holding a spear" in front (Benton and Potts 1994 figs. 32-33. Potts 1998 p. 189, fig. 4).

A few bronze finger rings (cf. Jasim 2003 fig. 3:13-14), a copper rivet and some copper or bronze fragments found scattered in the disturbed sediments of Tomb 1312 may belong in the Iron Age, as may also a large slender bead of intense red carnelian (fig. 280).

The glass beads found in Tombs 1037 and 1311 should probably be dated to the Iron Age.

Fig. 383. Square bead of heated steatite with sawing marks 1310.C, 4:1.

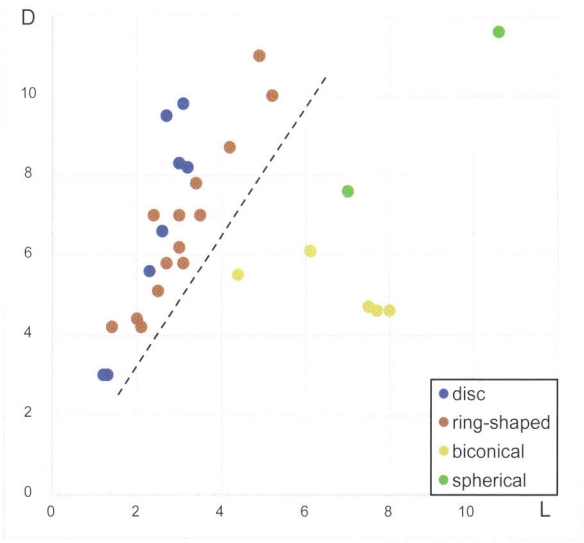

Fig. 384. Length and diameter in mm of hard stone beads from Hafit tombs.

12. Human skeletal remains

The excavated tombs showed several kinds of disturbances from reuse of the burial chamber to grave plundering and stone robbing. Only in some cases have major parts of the primary burial strata survived these activities.

Most skeletal material came from the tombs excavated in the 1971 campaign, i.e. from tombs on the western ridge, from the southern plateau and from the eastern side of Jebel Hafit. As mentioned previously, the first campaigns concentrated on the more damaged tombs with recent stone plundering, which were situated closer to the town of Al-Ain. Human skeletal material would not have been preserved unless covered by sediments. The reopening of the chambers in connection with both ancient looting and more recent stone robbing with exposure of the burial sediments no doubt speeded up the decay of the skeletal remains besides crushing them. In addition, the procedures of a fast salvage excavation may have played a role in the identification and the documentation of badly preserved bone parts. The skeletal material was always very brittle when encountered and in most cases fell apart when taken out of the sediments.

Of the 46 Hafit type tombs that were identified, 29 contained some, generally scarce, remains of identifiable human skeletal material. With respect to stratigraphic position the skeletal finds were located either in an upper secondary level as intrusive burials or were found at the floor level.

The best preserved skeletons, belonging to the Hafit period, came from Tomb 1309 (figs. 247, 250-252), Tomb 1311 (fig. 268), Tomb 1314 (figs. 307-308), Tomb 1315 (figs. 314-315) and Tomb 1317 (figs. 329-331), that all contained at least three skeletons, apart from Tomb 1309 which contained five or six. The evidence indicates that the burials have been successive, as there are no sign of paired or contemporary interments.

The dead were placed in a crouched or contracted position, on the left or right side. The arms of the dead were placed in a lifted position but there was no preferred orientation with respect to the cardinal points. The individual 1315.A may have been tightly wrapped up (fig. 315). To judge from the preserved material, all individuals seem to be adult or young adult.

A relocated burial was found in the outer, upper part of the entrance passage of Tomb 1031, above the blocking, with no indication of date (fig. 42).

The discovery of trepanned crania in two tombs in rather close vicinity (Tombs 1309 and 1315) is remarkable. On both crania the traces of the trepanations are placed on the top and in the back of the head and mainly on the left side of the skull (figs. 385-386). Two of the trepanations on the left side are actually mirrored between the two crania (Littleton and Frifelt 2006 p. 146) (fig. 387). The cranial operations on the two individuals from Hafit have been done by scraping the bone over in a limited area of c. 2 × 2 cm. In the case of Hafit Tomb 1309, a young adult, the patient had surgery in no less than nine places during at least two isolated episodes, as some of the lesions show signs of healing and others do not. One of the last incisions was left unfinished "either because the operation was aborted or because the patient died during the process" (Littleton and Frifelt 2006 p. 143).

Trepanation has more recently been identified in the skeletal material from the Jebel al-Buhais Neolithic cemetery, more than a millennium older than the Hafit tombs (Kiesewetter 2006 p. 197-198). As in the two calottes from Jebel Hafit a careful scraping technique has been applied to open a small hole through the cranial wall and reach the *dura mater*. Locally, trepanation thus seems to be an old practice and it was widespread during the Bronze Age in the Middle East, perhaps as a magical cure or therapeutically, to release pressure from the brain (Mogliazza 2009).

The Iron Age burials in four cases contained articulated to semi articulated skeletons in contracted position as seen in Tombs 1049, 1303 and 1307. The orientation of the head was in one case towards the north, one case towards the west and in two cases towards the east. The state of preservation of the bone material in the Iron Age burials was no better than in the Bronze Age burials, though the Iron Age burials were less disturbed.

Fig. 385. Fragment from the cranial roof with incisions from trepanation, from Tomb 1309, 1:1.

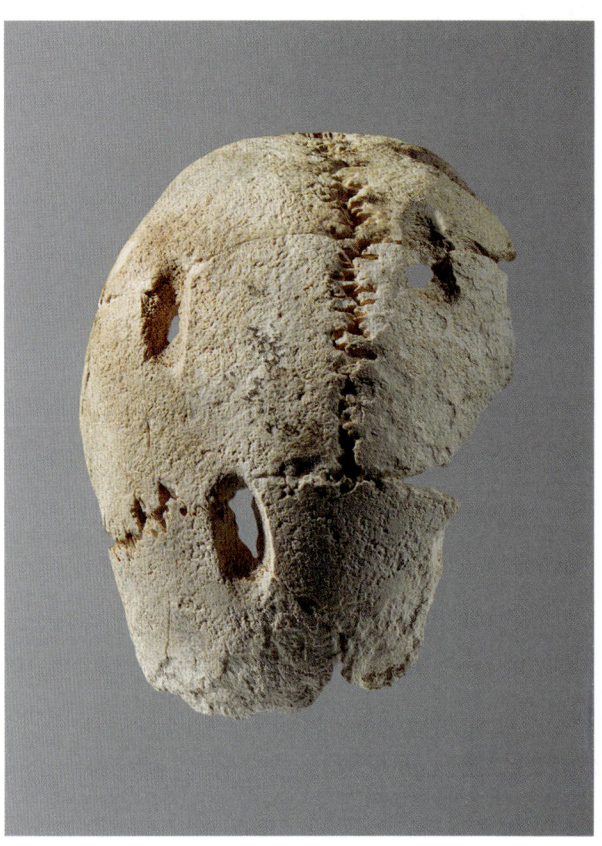

Fig. 386. The trepanned human calotte from Tomb 1315, 1:2.

Fig. 387. Comparison of the loci of trepanation on the two Hafit calottes (after Littleton and Frifelt 2006).

224

13. Funerary architecture

Of the 50 tombs that were investigated during the Danish campaigns 1961-1971 at Jebel Hafit, 46 shared a number of architectural and constructional elements that allow them to be grouped as Hafit type tombs. i.e. they are round tower-like structures built of rough stone covering a round, corbelled chamber with a narrow entrance passage. The rest were of different form, either elongated cists (Tombs 1053 and 1304) or small, rock shelter tombs of later date (Tombs 1301, 1307 and 1308), described in the next chapter.

During the early campaigns the excavated cairn burials were compared to hundreds of similar ruins of circular chambered tombs in the area, many of which had been opened by grave robbers or by recent stone removal exposing their inner corbelled construction. During surveys to the north and east of Al-Ain and Buraimi, while excavating the Hili Grand Tomb and the nearby mudbrick tower, large alignments of such cairns were also noted at Jebel Aghlah and further to the northeast. From their general appearance many were similar in size and construction method to the tombs of Jebel Hafit, although built from different raw materials.

In 1970-1972 a small group of similar tombs were identified at Qarn Bint Saud, an isolated rock outcrop in the desert 12 km north of Al-Ain. Some were investigated by excavators from Moesgaard Museum (Madsen forthcoming b) and subsequently by archaeologists from the Al-Ain Museum (Al Tikriti 1981).

After the preliminary presentation of the eponymous tombs from the foothills of Jebel Hafit, similar burial monuments were discovered in neighbouring Oman, not least in the important mound field at Bat a few years later (Frifelt 1975a, 1975b, 1975c, 1980 and 2002. De Cardi et al. 1982).

The diversity in this large group of burials, primarily caused by the availability of different kinds of building materials, has led to a division into a number of sub-types of questionable validity: pill boxes, tower tombs, beehive tombs etc. (Frifelt 1975a-b. Vogt 1985. Yule and Weisgerber 1998. Bortolini 2012).

Attempts have also been made to trace a typological development from tombs of Hafit type to the later tombs of Umm an-Nar type, and in this connection the cemetery of Bat has played a certain role (Frifelt 1975b, Al Tikriti 1981 and 2011a, Vogt 1985).

The group of tombs presented in this publication cannot, however, substantiate an idea of a gradual development from the Hafit type to the Umm an-Nar type. On the contrary, the tombs presented here are in every way a tight knit group, and the metric dimensions and proportions in the 43 measurable tombs constitute a continuum of sizes and shapes. Despite differences in their state of preservation and in the quality of the local limestone, the tombs at Jebel Hafit appear very uniform, and any distinction into sub-types would be difficult. The architectural homogeneity of this group of tombs is paralleled in the homogeneity of the funeral objects found in the tombs and supports the impression that these tombs were erected during a relatively short period.

State of preservation

Most of the early investigated tombs at Jebel Hafit had, to varying degrees, been altered by secondary activities, such as reuse with later interments, grave robbing and recent quarrying of stone from the outer construction. During these successive activities the original appearance of the monuments was gradually obscured. The remaining height gives a certain measure of their state of preservation. The best preserved structures were excavated in 1971. The average height of the tombs investigated in 1961 to 1963 was, across 21 tombs, 1.14 m, whereas in 1971 the average of 15 tombs was 1.6 m. Only seven tombs exceeded a height of 1.7 m. The best preserved tombs, Tombs 1317, 1318 and 1319, measured respectively: 2.1, 2.7 and 2.5 m.

Materials

Most of the rock in the foothills around Jebel Hafit comes from a relatively hard, occasionally silicified limestone which on some exposed surfaces has grey-brown crusts. Beneath the weathered surfaces lighter-coloured limestone and chalk are visible. The suitability of stones for building tombs varies very much with the degree of erosion and undercutting of the local outcrop, especially in high energy environments like the canyons leading down from the steeper mountain sides. Lower down in the relief the eroded material is composed of boulders and blocks intermingled with rubble, smaller debris and some waterborne sediments, often densely cemented, making the material difficult to quarry. Beyond the foothills and the plateaus, the terrain is generally plain and covered with finer sediments. Only occasional smaller stone blocks and pebbles are exposed in the washes a few hundred meters from the foothills.

In some locations, both on the eastern side of Jebel Hafit and at the northern ridges towards Al-Ain, local occurrences of more stratified limestone have been observed, which gradually exfoliates as regular stone slabs. As one moves further east and north of Jebel Hafit towards the Oman Mountains, the raised limestone gradually exposes more outcrops of stratified material, occasionally with horizons of nodular flint concretions which are characteristic of some of the Eocene beds. At Jebel Aghlah, north of Al-Buraimi, very regular beds of hard dune limestone (calcarenite) from the late Eocene are exposed for several km (Gagnaison et al. 2004). The many tombs in this area which were noted during the early Danish surveys were predominantly in the same family as the tombs of the Hafit area, but with more well defined wall faces. The finish of the construction evidently had benefitted from the favourable local outcrop.

All the tombs in the Hafit area have been constructed from unworked, but selected limestone blocks, in various sizes and shapes. There is a considerable variation to the degree that tombs were built of large, flat blocks, elongated narrow nodules or smaller slabs. The dominant building material was the local assortment, most often oblong sometimes relatively wide stone blocks with irregular surfaces. The local environment evidently influenced some of the features of the tombs. Near Tomb 1300 a source of fine-layered sandy limestone provided the slabs for the floor pavement of the chamber. In the same neighbourhood, a very large thin slab of this material was used as a lintel stone in Tomb 1052. The large Tomb 1317, which contained big flat stone blocks in its construction, was located near a distinct outcrop of hard layered limestone, exposed in the rock and eroded into a high-energy canyon or wadi as very large slab-like blocks.

There seems to be a tendency, to judge from the photos, that more gravel fill was used in the ring walls of tombs on low lying and more gravelly areas, e.g. the ring wall of Tomb 1316 contained much more soil than seen in the higher tombs in the western mountain ridge.

Dimensions in plan

The diameters of the ring walls were exaggerated in the early references to Hafit tombs mentioning diameters up to 11 m (Bibby 1965 p. 109). In the 1971 campaign the excavators deliberately chose to excavate a few of the largest cairns and found the true dimensions to be less, but with large volumes of stone lying in secondary position around the ring wall. 40 tombs were well enough preserved to measure or interpolate the outer diameter of the ring wall (fig. 388). As quite a number of tombs on uneven ground had a slightly ovate outline, they were measured at base level on the field plans and an average of two possible measures calculated. In some cases a major part of the ring wall periphery was preserved, and in many cases the ring wall thickness could be interpolated from the length of an intact entrance passage and/or remaining wall parts.

Most of the monuments measured were around 5 or 6 m in diameter (figs. 389); 7 tombs were around 7 or 8 m, and the smallest tombs encounted were around 4 m.

The diameter of the tombs from the Hafit area corresponds well to a similar sample of Hafit/Beehive/Tower tombs from Shir in Oman which range from 3.5 to 7.5 m, with most between 4 and 6 m (Yule and Weisgerber 1998 fig. 12).

In 43 cases the burial chambers were preserved to an extent which made it possible to measure their dimensions at the floor level. Only a few chambers approached a symmetrical outline. Some also had an inclined chamber floor, in which case the measurements were projected to the horizontal plane. The length (or depth) of the chamber was measured in line with the axis of the entrance passage and perpendicular to this, the width. Some of the chamber walls had a rather jagged outline at the floor level due to pointed stone blocks jutting out. In these cases, measurements have been taken to the average line of the wall face.

The length of the chambers ranges from 1.2 to 2.8 m with a median value of 2.0 m; their width ranges between 1.0 and 2.8 m with a median value of 1.9 m (fig. 390). Most of the chambers were slightly longer than wide.

The proportion between chamber size (length) and the diameter of the ring wall seems rather constant (fig. 391); the largest chambers are surrounded by thicker ring walls, which probably relates to the height-width dimensions of the corbelled vault.

Constructional elements

The chambered tombs at Jebel Hafit are defined by their ring wall surrounding the chamber. This rises into a corbelled construction like a thick shell of stacked stone arches over the deceased. The ring walls are mostly circular to slightly oval in plan. The lower part of the exterior profile rises almost vertically, but the continuation upward is not preserved. The outline plan seems, in some instances to be dependent on the terrain on which the tomb was constructed. As has been described, tombs have in some cases been constructed on the visually most prominent locations such as rocky peaks and crests. In several cases, the ring wall seems to have been made thicker or more inclined in order to distribute the weight of the stone. In the case of Tomb 1306, placed almost like a bird's nest at the end of a sharp crest, part of the ring wall was raised on a foundation built from large stone blocks. The lower stone courses were stabilized by an infill or shims of gravel and rubble.

The ring walls were generally around two meters thick and built from carefully arranged stones. There was a tendency that the largest or longest stones to be placed in the chamber wall face and in the exterior wall face, especially in the basal and the lower courses.

In several tombs it was noted, as in Tomb 1031, that the wall was made from predominantly elongated stones which were placed in concentric lines in each individual course, but with the stones interlocking and overlapping in between the lines. In no cases were any coffer work observed. In the chamber walls these courses were marked by the wedging corbel stones jutting out in horizontal lines. A similar ring pattern, superficially looking like stepped walls within the main ring wall, are seen in some of the five tombs excavated by the French team on the southern plateau in close proximity to the previous Danish excavations (Cleuziou 1977, 1978). Maybe these observations gave birth to the idea that all the Hafit graves are "made of two concentric ring walls of unshaped stones" (Cleuziou 1984, Vogt 1985, Cleuziou and Tosi 2007).

In only a few of the tombs presented here did a second wall circumscribe the ring wall. At Tomb 1319, a clear secondary wall was encountered as an independent shell around the primary ring wall covering and hiding the already blocked entrance to a level of 1 m above the base of the ring wall. In the case of Tomb 1318 there seemed to be a secondary shell stacked from the north-western side round to the eastern side where it integrated with the rest of the ring wall. In the quite ruined Tomb 1034 a secondary wall also surrounded the ring wall and seems similarly to have covered the entrance. The only grave furniture that survived here was a large sherd of an Umm an-Nar vessel indicating secondary burial activity and a possible dating of the secondary wall.

The interior chamber walls in most cases stood almost vertical to a level above the entrance passage, approximately 0.5-1 m above the floor, depending on the size of the chamber, from where the walls gradually curved inwards as a false dome. In a few cases, the chamber roofs were found almost intact.

The best preserved tombs were located on the eastern side of Jebel Hafit, especially Tombs 1317, 1318 and 1319 (fig. 391). The vaults in these three tombs reached heights of 2.1, 2.7 and 2.5 m above the chamber floor and illustrated the upper end of the Hafit tomb spectrum by the use of relatively tall ogival vaults. In the case of Tomb 1319 the vault probably reached almost 3 m in its centre. The original appearance of the upper exterior of the monuments was in no case preserved.

In all cases the chambers had levelled floors consisting either of a layer of gravel or rubble or of a pavement of stones. Sometimes several pavements were observed, often made from selected stone blocks with a flat side or from regular slabs.

The entrance passages were the same level as the chamber floor with the exception of Tomb 1305, erected on an uneven mountain crest, which had a step hewn into the bedrock, between the entrance passage and the chamber.

The dimensions of the passage were mostly uniform, from 0.5 to 0.6 m wide and from 0.7 m to 1.1 m high with either an A-shaped or angular/trapezoidal cross section. The average entrance had a width-height of approximately 1:2. The A-shape construction consists simply of the two flanking walls meeting in the top, possibly closed with a row of flatter stones. The angular version sometimes had very large cap stones or lintels that rested on the flanking walls and were carefully built into the chamber wall.

The flanking walls of the passage are in most instances made from stone blocks aligned with a flat, smooth facade to facilitate an unhindered passage. Normally, the entrance left just enough space for a person to climb in and allow the transport of the deceased into their resting place.

In most cases the tombs were sealed with a blocking of stones filling the entrance passage and normally great care was used to make the blocking of the entrance passage flush with both the inner side of the chamber (*sic!*) as well as the external face of the monument, so much that it often proved difficult to locate the entrance.

The orientation of the entrance passages could be determined in 34 tombs, and it varies from west-southwest to southsoutheast, with by far most entrances pointing south or southsoutheast (fig. 393). The orientation seems to be completely independent of the local topographical circumstances. In the case of Tomb 1315 situated on a narrow east-west orirented rocky crest, the entrance points due south into the empty space above the slope though it would have been more practical to enter the tomb from the east.

A small variant of the Hafit type tomb was encountered in the case of Tomb 1050, with the entrance continuing into a narrow elongated chamber which also had a rather low corbelled construction. A close parallel, which contained Jemdet Nasr type pottery, was excavated at Tawi Silaim (Cairn 4), north of the Wahiba Sands in Oman, 370 km from Jebel Hafit (de Cardi et al. 1977). Another narrow version of the Hafit-type chamber was observed at An Niba in Oman (Doe 1977 fig. 13).

At Tomb 1317 a meter-size stone block had been put in front of the entrance. This tomb was also remarkable because of its size and the very large and regular stone blocks used in the walls on both sides of the entrance. Outside this facade, a 0.7 m wide pavement of smaller stones was observed. The surrounding pavement and the more regular facade are paralleled in the Bat necropolis (Tombs 1137 and 1138) (Frifelt 1975a, 1975b).

The building technology

From a techno-economic view the burial monuments represent constructional knowledge, practical skills and, not least, a considerable investment of manpower. The idea of chambered tombs made as dry walling of unworked stones covered by capstones or corbelled is known in many versions and from several parts of the Arabian Peninsula and beyond (Yule and Weisgerber 1998). The single chambered round tombs with high corbelled construction have their centre in southeast Arabia. From an architectural viewpoint the Hafit tombs represent a uniform construction concept with no closely related predecessors yet known. They seem to be a prototype which marks the beginning of a long tradition of stone-built chambered tombs in the region.

The area of most chambers ranges from around 3.5 to 6 square meters. These dimensions were the basic parameters which influenced the dimensions of the whole construction. The length and regularity of the accessible stone blocks influenced the possible overlap of stones in the corbelled construction. This again influenced the curve of the false vault and together with the width of the chamber dictated the minimum height that the corbelling would reach.

There is a tendency amongst the excavated sample, for the chamber to be elongated along the same axis as the entrance passage. An explanation is probably constructional and may be an attempt to avoid too much outward loading or diagonal pressure on the area above the entrance, which is the weakest point in the lower ring wall. In relation to light entry, an elongated chamber also provides the best conditions.

From the ring walls and chambers sectioned during excavation or exposed by stone robbing it was possible to get an impression of the principles of construction. The chamber wall consisted of horizontal layers of selected elongated stones placed in a centripetal position, all more or less pointing towards the centre of the chamber; the successive courses constituted series of horizontal discs of stacked stone blocks. The weight from above provides a lateral thrust and strong friction in the contacting surfaces of the dry walling.

The exterior ring wall must have been the most sensitive part of the construction, especially in the lower part of tombs constructed on uneven ground. If just a few stone blocks were pushed or intentionally removed, part of the ring wall could easily destabilize. In several ring walls examples of what looked like ancient collapse were observed.

An assessment of the construction and its organization

To understand the complexity of a Hafit type tomb and the capacities lying behind the monument, it is useful to consider the construction process itself in order to reflect on the possible organizational parameters. These reflections are a hypothetical proxy and cannot substitute a real reconstruction made as a practical controlled experiment. The assessment may indicate the order of magnitude of the work invested. Some of the successive tasks to be encountered would be: collecting stone blocks, clearing and levelling the building ground, lay out, and stacking the ring wall.

After determining a suitable place and the orientation of the tomb, the outline of the chamber, the entrance passage and the ring wall would be indicated by placing stones of the first course as a base and template (fig. 394 upper).

The stacking of the ring wall up to the level of the top of the entrance passage would be a first major building phase, including the placing of eventual lintel blocks and merging the cover of the passage securely with the ring wall itself (fig. 394 middle).

The entrance proportions of the Hafit tombs are quite uniform. The dimensions very much resemble the dimensions of the tunnels in the traditional subterranean water channel-system, the *aflaj*. Traditionally, a *falaj* is around one *dhra'r* wide, the length of the forearm with stretched hand, c. 43-45 cm and approximately double this in height (Birks and Letts 1976). The determining factor in dimensioning the entrance passage of the Hafit tombs no doubt was similarly practical. The entrance passage had to allow the transport of a deceased into the burial chamber.

Stacking the upper ring wall and vault could have been carried out in a step-wise fashion to facilitate the movement of stone blocks by lifting, rolling and rocking the heavier blocks into their correct position (fig. 394 lower). The placing of the stones had to be done with care to ensure the optimal "setting" of the blocks. This is crucial when building by dry walling to ensure a maximum degree of friction between stones.

The corbel vault was closed with larger slabs or elongated blocks in order to bridge and anchor the apex of the chamber with the ring wall. During the final phase, an oblique ladder could have been made by wedging timber sticks in between the stone courses of the outer ring wall and use them as steps to walk up with the last stone blocks.

An estimate of the volume of a small tomb, 6 m wide and with a modest height of 3 m would reach around 12-14 cubic meters of stone when all hollows, including the volume of the chamber and entrance passage are subtracted. The rather dense limestone of Jebel Hafit is estimated to weigh nearly 2.5 tons per cubic meter, giving in the range of 30 ton or more for a small Hafit tomb. This volume had to be collected and stone blocks of a preferred form and dimension needed to be sought out. Many stone blocks would have been found on the surface, perhaps in a nearby wadi or taken from the scree of a nearby rock face. All stones had to be carried to the building site.

If one man each day succeeded in finding 30 loads of suitable stone weighing 15 kg in average and carried them cross-country to the site (450 kg per work day), the stones for the ring wall could be collected in 60-70 days or 2-2.5 months. We cannot calculate the distance to suitable stone nor the time of transport with any certainty, but distance and terrain in the uneven Jebel Hafit surroundings would have been time-consuming factors even for experienced workers.

A more likely possibility is that the transport of stone was organized on a collective basis where members of a local community, a tribal section or another corporate group joined. This type of organization is known from several ethnographic cases, where large groups move sometimes very large amounts of stone during prestigious festivals (Cotterell and Kamminga 1990 p. 216).

Added to the effort of assembling the stones for the ring wall comes also the transport of larger stones of specific dimensions for base and lintel, some in the range of 150-200 kg, where several men were needed. Hereafter, the building process could begin. We can only guess how the work was structured, but probably it was comparable to a work team involved in digging a traditional large well in more recent time where a few experienced men and even specialists directed the work (Birks and Letts 1976, Al Tikriti 2002). If the modest proxy above has any truth it must be assumed that the building of a small to average tomb would take at least 2 months of work of at least two workers including one experienced/specialist, but being 3-4 would have optimized efficiency.

If the workers were not full-time specialists but also had some herding or agricultural activities to tend to, the enterprise would take even longer. One can imagine it was done during a fixed season by an initiated group of adult males.

The Hafit tombs reflect an investment of work which, in the case of the medium to large monuments, extends beyond the capabilities of an extended family. We cannot determine how the work was organized, but it is possible to estimate the amount of work necessary to build such a monument. It must have called upon a certain level of organization within a local community and needed a yearly surplus of labour to be invested into such ceremonial and status manifestations. Graves were built in their hundreds in the mound fields at Jebel Hafit and east of Hili. In some traditional agrarian societies this sort

Tomb Number	Outer Diameter	Preserved Height	Chamber		Entrance Passage	
			Length	Width	Length	Width
1030	5.8	0.9	2.0	1.8	2.0	0.4
1031	5.7	1.3	2.4	2.2	1.8	0.7
1032	6.0	0.75	1.8	2.0	(1)	0.5
1033	(6.0)	1.5	2.3	1.9	(1.2)	0.6
1034	(6.0)	1.4	2.4	2.2	1.8	0.6
1035	8.0	2.0	2.6	2.2	2.5	0.5
1036	(6.0)	1.3	2.0	2.2	(1.3)	0.5
1037	(5.0)	1.3	2.0	1.8	(1.8)	0.5
1038	(5.0)	1.0	1.9	1.8	(1.4)	0.5
1039	(6.0)	1.0	1.8	1.9	(1.4)	0.5
1040	(4.5)	(0.7)	1.2	1.4	1.6	0.6
1041	(6.0)	1.22	2.0	2.2	(1.5)	(0.4)
1042	-	0.7	2.0	1.8	-	-
1043	(5.5)	1.1	2.0	1.7	(1.4)	(0.5)
1044	(4.5)	-	1.5	1.6	-	-
1045	(5.0)	1.2	(1.3)	(1.5)	-	-
1046	7.0	2.0	1.8	1.9	2.7	0.5
1047	(4.0)	0.8	1.4	2.2	(1.2)	0.6
1048	(4.0)	0.5	1.2	1.4	1.2	0.6
1049	(5.5)	-	2.0	2.2	(0.8)	0.5
1050	-	-	2.0	1.0	1.1	0.5
1051	(8.0)	1.0	2.6	2.8	2.0	0.6
1052	>5.5	1.3	2.0	1.9	(1.8)	0.5
1053/1	(6.5)	<1.0	2.2	1.8	(1.7)	-
1054	(6.0)	-	1.8	1.5	(1.2)	0.4
1055B	-	-	-	-	-	-
1055D	-	-	-	-	-	-
1055L	-	-	-	-	-	-
1300	>4.0	-	1.6	-	-	-
1302	6.0	(2.0)	2.0	1.8	-	-
1303	6.0	1.3	2.8	2.2	-	-
1305	5.2	-	1.7	1.4	1.6	0.5
1306	5.0	1.3	2.0	2.2	(1.9)	0.5
1309	8.0	1.8	2.6	2.4	2.8	0.5-1.0
1310	-	-	(2.0)	(1.6)	-	-
1311	8.5	1.5	2.4	2.5	2.5	0.5
1312	(6.0)	0.8	2.0	1.6	-	-
1313	6.0	1.6	2.0	1.9	2.2	0.5
1314	6.5	1.5	2.2	2.2	2.0	0.6
1315	6.0	1.5	1.6	1.4	1.8	0.4
1316	7.0	1.1	1.9	1.8	2.0	0.4-0.7
1317	7.0-8.0	2.1	2.5	2.5	2.5	0.6
1318	6.0-7.0	2.7	2.2	1.9	1.8	0.6
1319	6.0	2.5	2.1	2.0	1.6	0.6
1320	6.0	1.4	2.0	2.0	2.5	0.4-0.7
1321	6.0	1.0	2.2	1.8	2.2	0.5

of work was linked to the upkeep of reciprocity and social bonding as well as demonstrations of power and territory. The Hafit tombs have in this line of thought been seen as territorial markers (Carter & Al Tikriti 2004 p. 60. Cleuziou and Tosi 2007) linked to dwelling areas (Giraud 2010 p. 79).

«« Fig. 388. Metric data from Hafit tombs 1030-1321.

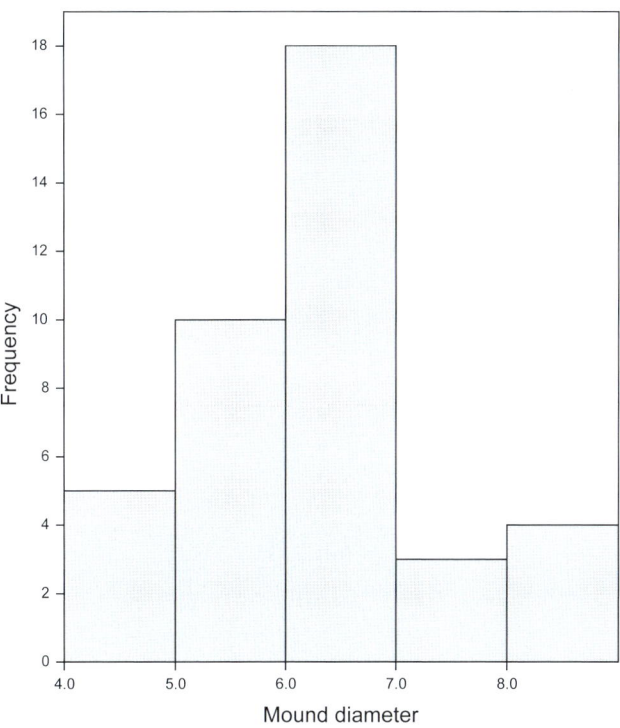

Fig. 389. Approximate diameters in m of Hafit tombs.

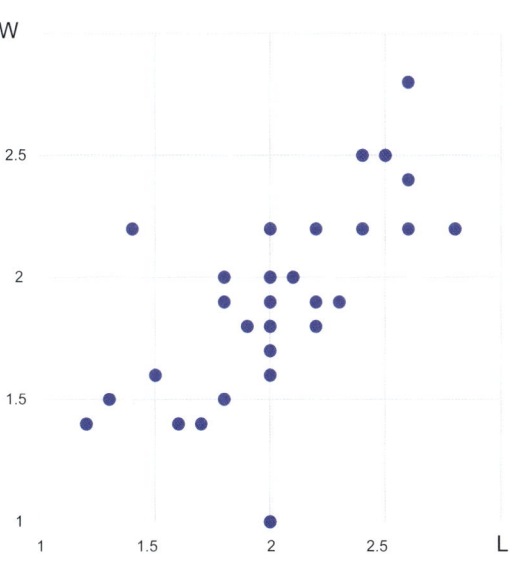

Fig. 390. Length-width relation of burial chambers measured at base level.

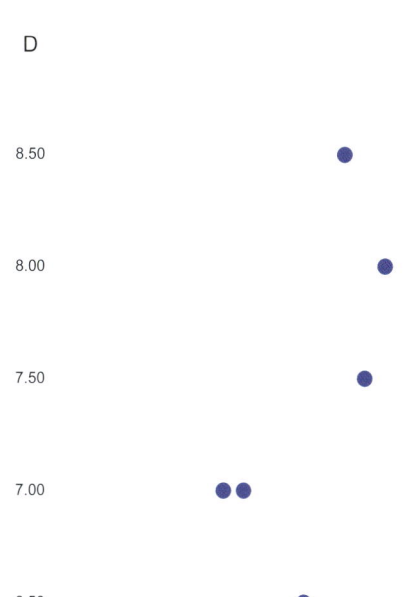

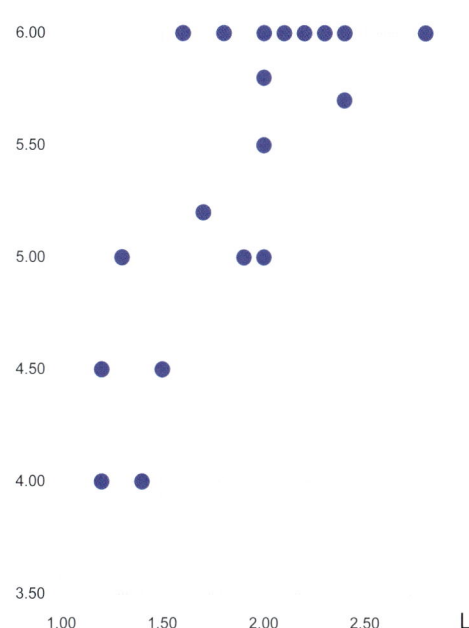

Fig. 391. Relation between ring wall diameter and length of burial chambers at base level.

231

Tomb 1317

Tomb 1318

Tomb 1319

Fig. 392. Plan and section of the three best preserved Hafit tombs, 1317, 1318 and 1319.

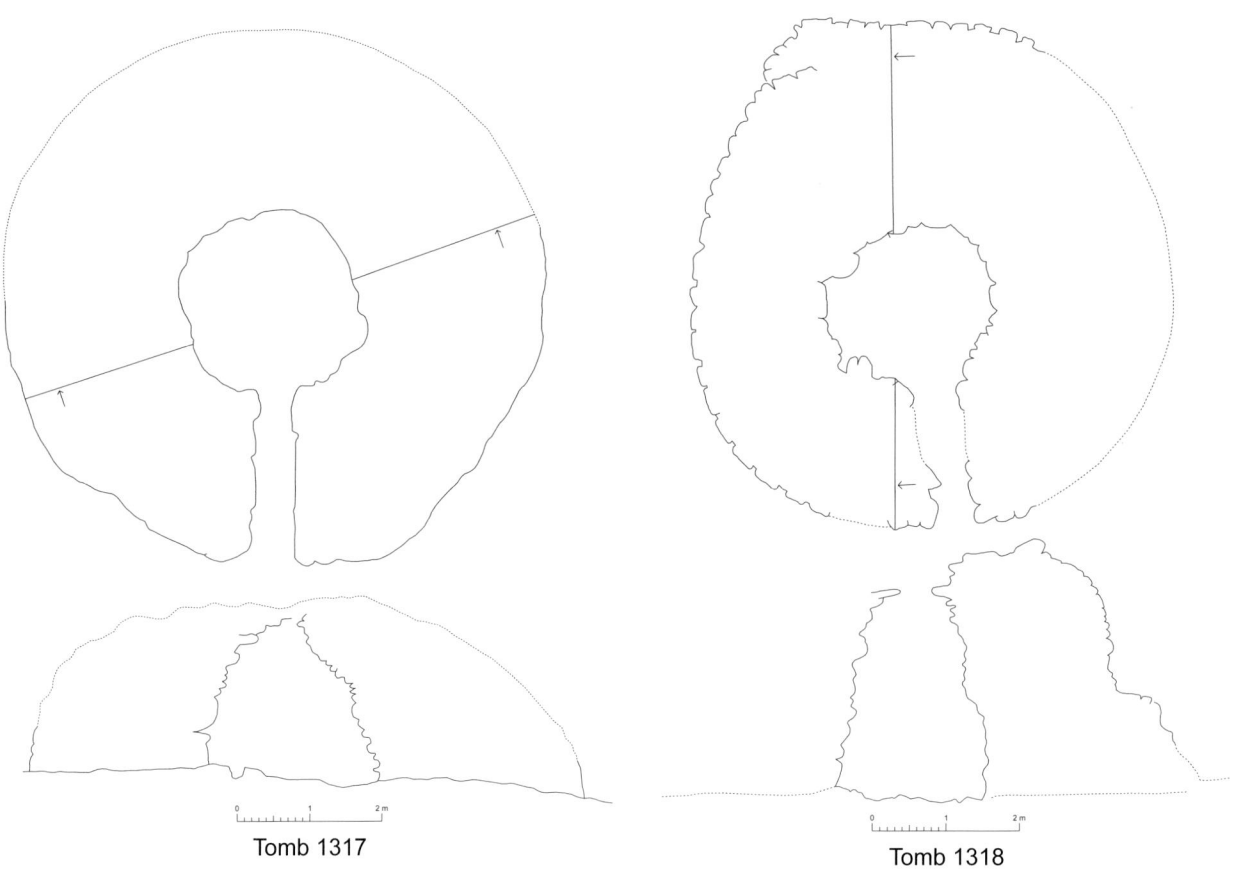

◯	WSW	1
◯	SW	0
◯	SSW	3
◯	S	19
◯	SSE	11

Fig. 393. Orientation of the entrance passage in 34 tombs.

232

Fig. 394. Hypothetical stages in constructing a large Hafit tomb (*BM del*).

14. Secondary burials and later burial forms

The relative stratigraphy of both the skeletal and artefactual remains in several Hafit tombs indicate a general pattern to the sequence of burial levels. On the chamber floor level are the primary burials, mainly defined by the presence of pottery with Jemdet Nasr affinities as observed in 21 tombs. In this lowest level of the chamber the skeletal material, though limited in number and often in a poor state of preservation, points to successive interments next to or on top of each other.

In other cases, the typology of the grave furniture points to a later reuse of the chamber, even though the grave furniture in some instances was placed on or just above the chamber floor. In Tomb 1317 part of a Jemdet Nasr vessel was found outside the entrance as an example of clearing of the primary burial. In the case of Tomb 1312 an Umm an-Nar type soft stone vessel was recovered at the floor level. In these cases, the chamber has probably been cleared of all primary burial furniture, except for scattered bone splinters.

Eleven out of 46 Hafit type tombs had evidence of secondary burials. The tendency was for the secondary burials to be placed in a higher position above the chamber floor, sometimes separated by a "sterile" sand layer or a secondary pavement. In many cases the chamber fill was very mixed by later intrusions, either from grave robbing or stone quarrying.

In the uppermost level of the burial chamber there are a few examples of burials which have been established by breaking through the corbelled roof or by making a shaft through the upper ring wall. These late intrusive burials, e.g. Tombs 1049, 1303, and 1306, are placed either at a level above the upper part of the entrance passage, or at a level too high to be accessed from it. Both Tomb 1049 and Tomb 1303 can be dated to the Iron Age.

In two instances the excavation of ruined cairns led to the recovery of later, non-Hafit type tombs. Tomb 1304 was a narrow chamber apparently without a passage and Tomb 1053.B was placed inside the ruined ring wall of a Hafit type tomb. In both cases no datable material was found, but their constructions have affinities to cists of Wadi Suq or early Iron Age form (Vogt 1994).

The unimposing rock shelter tombs (1301, 1307 and 1308) appeared on steep rocky slopes in small clusters with five to ten tombs, near groups of Hafit mounds. The three excavated rock shelter tombs all contained material dating to the Iron Age, a shell button with three V-shaped holes in Tomb 1301, an iron sword in Tomb 1307 and a camel in Tomb 1308.

The Hafit tombs from the 1961-1971 excavations, as concluded above, do not present any major constructional differences. No signs of looting of stone blocks for the construction of later nearby tombs were observed. This phenomenon occurs among the Umm an-Nar tombs on the island of Umm an-Nar, at Hili, Bat and similar mound fields. Hafit graves have elsewhere occasionally been used, or rebuilt, for later burials. At Jebel Al-Emalah in Sharjah it seems that Hafit tombs have been extended by a soil and stone built mound to serve as an Umm an-Nar period burial place (Benton and Potts 1994). As mentioned above, only Tomb 1317 at the eastern side of Jebel Hafit displayed a possible later addition, a pavement in front of the entrance.

The secondary burials indicate that the monuments continued as burial grounds throughout the Bronze Age. Small local communities continued to use the ancient graves while larger communal tombs were being built during the Umm an-Nar and Wadi Suq periods to the north, at the Hili plain. At the time of the Iron Age the burial reuse concept had changed, and the Hafit-chambers were sometimes entered through the roof. Besides, a new kind of tomb constructed up against a vertical cliff was introduced. In the case of Tomb 1311 a fireplace with a glass bead and some bronze fragments indicate an unusual, possibly non-burial episode from the Iron Age.

15. Concluding discussion

The 50 burials excavated in 1961-1971 by the Danish archaeological expedition and presented in this volume were part of an extensive spread of stone built monuments covering the landscape around Jebel Hafit in the eastern province of Abu Dhabi. 46 of these burials belong to a special type of monument named the Hafit type roughly dated to around 3000 BC and consisting of tower-like structures built of rough stone covering a round, corbelled chamber with a narrow entrance passage.

41 Hafit tombs were excavated north of Jebel Hafit between the West and the East Ridge (fig. 4: Areas A, B, C and D and figs. 23-25), where a total of 234 mounds were counted in 1961.[1]

5 Hafit tombs were excavated on the eastern slope of Jebel Hafit (figs. 4-5: Area E and fig. 26), where they are part of a mound field that consisted of 317 tombs (Al Tikriti 1981).

Besides the 46 Hafit tombs investigated by the Danish expedition, Al Tikriti excavated further 3 tombs of the same type at Jebel Hafit in 1975 (fig. 4: Area C) (Al Tikriti 1981 p. 63). In 1976-77 the French mission excavated 6 Hafit tombs located on the Southern Plateau (fig. 4: Area D)(Cleuziou et al. 2011 p. 13 ff). These 9 tombs and their contents do not distinguish themselves from those excavated by the Danish expedition. Further c. 40 Hafit tombs in the Jebel Hafit area have been excavated by the Department of Antiquities in Al-Ain in the period 1974-78, but they remain unpublished (Al Tikriti 1981 p. 61).

At the present moment a total of c. 55 Hafit tombs out of a population of 551 located around Jebel Hafit have thus been investigated and published, i.e. 10 %. The analyses that have been carried out in the present publication of these burial monuments and their grave goods point towards a high degree of uniformity. The construction and dimensions of the tomb buildings are very similar (p. 226-227), which is only partly due to the fact that in general the available stone material in the area is uniform. The Hafit graves make out a tight-knit group with no basis for division into subtypes and no indications for a typological evolution in burial architecture towards the Umm an-Nar graves that appeared around 2700 BC at Hili.

The pottery found in the graves was imported from Mesopotamia and is also quite homogenous (p. 217), as are the beads (p. 219) and the metalwork (p. 218).[2] The evidence seems to indicate that the Hafit graves excavated around the Jebel Hafit, that we are dealing with here, belong to a limited time period. The sporadic secondary use of the Hafit tombs has produced only a handful of objects that can be dated to the end of the 3rd millennium BC and later, but nothing that must be referred to the early part of the Umm an-Nar culture.

This picture is not in agreement with the very wide dating given to the Hafit graves by Cleuziou who has advocated a span of c. 31-3200 to 2700 BC and who has placed this phase contemporary with the first period of the settlement at Hili 8 lying to the north in the Al Ain oasis (1989 p. 49-53). However, none of the so-called Jemdet Nasr vessels diagnostic of the Hafit graves have been found in the Hili 8 settlement, and there does not seem to be any compelling reason why the only reasonably well preserved Mesopotamian pottery vessel from Hili 8 period 1 (Cleuziou 1989 fig. 1:2. Méry 2000 fig. 105) could not post-date the so-called Jemdet Nasr vessels.

The available stratigraphic evidence from Mesopotamian excavations is far too poor to date the Mesopotamian imports to Abu Dhabi with any precision (cf. Potts 1986), and for that reason caution should be exersised when referring the Hafit tombs to a similar very long period. To mention a hypothetical possibility, the Jemdet Nasr vessels could easily belong only to the Jemdet Nasr period or perhaps extend into the ED I period, whereas the Hili 8 vessel might be quite at home in the ED III period. The radiocarbon dates

---

[1] According to Thorvildsen's field notes, he and his team systematically field-walked Area A, B, C and D in 1961 and counted 234 mounds. In 1980 Al Tikriti counted some 163 tombs in the same area, but he estimated the original number to around 210-250 tombs (without having access to Thorvildsen's count) (Al Tikriti 1981).

[2] The 16 Hafit graves excavated at Qarn Bint Saud by the Danish expedition (Madsen forthcoming b) and by the Department of Antiquities in Al-Ain (Al Tikriti 1981 p. 71-75) are also very similar to the Hafit graves published in this volume, both with respect to architecture and finds.

are, at any rate, far too few to decide the relationship between the Hafit graves and Period I at Hili 8.

The tombs found around Jebel Hafit were placed in marked positions in the landscape that could be seen from far away: on escarpments along the plain, along the dry washes, on isolated hillocks, on small terraces on rocky foothills, in saddles and passes as well as on the lower visible crests or on small peaks. Their altitudes varied 70-80 m in height from about 290 m above sea level at the western ridge (Tomb 1300) to around 368 m on the high pediment of eastern Jebel Hafit (Tomb 1319).

The exact nature of human settlement at this time is uncertain, but the location of tombs may in some way reflect ownership to land and ressources (Cleuziou 1997. Cleuziou & Tosi 2007 p. 111-123). A certain difference in subsistence economy should therefore be expected between the Hafit period and the Umm an-Nar period in view of the stark contrast between the distribution of Hafit graves, which in several bounded areas cover an extended area from the east side of Jebel Hafit and 40 km to the north to Qarn bint Saud, and the concentration of Umm an-Nar graves in one area immediately east of Hili (figs. 1 and 4).

Based on his investigations of Hili 8, Cleuziou has argued that date-palm oases were established already in period 1 (Cleuziou 2002 p. 200-201. See though Power & Sheehan 2012), but as suggested above, period 1 at Hili 8 may post-date the Hafit tombs that we are dealing with here. Others have argued that the distribution of Hafit graves rather suggests that the Hafit population "did not farm at all and were primarily animal herders" (Deadman & Al-Jahwari 2016 p. 27).

It has been suggested that the location of the Hafit graves may mark trade routes (Gentelle & Frifelt 1989 p. 124-125). On the maps from the 1950's and 1960's the major traditional trails were indicated, leading from the oases of Dank, Ibri and Bat in present day Oman along Jebel Hafit and its two northern ridges towards the Al Ain/Buraimi oases and further north to the coast (Hunting Surveys Limited 1969. Walker 1959). The old trails were still easy to identify in 1971 as narrow footpaths on the gravelly and rocky surfaces, and they were occasionally still used by camel herdsmen and small caravans (fig. 19). As the rocky terrain, contrary to the desert, has not changed during millennia it is believed that the major trails would have been in existence for a very long time.

The Jemdet Nasr pots and perhaps some of the beads found in the Hafit graves show that these lines of communication and exchange reached all the way to Mesopotamia, a distance of c. 1000 km. The scarcity of similar pottery on the coast along the route suggests that this connection was seaborne.[3]

As has often been speculated the reason for establishing this close connection between Mesopotamia and Southeast Arabia may very well have been a desire on the part of Mesopotamia to obtain copper from the Oman mountains. The relationship was therefore probably organized from Mesopotamia, like in the Ur III period by the end of the 3rd millennium BC (Laursen & Steinkeller in press). The painted Jemdet Nasr vases and perhaps also beads of faience, heated steatite, carnelian and rock crystal may have been amongst a range of goods brought by traders from southern Mesopotamia to be exchanged for copper. It is evident that these goods came to play very important roles in the local value system, essential for status communication and rituals related to the passage to the afterlife.

---

[3] From a burial mound (Tomb SBH-16) at As-Sabbiya in Kuwait, comes a Jemdet Nasr type pot similar to the most frequent type at Jebel Hafit (Carter 2013 fig. 30.4 right side). A sherd from a Jemdet Nasr pot was encountered out of context at the Barbar temple in Bahrain (Andersen & Højlund p. 219, fig. 392) and at Hamad Town, also in Bahrain, two Jemdet Nasr type vessels have been found in a grave (Laursen 2013).

Bibliography

Anon. 2011: *The Dawn of History. Revealing the Ancient Past of Abu Dhabi*. An exhibition at Al Jahili Fort, Al Ain, arranged by ADACH & Moesgaard Museum.

Al Tikriti, W.Y. 1981: *Reconsideration of the Late Fourth and Third Millennium B.C. in the Arabian Gulf, with Special Reference to the United Arab Emirates*. PhD thesis. Trinity College, University of Cambridge.

Al Tikriti, W.Y. 2002: The south-east Arabian origin of the falaj system. *Proceedings of the Seminar for Arabian Studies* 32 p. 117-138.

Al Tikriti, W.Y. 2011a: *Archaeology of Umm an-Nar Island 1959-2009*. Abu Dhabi Culture & Heritage. Department of Historic Environment.

Al Tikriti, W.Y. 2011b: *Archaeology of the Falaj. A field study of the ancient irrigation systems of the United Arab Emirates*. Abu Dhabi Culture & Heritage. Department of Historic Environment.

Andersen, H.H. & Højlund, F. 2003: *The Barbar Temples*, vols. 1-2. Jutland Archaeological Society Publications 48. Moesgaard Museum. Aarhus.

Aspinall, S. and Hellyer, P. (eds.) 2004: *Jebel Hafit, A Natural History*. Emirates Natural History Group.

Begemann, F., Haerinck, E., Overlaet, B., Scmitt-Strecker, S. & Tallon, F. 2008: An Archaeometallurgical study of the Early and Middle Bronze Age in Luristan, Iran. *Iranica Antiqua* 43 p. 1-66.

Benton, J. N. 1996: *Excavations at Al Sufouh. A Third Millennium Site in the Emirate of Dubai*. Abiel I. Brepols.

Benton, J.N. and Potts, D.T. 1994: *Jebel al-Emalah 1993/4*. Report compiled for the Department of Culture and Information. Government of Sharjah, United Arab Emirates.

Bibby, T. G. 1954: Five among Bahrain's Hundred Thousand Grave-mounds. *Kuml 1954* p. 116-141.

Bibby, T. G. 1965: Arabian Gulf Archaeology. *Kuml 1964* p. 86-111.

Bibby, T. G. 1969: *Looking for Dilmun*. Reprinted by Stacey International, London 1996.

Birks, J. S. and Letts, S. E. 1976: The Awamir: Specialist Well- and Falaj-diggers in Northern Interior Oman. *Journal of Oman Studies*, vol. 2 p. 93-100.

Blau, S. 2004: Out of anonymity – A central location for "peripheral" places through people: The contributions made by Karen Frifelt and Beatrice de Cardi to an understanding of archaeology of the United Arab Emirates. *Arabian Archaeology and Epigraphy* 15 p. 11-19.

Bortolini, E. 2012: The Early Bronze Age of the Oman Peninsula: from Chronology to Evolution. In: J. Giraud and G. Gernez (eds.), *Aux Marges de l'archéologie: Hommage á Serge Cleuziou*. Paris: De Boccard, Paris, *Collection Travaux de la Maison René-Ginouves*, vol. 16 p. 353-369.

Carter, R. 2013: The Sumerians and the Gulf. In: Crawford, H. (ed.), *The Sumerian World*. UK, Routledge, p. 579-599.

Carter, R. & Al Tikriti, W.Y. 2004: The Archaeology of Jebel Hafit. In: *Aspinall & Hellyer (eds.) 2004*, p. 48-64.

Chevalier, J., Inizan, M.-L & Tixier, J. 1982: Une technique de perforation par percussion de perles en cornaline (Larsa, Iraq), *Paléorient* 8/2 p. 55-65.

Cleuziou, S. 1977: French Archaeological Mission. First Campaign. December 1976/February 1977. *Archaeology in the United Arab Emirates*.

Cleuziou, S. 1978: *Économie et Société de la Péninsule d'Oman au IIIe Millénaire: Le Role des Analogies interculturelles*. Collogues Internationaux du CNRS, no. 580 p. 343-359.

Cleuziou, S. 1984: The Oman Peninsula and its relations eastwards during the Third Millennium BC. In: Lal, B.B. & Gupta, S.P. (eds), *Frontiers of the Indus Civilization. A Sir Mortimer Wheeler Commemoration Volume*. New Delhi p. 372-394.

Cleuziou, S. 1989: The chronology of protohistoric Oman as seen from Hili. In: Costa, P.M. & Tosi, M. (eds), Oman Studies. *Papers on the archaeology and history of Oman*. IsMEO, Serie Orientale Roma, vol. LXIII, p. 47-78.

Cleuziou, S. 1997: Construire et proteger son terroir: les oasis d'Oman a l'âge du bronze. In: *Burnouf, J., Dynamique des Paysages Protohistoriques, Antiques, Medievaux et Modernes*. XVIIe rencontres internationales d'archeologie et d'histoire d'Antibes. Paris, CNRS, p. 389-412.

Cleuziou, S. 2002: The Early Bronze Age of the Oman Peninsula: from Chronology to the Dialectics of Tribe and State Formation. *Essays on the Late Prehistory of the Arabian Peninsula*. Ed. Is. I. A. O. Serie Orientale Roma, vol. XCIII, p. 191-236.

Cleuziou, S., Méry, S. and Vogt, B. (eds) 2011: *Protohistoire de l'oasis d'al-Aïn, Travaux de la Mission archéologique française à Abou Dhabi (Emirats arabes unis). Les sépultures de l'âge du Bronze.* BAR International Series 2227.

Cleuziou, S. and Tosi, M. 1989: The South-eastern Frontier of the Ancient Near East. *South Asian Archaeology 1985*. Nordic Institute of Asian Studies Occasional Papers No. 4, p. 15-47.

Cleuziou, S. and Tosi, M. 2007: *In the Shadow of the Ancestors. The Prehistoric Foundations of the Early Arabian Civilization in Oman.* Ministry of Heritage and Culture. Sultanate of Oman.

Cotterell, B. and Kamminga, J. 1990: *Mechanics of pre-industrial technology.* Cambridge University Press.

Daems, A. and De Waele, A. 2010: Camelid and equid burials in pre-Islamic Southeastern Arabia. Death and Burial in Arabia and Beyond. BAR International Series 2107. *Society for Arabian Studies Monographs* 10 p. 109-113.

Deadman, W.M. & Al-Jahwari, N.S. 2016: Hafit tombs in ash-Sharqiyah, Oman: assessing the accuracy and precision of Google Earth remote-sensing survey and analysing their distribution in the landscape. *Arabian Archaeology and Epigraphy* 27 p. 19-30.

de Cardi, B., Doe, D.B. & Roskams, S.P. 1977: Excavation and Survey in the Sharqiyah, Oman 1976. *Journal of Oman Studies*, vol. 3, part 1 p. 17-33.

de Cardi, B., Bell, R. D. & Starling, N. J. 1982: Excavations at Tawi Silaim and Tawi Sa'id in the Sharqiyah, 1978. *Journal of Oman Studies*, vol. 5, 1979 p. 61-94.

Delougaz, P. and Lloyd, S. 1942: *Pre-Sargonid Temples in the Diyala Region.* Oriental Institute Publications, 58. Chicago: The University of Chicago Press.

Doe, D. B. 1977: Gazetteer of sites in Oman; 1976. *Journal of Oman Studies*, vol. 3, part 1 p. 35-57.

During Caspers, E. C. L. 1971: New Archaeological Evidence for Maritime Trade in the Persian Gulf During the Late Protoliterate Period. *EAST AND WEST, New Series* Vol. 21. Nos. 1-2. IsMEO, Rome p. 21-44.

Dyson, R.H. Jr. 1964: Notes on Weapons and Chronology in Northern Iran around 1000 B.C. In: *Mellink, M.J. (ed.), Dark Ages and Nomads c. 1000 BC.* Leiden p. 32-43.

Frifelt, K. 1971: Jemdat Nasr Graves in the Oman. *Kuml 1970*, p. 355-383.

Frifelt, K. 1975a: On Prehistoric Settlement and Chronology of the Oman Peninsula. *EAST AND WEST, New Series* Vol. 25. Nos. 3-4. IsMEO, Rome, p. 359-424.

Frifelt, K. 1975b: A possible Link between the Jemdet Nasr and the Umm an-Nar Graves of Oman. *Journal of Oman Studies* 1, p. 57-80.

Frifelt, K. 1975c: Archäologische Forschungen am Persischen Golf. *Antike Welt. Zeitschrift für Archäologie und Urgeschichte* no. 2, p. 15-24.

Frifelt, K. 1979: The Umm an-Nar and Jemdet Nasr of Oman and their Relations abroad. *South Asian Archaeology 1975*, Leiden p. 43-57.

Frifelt, K. 1980: "Jemdet Nasr Graves" on the Oman Peninsula. *Mesopotamia: Copenhagen Studies in Assyriology 8*, p. 273-279.

Frifelt, K. 1985: Further Evidence of the Third Millennium BC Town at Bat in Oman. *Journal of Oman Studies* 7, p. 89-104.

Frifelt K. 1991: *The Island of Umm an-Nar, vol. 1. Third Millennium Graves.* Jutland Archaeological Society Publications 26 (1), Aarhus.

Frifelt K. 1995: *The Island of Umm an-Nar, vol. 2. The Third Millennium Settlement.* Jutland Archaeological Society Publications 26 (2), Aarhus.

Frifelt, K. 2002: Did the Umm an-Nar Graves Originate in Oman? *Essays on the Late Prehistory of the Arabian Peninsula.* Ed. Is. I. A. O. Serie Orientale Roma, vol. XCIII p. 317-335.

Frohlich, B. 1986: The human biological history of the Early Bronze Age population in Bahrain. In: *Bahrain through the Ages: the Archaeology.* London p. 47-63.

Gagnaison, C., Barrier, P., Méry, S. & Al Tikriti, W. Y. 2004: Extraction de calcaires éocènes à l'Age du Bronze et architecture funéraire á Hili (Emirat d'Abou Dhabi). *Revue d'Archéométrie* 28 p. 97-108.

Gebel, H.G., Hannss, C., Liebau, A., Raehle, W. 1989: The Late Quaternary Environments of Ain al-Faidha/Al-Ain. Abu Dhabi Emirate. *Archaeology in the United Arab Emirates*, vol. V 1989, p. 9-48.

Gensheimer, T. 1984: The role of shell in Mesopotamia. Evidence of trade/exchange with Oman and the Indus Valley. *Paléorient* 10 (1) p. 65-73.

Gentelle, P. and Frifelt, K. 1989: About the Distribution of Third Millennium Graves and Settlements in the Ibri area of Oman. In: Costa, P.M. & Tosi, M. (eds.), *Oman Studies. Papers on the archaeology and history of Oman.* Ed. IsMEO, Serie Orientale Roma, vol. LXIII, p. 119-126.

Giraud, J. 2010: Early Bronze Age graves and graveyards in the eastern Ja'alan (Sultanate of Oman): an assessment of the social rules working in the evolution of a funerary landscape. *Death and Burial in Arabia and Beyond.* BAR International Series 2107. Society for Arabian Studies Monographs 10 p. 71-84.

Glob, P.V. 1959a: Reconnaissance in Abu Dhabi. *Kuml 1958* p. 162-165.

Glob, P.V. 1959b: Archaeological Investigations in Four Arab States. *Kuml 1959* p. 233-239.

Glob, P.V. 1968: *Al-Bahrain. De danske ekspeditioner til oldtidens Dilmun.* Gyldendal, Copenhagen.

Haerinck, E. 2001: *The Tombs. The University of Ghent South-East Arabian Archaeological Project. Excavations at ed-Dur (Umm al-Qaiwain, United Arab Emirates,* vol. II). Leuven: Peeters.

Hunting Surveys Limited (1969): *Photogrammetric Maps from Air Photographs 1:10.000*. Abu Dhabi State. Al-Ain and district.

Højgaard, K. 1980a: Dentition on Umm an-Nar (Trucial Oman), 2500 B.C. *Scandinavian Journal of Dental Research* 88, p. 355-364.

Højgaard, K. 1980b: Dentition on Bahrain, 2000 B.C. *Scandinavian Journal of Dental Research* 88 p. 467-475.

Højgaard, K. 1985: SEM (Scanning Electron Microscopic) examination of Teeth from the Third Millennium B.C. Excavated in Wadi Jizzi and Hafit. *South Asian Archaeology 1983.* Naples p. 151-156.

Højlund, F. 2013: The first excavations in the UAE: Glimpses into the archives of the Moesgård Museum. In: *Proceedings of UAE 50th anniversary of Umm an-Nar excavations conference 2009,* p. 12-19.

Højlund, F. & H.H. Andersen 1994: *Qala'at al-Bahrain vol. 1. The Northern City Wall and the Islamic Fortress*. Jutland Archaeological Society Publications 30:1. Moesgaard Museum. Aarhus.

Jasim, S. A. 2003: The Third Millennium Culture in the Emirate of Sharjah. In: Potts, D.T., Al Naboodah, H. & Hellyer, P. (eds), *Archaeology of the United Arab Emirates. Proceedings of the First International Conference on the Archaeology of the U.A.E.* Trident Press, London, p. 86-99.

Jasim, S.A. 2012: *The Necropolis of Jebel al-Buhais. Prehistoric Discoveries in the Emirate of Sharjah, United Arab Emirates.* The Department of Culture & Information, Government of Sharjah, UAE.

Kiesewetter, H. 2006: Funeral monuments and human remains from Jebel Al-Buhais. In: Uerpmann, H.-P., Uerpmann, M. and Jasim, S.A. (eds.), *Funeral Monuments and Human Remains from Jebel Al-Buhais,* vol. 1. Tübingen: Kerns Verlag, p. 103-380.

Kunter, M. 1991: Die menschlichen Skelettreste aus den Gräbern von Umm an-Nar, Abu Dhabi, U.A.E. (3. Jt.v.Chr.). In: Frifelt K. 1991: *The Island of Umm an-Nar, vol. 1. The Third Millennium Graves.* Jutland Archaeological Society Publications 26 (1), Aarhus, p. 163-179.

Laursen, S.T. 2013: A late fourth- to early third-millennium grave from Bahrain, c. 3100-2600 BC. *Arabian archaeology and epigraphy* p. 125-133.

Laursen, S.T. & Steinkeller, P. in press [2017]: *Babylonia, the Gulf Region and the Indus: Archaeological and Textual Evidence for Contact in the Third and Early Second Millennia BC.* Eisenbrauns, Winona Lake.

Littleton, J. and Frifelt K. 2006: Trepanations from Oman: A case of diffusion? *Arabian archaeology and epigraphy* 17, p. 139-151.

Madsen, B. forthcoming a: *The Hili Grand Tomb. A monumental Bronze Age tomb in Abu Dhabi. Investigations 1964-1970.*

Madsen, B. forthcoming b: *Archaeology from Qarn Bint Saud. Investigations at a rock outcrop in the eastern desert of Abu Dhabi. The results of the fieldwork 1970-1972.*

Mallowan, M.E.L. 1966: *Nimrud and its remains*, vol. I. London.

Mann, C. C. 1969: *Abu Dhabi. Birth of an Oil Sheikhdom.* Khayats, Beirut.

McSweeney, K., Méry, S. and Macchiarelli, R. 2008: Rewriting the end of the Early Bronze Age in the United Arab Emirates through the anthropological and artefactual evaluation of two collective Umm an-Nar graves at Hili (eastern region of Abu Dhabi). *Arabian Archaeology and Epigraphy* 19 p. 1-14.

Méry, S. 2000: *Les céramiques d'Oman et l'Asie moyenne. Une archéologie des échanges à l'Age du Bronze.* CRA Monographies 23. CNRS ÈDITIONS, Paris.

Miles, S. B. 1919: *The Countries and Tribes of the Persian Gulf.* Frank Cass and Co. Ltd. London 1966.

Mitchell, T. C. 1972: A review of acquisitions 1963-70 of Western Asiatic Antiquities (I). *British Museum Quarterly* 36: 3-4. London, p. 131-146.

Mogliazza, S. 2009: An example of cranial trepanation dating to the Middle Bronze Age from Ebla, Syria. *Journal of Anthropological Sciences* Vol. 87 p. 187-192.

Mouton, M. 1992: *La Peninsule d'Oman de la Fin de l'Age du Fer au Debut de la Periode Sassanide.* These de Doctorat. Universite de Paris 1.

Panei, L., Rinaldi, G. & Tosi, M. 2005: Investigations on ancient beads from the Sultanate of Oman (Ra's al-Hadd – Southern Oman. *ArcheoSciences* vol. 29 p. 151-155.

Piesinger, C.M. 1983: *Legacy of Dilmun: The Roots of Ancient Maritime Trade in Eastern Coastal Arabia in the 4th/3rd Millennium B.C.* Ph.D. dissertation. University of Wisconsin-Madison.

Potts, D.T. 1986: Eastern Arabia and the Oman Peninsula during the Late Fourth and Early Third Millennium B.C. In: Finkbeiner, U. & Röllig, W. (eds), *Gamdat Nasr. Period or Regional Style?* Papers given at a symposium held in Tübingen November 1983. Beihefte Zum Tübinger Atlas Des Vorderen Orients. Wiesbaden, p. 121-170.

Potts, D.T. 1990: *The Arabian Gulf in Antiquity, vol. I-II.* Clarendon Press. Oxford.

Potts, D.T. 1996: Atacamite pigment at Tell Abraq in the early Iron Age. *Arabian Archaeology and Epigraphy* 7, p. 13-16.

Potts, D.T. 1997: Rewriting the late Prehistory of South-Eastern Arabia: A Reply to Joycelyn Orchard. *Iraq*, vol. LIX p. 63-71.

Potts, D.T. 1998: Some issues in the study of the pre-Islamic weaponry of southeastern Arabia. *Arabian Archaeology and Epigraphy* 9 p. 182-208.

Power, T. & Sheehan, P. 2012: The origin and development of the oasis landscape of Al-Ain (UAE). *Proceedings for the Seminar for Arabian Studies* 42 p. 291-308.

Rahim, F. 1979: Al Ain Museum. In: *Archaeology in the United Arab Emirates. Vol II-III.* Department of Antiquities and Tourism. Al-Ain.

Reese, D. S. 1991: Shells from the Umm an-Nar and Hafit graves, Abu Dhabi. In: *Frifelt 1991*, p. 184-186.

Thorvildsen, K. 1962: Burial Cairns on Umm an-Nar. *Kuml 1962* p. 191-219.

Tosi, M. 1989: Protohistoric Archaeology in Oman: The First Thirty Years (1956-1985). In: Oman Studies. *Papers on the Archaeology and History of Oman.* Ed. IsMEO, Serie Orientale Roma, vol. LXIII, p. 135-161.

Vats, M. S. 1940: *Excavations at Harappa.* Delhi: Manager of Publications.

Velde, C. 2003: Wadi Suq and Late Bronze Age in the Oman Peninsula. *Archaeology of the United Arab Emirates.* Trident Press, p. 102-113

Vogt, B. 1985: *Zur Chronologie und Entwicklung der Gräber des Späten 4.-2. Jtsd. V. Chr. auf der Halbinsel Oman: Zusammenfassung, Analyse und Würdigung publizierter wie auch unveröffentlichter Grabungsergebnisse.* Dissertation. Göttingen.

Vogt, B. 1994: *Asimah. An Account of Two Months Rescue Excavation in the Mountains of Ras al-Khaimah, United Arab Emirates.* Department of Antiquities and Museums, Ras al-Khaimah. Shell Markets Middle East, Dubai. UAE.

Walker, J. F. 1959: *Hand drawn topographic map of the Al-Ain, Buraimi and Jebel Hafit area 1:100.000.* (The map comprises main topographic features, tribal pasture names and place names in English spelling. A copy of the map is on file in the Oriental Department Archive at Moesgaard Museum).

Williams, K. & Gregoricka, L. 2013: The social, spatial, and bioarchaeological histories of Ancient Oman project: the mortuary landscape of Dhank. *Arabian archaeology and epigraphy* 24 p. 134-150.

Williamson, A. 1973: *Sohar and Omani Seafaring in the Indian Ocean.* Petroleum Development of Oman LTD, Muscat.

Yule, P. and Weisgerber, G. 1998: Prehistoric Tower Tombs at Shir/Jaylah, Sultanate of Oman. *Beiträge Zur Allgemeinen Und Vergleichenden Archäologie*, Band 18. Mainz, p. 183-241.

Yule, P. and Weisgerber, G. 2001: The Metal Hoard from Ibri/Selme, Sultanate of Oman. *Prähistorische Bronzefunde*, Abteilung XX, Band 7. Stuttgart.

Appendix. The camel bones from Tomb 1308

by Margarethe Uerpmann & Hans-Peter Uerpmann

An amount of 5,761 kg of bone fragments from the Danish excavation of a rock shelter (Tomb 1308) on Jebel Hafit (UAE) (cf. above p. 148) were examined with regard to the animal species and the represented parts of their skeletons. A particular focus was on the occurrence of camel burials.

The bone finds were badly preserved and highly fragmented. It was considered inappropriate to quantify the bones by fragment-counting. Thus, the quantities provided in the following table are bone-weights in gram (g).

Animal bones from Tomb 1308 at Jebel Hafit (1308.A)

Camel (Dromedary)	bone weight (g)	totals (g)
skull (base)	200	
zygomaticum	7	
dist. Humerus	230	
mandib. Frag.	11	
mandib. Frag.	13	
Radius, Epiphys. dist. open	168	
prox. Ulna frag. Re.	39	
carpal	21	
carpal	15	
dist. Femur epiphysis of 1st indiv.	35	
dist. Femur epiphysis of 2nd indiv.	104	
Tibia left, young	123	
dist Epiph tibia	16	
dist. Tibia fused	46	
left Calcaneus – Indiv. 1	47	
right Calcaneus – Indiv. 1	48	
left Calcaneus – Indiv. 2	58	
right Calcaneus – Indiv. 2	43	
tarsal	22	
fragments of long bones	252	
metapodial fragments	143	
dist. Metapodium epiph.	12	
Dromedary, total:	1653	
spongious bone fragments (large camel Indiv. 3)	525	

Camel (Dromedary)	bone weight (g)	totals (g)
Camel, including Indiv. 3:	2178	2178

Cattle	bone- weight (g)	
Zygomatic*	5	
Incisivum	8	
Molar (max.)	5	
Molar (mand.)	10	
Calcaneum	25	
Os tarsale	8	
Metatarsal	61	
Cattle, total	122	122

Sheep or Goat	bone-weight (g)	
mandible	5	
Sheep/Goat, total	5	5

Donkey (min. 2 individuals)	bone-weight (g)	
Metacarpal	6	
3 mand. Teeth – (Indiv. 1)	47	
3 mand. Teeth – (Indiv. 2)	52	
Sacrum	9	
Tibia dist.	2	
Donkey, total	116	116

Gazelle	bone-weight (g)	
Pelvis	2	
Pelvis	2	
Gazelle, total	4	4

Oryx (?)	bone-weight (g)	
Tibia dist.	1	
Oryx (?), total:	1	1

Dog (min. 2 individuals)	bone-weight (g)	
Mandible corpus (Indiv. 1)	14	
Mandible corpus (Indiv. 2)	13	
Tibia dist.	2	
Dog, total:	29	29
Total identified	2455	2455

Unidentified:		
Large animals	2116	
medium-sized animals	1190	
Total unidentified:	3306	3306
Total:		5761

Camel

As documented in the above table the majority of the bone finds, 1653 g, are definitely dromedary bones. Where morphological criteria are well enough preserved, they clearly indicate the exclusive presence of Camelus dromedarius. None of them was large enough to be considered as representing a wild dromedary or a hybrid between one-humped and two-humped camels. At least two domestic dromedary individuals are represented. Both of them were subadult, one slightly smaller than the other. The excavated bones cover the whole skeleton, probably indicating that both animals were complete when they entered the archaeological context.

Apart from the remains of these young dromedaries there are three finds of very large bones, listed separately in the above table. One of them is from a distal tibia with an open epiphysis and can be identified as camel. The other two finds are very badly preserved and only represent the spongious inside of large bones. Size wise these finds might represent wild dromedaries or hybrids between dromedaries and Bactrian camels. Up till now the earliest finds of camel hybrids are from Late Preislamic contexts (Uerpmann & Uerpmann 2012 p. 118). Most probably these large bones represent fully grown male dromedaries.

Other animals

Whereas the dromedary bones seem to represent whole skeletons, the remains of other animals obviously are kitchen offal. They derive from domestic animals – cattle, sheep and goat, donkey, and dog. Gazelle and Oryx antelope represent the local wild fauna. As a particular feature it should be pointed out that the find of a cattle zygomatic has zebu characteristics. The donkey and dog remains each are from two different individuals. From the dog there are two almost identical finds of right mandibles of middle sized animals.

As a final remark it should be pointed out that the camel remains as predominant constituents of the faunal remains from Tomb 1308 and its surroundings are well compatible with the assumption that the site represents a burial context. However, the other animals remains are typical settlement debris. It should be discussed how the features of the site might have contributed to this particular situation.

Literature

Uerpmann, M. & Uerpmann, H.-P. 2012: Archaeozooology of Camels in South-Eastern Arabia. In: Knoll, E.-M. & Burger, P. (Eds.): *Camels in Asia and North Africa*. Österreichische Akademie der Wissenschaften, Denkschriften Bd. 451, p. 109-122.